Armed and Dangerous

**Memoirs
of a Chicago Policewoman**

Gina Gallo

A Tom Doherty Associates Book • New York

Note to Readers: This is a true account. The incidents portrayed are all based on actual events, but many are composites, and names and certain other identifying characteristics have been changed.

ARMED AND DANGEROUS: MEMOIRS OF A CHICAGO POLICEWOMAN

Copyright © 2001 by Gina Gallo

All rights reserved.

A Forge Book
Published by Tom Doherty Associates
175 Fifth Avenue
New York, NY 10010

www.tor-forge.com

Forge® is a registered trademark of Macmillan Publishing Group, LLC.

ISBN 978-0-7653-9800-0

Our books may be purchased in bulk for promotional, educational, or business use. Please contact your local bookseller or the Macmillan Corporate and Premium Sales Department at 1-800-221-7945, extension 5442, or by e-mail at MacmillanSpecialMarkets@macmillan.com.

First Edition: March 2001
First Mass Market Edition: February 2018

Printed in the United States of America

0 9 8 7 6 5 4 3 2 1

For the men of Company G

Contents

Preface

It wasn't something I'd planned on. Not as an adult, and never in my wildest fantasies as a daydreaming child, did I consider becoming a cop. Back in those childhood days, it wasn't an occupation considered suitable for little girls. At that time, the placid days of the Eisenhower administration were winding down, JFK was gearing up for his reign in Camelot, and little girls still dreamed of being ballerinas, or nurses, or princesses. Aspirations for the "masculine" professions, like police, firefighters, and doctors, were considered strictly a part of the male domain. Men could become any of these things; women could be their assistants. In that prefeminist era, it was considered correct and appropriate for women to adopt the age-old social role of admirer and supporter of the men who performed these males-only occupations. We were still light-years away from the feminist movement, and the changes that occurred in what were once "gender-specific" occupations. Back then, there were no female firefighters, and no such thing as "policewomen," unless you counted the crossing guards who hovered like uniformed mother hens near school intersections.

So my becoming a cop seemed as likely as going to the moon. But time and circumstances were to prove that, just like the "giant leap for mankind" in the space program, the day was fast approaching when anything was possible.

It wasn't that I didn't know about a cop's life. My dad was a cop—a thirty-year veteran of the Chicago Police Department, who worked the gamut of assignments from citywide traffic, to patrol, to task-force assignments to the rarefied air of the Detective Division. Being a cop's kid gave me special insight into that clandestine brotherhood. I heard all my father's war stories, learned more from them about the strange quirks of human behavior than anything contained in my college psychology courses later on.

I learned about courage from the unknown dangers my father faced daily, and from the silent strength of my mother, who lived with the knowledge that any night might be the one when he didn't return home. I remember the funny stories, the outrageous ones, and the somber memories that replay with a clarity that time has not diminished.

Like the Easter Sunday when our family was preparing for the trip to church and Easter mass. Dad was on the midnight watch and wouldn't be home until we returned. By that time, the Easter bunny would have visited, and we'd get to rip into our respective baskets, stuff ourselves with candy, and then wait for all our relatives to arrive later for a sumptuous Easter dinner. I remember my mother adjusting my Easter bonnet—a much-hated frilly thing with entirely too many ribbons and bows for a fidgety six-year-old. While I was trying to squirm away, the doorbell rang, unusual for such an early hour. It was the police chaplain and my father's field lieutenant, bearing grave news. Caught behind my older sister's protective arm, I couldn't hear their whispered words, only saw the bloodied uniform they handed my mother, and heard her gasp. And instead of chocolate bunnies and a baked ham dinner, Easter that year was the sterile smells of the hospital waiting room, while my father hovered near death.

Cops' kids are raised to understand and accept the inevitable: that the duty their parent performs is a dangerous one that someday might require the "supreme sacrifice." But words like "hero" and "bravery" mean nothing when you watch machines pump air and life into your own father as he lies gray and still before you. Or when you watch your mother sit, motionless, too frightened to cry, lips moving silently in fervent prayer. That's when you learn how capricious life can be—especially a cop's life. One incident, a single bullet, can alter a life—a family of lives—forever.

I didn't understand it at the time. I knew *how* it happened, but couldn't figure out *why*. Why my father would continue to work a job that was so dangerous; why he would put his life in constant jeopardy when there were other occupations that were safer. And it never got any easier to understand, through more injuries, more bedside vigils, more cadres of physicians who lingered outside the intensive care unit with a guarded prognosis. It never got easier, but we learned to deal with it. And developed a "game face" just like cops do, a stony stoicism that hid our fear, the spiraling panic that gripped us while we watched and waited. And each time my father recovered, there was relief, and prayers of thanksgiving, and the inevitable sense of dread and anticipation of "the next time."

There were a lot of other things that made a cop's life, and that of his family, different than the average citizen. At that time, cops were expected to rotate shifts every twenty-eight days. Which meant that while other dads were home for the evening, mine might be working, or grabbing a catnap just before work. Criminals don't call, "Time out!" during holidays or birthdays, and cops have to work through them. Christmas dinners, family celebrations, school functions all had to be scheduled around Dad's work, or else relegated to my mother. In many ways, ours was like a single-parent family. And, as we learned to be independent, to function without his presence or input, he became almost like a stranger among us.

Although Dad shared his work stories with us, we had no idea what the job was like for him. When he put on his uniform, strapped on his gun belt, there was no way we could understand the feelings attached to those acts. He never talked about fear, or panic, or the misery of the things he saw. He could speak of the grisliest crimes with the same level of detachment as one discussing the weather: strictly an objective observation with no obvious emotion. In fact, there was a stoicism there that could have been interpreted as apathy. Or coldness. My father, the unfeeling cop. I didn't understand then what the job really was, what it made my dad. But as I moved through my teenage years, I was certain of one thing: being a cop was a loser's game. I saw what it did to my father, and was fairly certain that anyone with a shred of intelligence or self-respect would never make the mistake of becoming a cop. Not me, anyway. But remember what they say about "never say never"?

It wasn't until I was in my twenties that reality struck in a big way. I'd finished a master's degree in psychology, was enjoying a career as a therapist in a state facility, was married with one child and another on the way. All happy events and, unfortunately, all situations that were critically altered or reversed within the same short period of time.

It all happened within a year. Federal cutbacks in mental-health programs, instigated by the Reagan administration, meant that jobs in my facility were downsized or virtually eliminated. I was one of the "lucky" ones: I could keep my job, if I accepted a significant pay cut and loss of medical benefits. Not a viable alternative, since I'd just divorced and now had two kids to support.

Enter the "critical incident"—the one that comes at some point in everyone's life and changes its entire course. A friend who worked at City Hall told me of the upcoming Chicago Police exam, an announcement I met with a few giggles. My father had been a cop, I said. I saw what it did to him, and having to grow up with that had been quite enough, thanks. Besides, I wasn't cop material. I was a *pacifist,* for God's sake! Had no desire to march around in uniform toting a gun. Even less interest in being a target for bad guys intent on adding a few "cop notches" to their belt. So no, thanks; being a cop was out of the question.

My friend mentioned a starting salary that was considerably more than my current one. Although it required advanced degrees and years spent slogging through research and study, I'd discovered psychology was *not* a particularly lucrative profession. So when my friend started quoting benefits packages, comprehensive medical and dental plans for employee *and* family, I was swayed. And when it was suggested that, with my education, I could go directly from the Training Academy to the Department Counseling Center, where I could utilize my therapist's skills within the department, I was sold. The only difference in what I'd be doing, I reasoned, would be the addition of another title: Officer.

The next day, I applied for the job. The only one more shocked by my decision than my family was me. Becoming a cop was completely at odds with what I perceived to be my nature, my basic personality. There was no way I could fit in with what I thought of as "the cop mentality." I assured myself I wouldn't have to fit in, that once I was assigned as a therapist at the counseling center, I could assume my clinical duties and detach from the rest. And I told myself that, as a cop's kid, I had at least enough insight to understand the job from the beginning. Forewarned is forearmed, right?

I was certain that I had all the answers. Was positive that I knew myself, and what I was getting into. And told myself that it was a temporary gig—just something to support my family paycheck-to-paycheck, until something better came along. And swore to God and all the saints in heaven that I would *never* allow the job to change me, the way it had my father.

Today, sixteen years later, I can see that I was wrong on all counts.

Introduction

Ever wonder what it's like to be a cop? You sit at home watching the latest cop show on the tube and wonder if it's really like the way they portray it: lots of excitement, plenty of action, enough cop groupies to keep your libido within manageable levels—yeah, that's what it must be like. And if you thought that, you'd be right . . . partially. It's much more—and less—than that, so much so that you can never really grasp it unless you've been there, done it, and lived to tell about it. And then learned to live with yourself while you're doing it.

What does it take to be a cop? Forget all that bull the police recruiters promote as being "desirable characteristics." As a sixteen-year veteran of the Chicago Police Department, I can tell you the real deal. In a city like this, it takes more than ideals, more than guts. It takes a knowledge of yourself, the people you serve, and the city you call home.

Chicago sprawls along the southwestern edge of Lake Michigan, so large that an ongoing rivalry exists between North Side and South Side residents.

"You mean there's life south of the Loop?" some North Siders will sneer. To which South Siders reply, "I get a nosebleed whenever I go north of Madison." (Madison Street is the geographical center of Chicago.)

North Siders promote their baseball field (Wrigley Field, home of the Chicago Cubs), the booming nightlife of Rush Street and River North, the educational excellence of universities such as DePaul, Loyola, and Northwestern.

With typical in-your-face bravado, South Siders have a ready reply. What about Comiskey Park, bastion of the White Sox? Or Chinatown, Bronzeville, and Hyde Park, all cultural treasures? Toss in the Museum of Science and Industry, the DuSable Museum, and finish with the University of Illinois's Circle Campus and the venerable University of Chicago for a one-two KO punch.

Each part of the city has its treasures, its nuances which make it special, make its residents certain their neighborhood is the best. Chicago is a city of neighborhoods, with ethnic pockets from nearly every culture represented in its demographic spread. To best serve each neighborhood, the police department must be aware of the cultural differences of the city's diverse population, and adjust policing techniques accordingly. From the predominantly Swedish population of Andersonville to the largely Jewish enclave of Edgewater, the African-American neighborhoods of the West Side, Greektown, the Hispanic community of Pilsen—each neighborhood requires a police department that understands their culture, and their particular needs.

Unlike other large cities, Chicago's police department is divided into districts rather than precincts. There are twenty-five police districts here, with Police Headquarters diplomatically located on State Street, at midpoint between North and South Side districts. The police superintendent heads the force. Outside of the mayor, the superintendent is considered to be the final authority on all police-related issues.

Ask any Chicago cop what makes policing the Windy City special, and the answer will be basically the same. It's the people. From North Side to South, the diversity of the population means that working in any particular district will be different than another. Transfer from the Eighteenth District, home to both the fearsome Cabrini-Green Housing Projects and the glitz and glitter of Rush Street nightlife, to the blue-collar neighborhoods of the Ninth District's Bridgeport area, and you'll swear you're in another city. Make a more radical move to a specialized unit like Prostitution, Organized Crime, or Gangs, and you'll think you're in another dimension.

Each police district is a community unto itself, with different requirements of its personnel. Cops in the First (Central) District, which is located in the same building as Police Headquarters, patrol the downtown business district, the posh hotels, tourist attractions along the pristine Lake Shore Drive—all the high-profile places that require a spit-and-polish image. In this district, certain cosmetic requirements are important: your hair cut well within the limits of department mandates, a high-gloss shine on your shoes and your uniform inspection-ready. Cops assigned to the Central District are expected to be savvy in handling tourists, the press, judicial bigwigs, and all manner of VIPs. In the First District, image counts as much or more than standard police skills. You dress to impress and jump through the hoops, because the eyes of the public are on you, from the department brass (hobnobbing on the upper levels of Headquarters), to hungry media reporters tired of another fruitless afternoon spent hanging out in the department's press office. This is the district of the "poster cops" whose pictures grace the newspapers as representatives of those honorable and noble among the ranks who still uphold the department's proud traditions. Which is to say that image is everything, which anyone wearing a star would do well to remember.

It's a far cry from the high-crime, combat-zone districts, like the notorious Fillmore (Eleventh) District on the West Side, or "the Deuce," the Wentworth (Second) District on the South Side. Cops in these districts are more likely to say *"Freeze!"* than "cheese," because there's no media here, unless they arrive, accompanied by armed guards, to cover a story on the latest police brutality rap, or some especially grisly gang murder. The uniform du jour in these parts is open to interpretation, except for a bulletproof vest, which is absolutely nonnegotiable. Here, it's about survival of the fittest, which means razor-sharp instincts instead of creases, fully functional weaponry, and an encyclopedic knowledge of the patterns of a large and very cunning criminal population. Where spit and polish might go a long way in some districts, in others it's about blood and guts.

And while each district has its own idiosyncrasies, the department as a whole is a culture unto itself, with its own practices, traditions, even an arcane language indigenous to Chicago cops. In Chicago, nobody calls the bad guy "the perpetrator"—a term that's a little too Hollywood for Midwestern tastes. Why complicate things? The bad guy is called "the bad guy" or, for report writing, the "offender." The police car is a "squad," not a "cruiser" or a "prowler" or even a "blue-and-white." Prisoners are transported via "squadrol" or, if you're on the South Side, a "paddy wagon," a term derived from the early days of the department, when most of the force was of Irish extraction. Chicago cops use "billy clubs," although the image-conscious department has finally recognized the brutal implications of that term, and is now asking that we call them "nightsticks" instead. And Chicago cops pin a star on their chest, not a badge or a shield. A star on the chest, with a corresponding numbered shield on the uniform hat.

Chicago police don't use number codes in their communications, other than to say, "Ten-four" (for acknowledgment of a message received), or "Ten-one," which is a distress call asking for all available manpower immediately. Unlike other police departments, we don't respond to a two-eleven, decide where we'll eat our ten-fifty-three, or write tickets on a ten-ninety-three. In a rare flash of wisdom, the departmental powers that be decided that memorizing number codes was less important than watching our butts out on the street, and so they opted for simplicity in all radio communications.

During a visit to Chicago, one Los Angeles cop was fascinated by our lack of number coding.

"How do you tell the dispatcher you're going to lunch?" he wondered.

"We say, 'We're going to lunch.'"

"Wow! That's so *weird*!"

However quirky Chicago cops seem, they begin their career just like law-enforcement officers everywhere—with a grueling, intensive program at the Training Academy. It's a place designed to turn reasonably normal young men and women into cops, a place where dreams die and are born again, where illusions are trashed and replaced with a tenuous hold on reality, or *what's real in the eyes of the police department.*

Most recruits start out armed with resolve, bearing their polished morals as a weapon guaranteed to vanquish the evils of the world. They intend to be supercops: catch the bad guys, help the downtrodden, uphold truth, justice, and all that good stuff. Forget the lard-assed, cynical, doughnut-gulping slobs you see waddling around like paramilitary Pillsbury doughboys—the ones who'd write their own grandmothers a ticket if their wheelchairs went out of control.

Recruits begin their careers as a new breed. They aim to be the creme de la cops, find the lost kids, save hapless victims, receive a few thousand commendations, and annihilate all crime as we know it on planet Earth. *And* dazzle every uniform-loving coffee-shop waitress and cop groupie while they're doing it. Everyone loves a hero, right?

But what happens when you get out on the street and find out there's a whole different set of standards and rules than the ones they preached in the Academy? No one's playing fair out there—not even your brothers in blue—and you have to shift your game plan accordingly. All the clear-cut, black-and-white concepts of right and wrong that you've embraced all your life start to bleed together, shift from absolutes into confusing blobs.

You hit the streets a rookie virgin, secure in your grip on what's real, what's right. Three months into the job, you begin to question. One year later, you haven't a clue.

The job is an adventure: an adventure in staying alive, in keeping your sanity as well as a sense of humor, and in clinging to some last shred of hope that people are basically good—hard to do when you're up to your ass in the slime of humanity on a daily basis.

A cop's life has pathos and humor, danger and tragedy, slapstick comedy and situations so incredible that the average person would swear they were fiction.

I'm here to tell you they're not.

Part One

Learning

1

Twenty Years of Vaudeville and a Pension

1211:	1211.
Dispatcher:	1211 coming in?
1211	Yeah, Squad. Looks like we got a new bunch of recruits coming in. I'm parked outside the Academy, and there's a whole swarm of 'em standin' around outside.
Dispatcher:	How do you know they're recruits? Maybe there's an awards presentation going on or something.
1211:	Negative, Squad. These are definitely recruits. They all look too excited to be *real* police, and none of 'em are wearin' a piece.

Chicago's Near West Side, Spring 1982

The crowd packed in the gym bleachers is silent, all eyes focused on center court. A static apprehension rises up from several hundred too-warm bodies pressed together in mute anticipation. An NBA playoff game perhaps, in which the Bulls are preparing to gore their opponents? No. This is the Chicago Police Training Academy gym, and there's only one player on the floor: a tall man in a white uniform shirt who wears a gold star and a decided smirk and who, he tells us, is Sergeant Woods.

This is recruit orientation, day one of the twenty-three-week intensive training program designed to turn some of those huddled in the stands into police officers, flush out the unworthy, and provide everyone the experience of a lifetime. Sergeant Woods looks like just the guy to make it happen. A tall, tightly muscled man with a menacing grin and forearms that hint of an off-duty hobby of bench-pressing Buicks, he could be the poster boy for "The Good, the Bad, and the Malevolent."

He's taken it upon himself to pass along some tips and clues about being the *po*-lice. And promises to be there every step of the way, helping to turn this motley crew into bullet-biting, vinegar-pissing, kick-ass-and-take-names *real police,* aka "Chicago's Finest." As his captive audience, we're all ears as he offers the first Recruit Class of 1982 some words of welcome.

"All you muthafuckas, *listen up*!" he bellows, by way of opening remarks. "We ain't no babysitters here, so if any of y'all are babies, take your sorry asses outta here right now. And the only pussy I like is the kind I fuck, so if you the other kind, get out while you can."

Dead silence. No one dares to breathe.

"Awright, then. I assume the rest of you feel you the man for the job. Now I know we got some females in the bunch, so don't think you been overlooked. But on this job, there are no pussies, male or female. No police*men* or police*women*. Only thing we turn out here is police *officers;* and by the time you're finished with this program, *if* you finish it, you will all be trained to perform the job equally." He rocks back on his heels and allows this news to sink in.

"One thing you need to understand now, and for the rest of the time you on this job, is that you the

Man. And as long as you the Man, you a target. People gonna call you for help, but they gonna resent you while you helpin' 'em. Most folks don't like us; lot of 'em hate us. Get used to it. This job ain't no popularity contest. If you wanted that, you shoulda joined the fire department.

"And one thing you can take to the bank: Bullets are not gender specific. Bullets cross all racial barriers. If someone be shootin' at you, don't matter if you a man, woman, black, white, brown, ugly, cute, pretty—you are still in danger. You are still the *police*. There's a lot of folks out there want to see us dead and put considerable effort into makin' that happen."

Sergeant Woods is pacing now, scanning the rows of recruits. He stops and glares at a vampish Latina in the third row, improbably dressed in a red-sequined hoochie-mama dress. Miami Beach comes to the Heartland.

"For those of you who expect special consideration because you're female, I got news," he rumbles. "You can forget that shit right now. When you're out on the street with your partner, it ain't no date. You there to do a job, and you goddamn well better do it. When the shit starts flyin' out there, don't matter if you on your period, or you just had your nails done, you are in it together. Is that understood?" The sequined princess nods so hard her spangles rattle.

The sergeant's booming voice bounces off the gym walls as the "opening remarks" continue. We're informed that, in the police department hierarchy, recruits are lower than snake shit. We're the lowest of the low, the slimiest of the slime. If by chance we commit some infraction, we can be tossed out on our asses without a second chance. As recruits, we have no rights. The contract upheld by the police union [Fraternal Order of Police] can't protect us until we sweat through our one-year probationary period.

"From now on, anybody asks what you do for a living, tell 'em you a garbage collector." Woods smiles and makes a sweeping motion. "Cuz that's what we do. We clean up the garbage. Which is where your job security comes in, because there will *always* be garbage. You'll be called Nigger, Honky, Spic, Dago, Pork Chop, Kike, Polack, Muthafucka, and some names you never even heard before. Don't matter. It ain't nothin' personal. To civilians, you just a uniform and a star. So if any of y'all are sensitive types, best to drop that shit right now." His eyes narrow as he scans the crowd again.

"Here's some statistics for you to think about. Twenty-three weeks from now, only about sixty percent of you will still be here. So take a good look at the folks sittin' next to you, cuz they might not be here later on. For those of you who do make it, some will be promoted to sergeants, lieutenants, captains, even superintendent. Some may spend your whole career in a beat car. Of those who do make it outta here, about twenty-five percent of you won't live to retirement age. Some of you will be shot, stabbed, and most of you, if you out there doin' your job, can expect a few broken bones along the way. And from every recruit class, a few of you will get yourselves killed in the line of duty."

He pauses to let this somber news sink in.

"In case you had any doubts, this job can be a mother. It's dangerous, it's stressful, and it ain't like what you see on TV. Yeah, sometimes there's car chases and shoot-outs and chasing the bad guys, but there's also long stretches where it's boring as hell. A lot of nights where you go home and don't want to see another human being cuz you think they *all* full of shit. This job's gonna change the way you walk, the way you talk and think, even something as simple as sittin' in a restaurant. Your family and friends'll notice it at first, but when they tell you about it, you won't believe it. Cuz you can't see it. It's what the job does, and you don't even notice. But y'all are gonna see a whole different side of human nature that most folks just wouldn't believe, and that's a show in itself. What y'all just got yourself is twenty years of vaudeville and a pension!"

Sergeant Woods instructs us to line up to receive our star numbers and turn in our health forms. It's a chance to check out some of my fellow recruits, get an idea of the people with whom I'll be sweating through the next few months. We're a disparate bunch, to say the least.

Hulking, tattooed bodybuilders lumber along with pinstriped, bespectacled types who look fresh out of the halls of academia. Women who could be librarians, housewives, waitresses, exotic dancers. Some tough-guy wannabes in torn T-shirts, sizing up the room while they chomp on toothpicks. Quite a few of these people look like they're on work release from Cook County Jail.

This is the only day we're allowed to wear street clothes. Starting tomorrow, we'll all be in the khaki twill uniform shirt and pants of the Academy recruit. On this last day of fashion freedom, some of the assembled have decided to make a statement. I see dapper suits, torn jeans, prim dresses straight from June Cleaver's wardrobe. Stained sweats, cleavage-baring tops, and enough miniskirts to look like "the

Rockettes do the Midwest." Stiletto heels mix with wingtips, knee-high boots clomp along behind the latest in athletic shoes. Last chance to grandstand, since tomorrow begins uniforms, unisex, unidrab.

Sergeant Woods is seated at a folding table now with Officer Vestry, his blue-shirted, buck-toothed assistant. In case his opening remarks didn't do the trick, Woods offers a few personalized comments to each recruit, just to make us feel at home.

He glares at the paperwork offered by the bookish young man in front of me.

"You got sickle-cell, nigger?"

The nervous recruit almost pees his pants.

"N-no, sir."

"Look like one of them sickle-cell muthafuckas to me. Why you wanna be the *po*-lice, man?"

"I . . . I want to help people, sir."

"Look like the type been helpin' yourself to other people's shit for years. You ever do time for any burglary?"

"No, sir."

"So if I run your prints, you ain't gonna come back wanted in fifty-two states?"

"No, sir."

"I can't hear you!"

"*No, sir!*"

"No, sir, *what*?"

"No, sir, I ain't gonna come back wanted in fifty-two states!"

The sergeant smirks. "Well, man, that was your first test in bein' the *po*-lice, and you flunked. Everybody knows there's only fifty-one states in the union."

I step up to the table. And notice the fearsome scar that claws its way down the sergeant's left cheek from ear to chin.

"This here your correct weight?"

"Yes, sir." Does he think I'd have the nerve to lie? This isn't the DMV!

"And you five-feet-nine?"

"Yes, sir."

Woods and Vestry exchange a look.

"You one tall drink of water. Mostly in the legs, looks like. Y'all got some long legs, girl."

Yawning silence. I'm beginning to fidget under their Neanderthal scrutiny.

"You married, Officer?"

"Divorced, sir."

"Why come? You don't like dick?"

". . . Sir?"

"You a muff diver? You go down that beaver trail?"

"No, sir."

"Good. Be a shame to waste all that talent." He adds my forms to the pile and winks. "You'll do okay, Officer. Just remember it ain't nothin' but a party, long as you know how to play the game. Keep your eyes open and your mouth shut. What you do with your legs is up to you."

As I walk away, I overhear a recruit talking to one of the friendlier officers who's slouched in the bleachers, checking out the new blood.

"That's a hell of a scar the sergeant has!" the recruit says. "Must have seen a lot of rough duty, huh?"

"Yeah. He got that from a ten-dollar whore."

"Tough Vice arrest?"

"Nah. He just forgot to pay her."

2

How to Build a Cop

Dispatcher:	1212? Beat 1212?
1212	'12.
Dispatcher:	'12, take a ride over to the Training Academy, transport an injured person to U. of I. Hospital ER. Name is Dawson.
1212:	They beating up the recruits again?
Dispatcher:	Ten-four. Says here he'll be waiting for you by the front desk.
1212:	They're really goin' easy on the new kids these days.
Dispatcher:	How's that?
1212:	Back when I was going through, the only ways we got taken out were by ambulance—or undertaker!

The Police Academy Training Program lasts for twenty-three weeks. Any illusions the recruits harbor about their new profession are shot to hell in considerably less time. The program is meant to be a combination crash course in street survival tempered with a heavy dose of criminal and municipal law classes so that, in the event you have a clue which law's been violated, you'll have a fair-to-middling chance of effecting the arrest and living to tell about it. Hopefully.

The task of devising the curriculum for building a

cop belongs to the guys in Research and Development. Imagine the brainstorming they must have done before they came up with a game plan. The program should be realistic enough to represent the same situations cops encounter on the street. Gritty, fast-paced, with enough macho esprit de corps thrown in to give an elitist flavor to the grunt work you're doing—like the Marines, only here, no one's running around yelling, "Semper fi!"

There should be equal amounts of scholarship (endless law classes and exercises in report-writing class, to make sure everyone knows how to write a complete sentence) and physical conditioning—gotta make sure these young pups are in shape when they hit the streets, and, oh yeah, better see that they know which end of a weapon is up, so throw in some firearms training and plenty of hours on the shooting range. And for those sticky situations when you run into some crazed three-hundred-pound felon who's amped out of his mind on crystal meth, some defensive-tactics classes might be a good idea.

On paper, the program looks good. In theory, it sounds great. And, to the credit of the department, it answers a lot of questions about the job. But the only real way this stuff will stick is to experience it on the streets. You can memorize theories and techniques ad nauseam but when someone's up in your face and terror is clawing at your back, it's a whole different story.

In the Academy, the closest thing to actual street experience is the veteran cops who swagger through the halls, bragging and griping and always, always telling improbable war stories—the police version of the fish story. In each telling, the bad guy gets a little bigger, a lot meaner, armed with enough weaponry to make Operation Desert Storm a one-day war game. The cop in question is always heroic, fighting to the finish, and always incurs some heinous injury so unspeakable that he's given little chance to survive, much less recover. But, what's a little maiming, a few crushed internal organs when you're the *real po*-lice? It's all part of the job, so you take it like a pro, and not only recover, but have some nifty scars to flash next time you're tipping suds in some cop bar and the war stories start spinning. (*"Oh, yeah? You think that's bad? Take a look at this one—three hundred forty-seven stitches and a metal plate!"*)

As recruits, we have nothing to add since we've never been there, and our comments are neither invited nor welcome. The only thing we can do is bide our time, watch these guys and listen, and heed Sergeant Woods's excellent advice: "Keep your eyes open and your mouth shut."

The teaching positions at the Academy are filled by police sworn personnel—officers, sergeants, an occasional lieutenant or two, who've been on the street at some point in their careers but are now assigned to the Academy. It's a much-coveted and cushy gig—straight days, weekends and holidays off, the kind of dream assignment where you can actually have a life outside the job. There's no mandatory court appearances, no depositions or grand-jury testimonies you're obligated to give on what's supposed to be your own time, no dealing with the unsavory elements of the public we serve. The only injuries instructors encounter within the Academy walls are paper cuts, the bane of desk jockeys everywhere, or the occasional pulled muscle from a lunchtime basketball game in the Academy gym. As we're quick to learn, departmental dream assignments don't fall like manna from heaven. Forget education or qualifications—for this type of assignment, you have to be "heavy," i.e., have some serious clout. In the New York City Police Department, it's called "having a rabbi." In Chicago, the question is, "Who's your Chinaman?"

A "Chinaman" is a sponsor, someone of considerable influence, like a politician, district commander, deputy superintendent, who's reached out to put you in a favored position. That's the polite definition. The actual answer is someone you're related to, have bought votes for, have fucked blind, or caught in such a compromising position that public exposure would be the end of their career; so they'll do whatever it takes to keep you happy. And silent.

Generally, the Academy staff is a self-satisfied, privileged lot who are willing to be congenial with the newest batch of recruits. Who wouldn't be? Most days they can come to work in a Hawaiian shirt and jeans if the mood strikes, have a captive audience for their bad jokes and war stories, get to play basketball or work out in the Academy gym, *and* select from any number of nubile young female recruits who learn early that the penis is a useful lever with which to propel themselves upward through the ranks. (More on that later.)

From this seasoned group of instructors, we learn the important stuff that somehow didn't make it into the curriculum syllabus. Like the most important law of the Department: "CYA" (Cover Your Ass). For all screwups, great and small, you should have the facility to cover yourself and, hopefully, your partner, and explain your way out of *anything*, no matter what the circumstances. In short, if you step in shit, you'd better be able to dance your way out of it.

There's a catch-all violation in the Department General Orders (that's your basic rules and regs) called "conduct unbecoming a sworn officer." When all else fails and some boss wants to nail you, that's the one they'll cite. It can apply to anything from being seen in a bar in uniform to instructing an overamorous instructor to go take a flying fuck. And if there's a complaint made by a citizen, such as the public's favorite, "police brutality," you might be seeing some suspension time or worse. Who wants an indictment when you can model yourself after the veteran cops who have developed a talent for "creative imagining." Cover your ass.

When it comes time to write the first of many reports explaining your actions (to your immediate supervisor, the district commander, even the fun folks from Internal Affairs), the prudent officer will begin with the time-honored statement: "Reporting officer has no knowledge . . ." That means no knowledge of the incident, no knowledge of any guilty action, especially your own. The concern is not how plausible your alibi sounds but rather, whether the powers that be will buy it. Best-case scenario is writing a report that will exonerate you from all pending charges, even if it means relating that you went into a fugue state and your memory has been out to lunch from the Reagan administration to the present. Covering your ass has nothing to do with honesty, integrity, or even conscience. It's simply a way to steer clear of bullshit and make it through to collect your pension more or less intact.

We learn firsthand that sex is a negotiable form of currency within the department. Faith may move mountains, but on this job, we discover that there are some officers who believe it doesn't hurt to offer additional . . . qualities. And they rationalize it by saying it's all about looking at the big picture: the span of an average police career. If the police department is a family, there are those of the opinion that "incest is best" judging by the untold number of officers who've been promoted, decorated, or, in general, managed to keep their butts out of a sling by resorting to a few close encounters of the most personal kind. We're not talking about sex with co-workers, a lateral move that would fall into the category of a "recreational" or "buddy" fuck. Just like other major business arenas, the sheer number of people employed by the department means that there will be a percentage who choose to curry favor and guarantee career boosts by interaction of the most intimate nature. These people believe that, if you want to move up, you have to go down first, on your knees or your back, and preferably with someone wearing enough bars to open doors for you. This does not fall into the category of sexual harassment, since the favors are offered freely by opportunistic officers eager to get ahead. And the percentage of those who do is high enough to cast a dispiriting pall on those of us who struggle for career advancement the old-fashioned way—by working for it.

In the interest of preserving the department's equal-opportunity policy, it's not just the females on their knees. The play-for-pay policy applies to all genders—even those unspecified. Some male cops have no qualms about hitting on female supervisors, if it would be to their professional benefit. There are a lot of women in supervisory positions who've been offered the same sexual perks as their male counterparts. Since female officers have only begun to obtain positions of significant rank (at the rank of commander or above) within the past ten years, this type of situation is both novel and unsettling. Just when female cops have come to grips with what it takes to function in a "man's profession," *and* made rank besides, they're faced with the same sexual land mines men have faced for years. Whether or not they accept is less important than the message conveyed: Sex can be a strong persuader, as powerful as money and less expensive. Whether motivated by desperation, greed, or lust for power, some officers believe it's the last-ditch ticket to get ahead.

During the Academy's intensive physical-training program, the recruits are required to complete, within a certain time limit, an obstacle course that includes scaling a 6'6" wall. It's made of flat, smooth wood with no foothold-friendly niches anywhere on its surface. The men simply run up to it, jump high, and use their arms to vault themselves over. But for some of the women, who are shorter, or bottom-heavy, or don't have much upper-body strength, the wall presents a problem. If you don't get over the wall, you don't complete the obstacle course. And if you don't complete the obstacle course, you don't graduate. That's what it says on the books.

There are ways to beat it, of course. A lot of women commit to arriving at the gym every morning at 6:00 A.M. for the "Breakfast Club": two hours of weight training and exercises designed to build enough strength to get them over the wall. It's a grueling schedule and punishing work—especially when you're expected to be showered, dressed in full uniform, and assembled, at attention, for morning roll call at 0800 hours—when the day begins officially—a day that will include a full complement of regular physical training, with a guaranteed three- to five-mile run thrown in just to keep you on your toes. And when the day grinds to an end at 4:00 P.M., these same determined Breakfast Clubbers will head back to the gym for another hour or two of workouts, and practice runs on the wall. It requires a lot of sweat, determination, and endurance, but nobody ever said it was going to be easy. If sweat and grit are what it takes, so be it.

For some people.

Others try a New Age approach. They opt for meditation, mental visualization, and some even go for hypnosis. It works for smokers, why not the wall? And then there are those who decide on what, for them, seems to be the easiest method. They get down on their knees, but not to pray for a miracle. And offer something a bit more personal, considerably less sweaty, and guaranteed to win friends and influence erections. And come graduation day, everyone makes it through.

A lot of the subject matter included in the training program can be somber and downright frightening. So much of it is crammed into such a short period of time, attention spans have been known to short out. It's easy to glaze over, become numbed by the onslaught of information, especially in the classes scheduled right after physical training, when your body's dragging and your mind is not far behind. With this in mind, the teaching staff makes an effort to present the material in creative ways. Whatever works as long as the point is made.

During a class discussion on street stops and searches, the instructor asks for three volunteers. By now, most of us have learned the first unwritten law of all military organizations: "*Never* volunteer."

Since the department considers itself a paramilitary organization, the same rule applies. But there are still a few recruits whose eagerness, or desire to preen overshadow lessons learned. When they join him at the podium, he produces three glass vials containing a white substance.

"You've just stopped Joe Citizen on the street," the instructor says gravely. "You search him and find these vials of powder. How do you identify the substances?" He places the vials on the desk and points to the first volunteer.

"You think you can identify these substances, Officer?"

"Yes, *sir*!" The recruit uncaps the first vial and, in his best *Miami Vice* imitation, dips his pinkie dramatically into the powder, and then licks it.

"This one's salt, sir." He repeats the process with the second vial.

"This one's sugar." By now the recruit's face is bloated with pride in his investigative prowess. But a taste of the third vial has him frowning. He tastes once, twice, and then again, but he still looks puzzled.

"I can't place this one," he admits finally. "Baking soda, maybe?"

The second and third volunteers repeat the process. They both taste the salt and sugar, but repeated licks of vial three's substance are inconclusive.

Throughout this testing, the instructor remains silent, impassive. And waits until all three recruits have finished before returning to the podium.

"First, I want to thank the volunteers who were brave enough to come up here. It takes courage to show your stupidity to a crowd." His smile stretches into a grimace as he glares at the class.

"Never, never, *never* taste anything!" he screams,

pounding the table for emphasis. "You don't know what kind of shit it is—for all you know, it could be poison, and you'd be three dead motherfuckers right now!" His eyes sweep the aisles. "This ain't Hollywood, people. Forget what you see on TV. Nobody with half a brain's going to taste *anything*—that's what the police lab is for. A very important thing to remember, if you want to stay alive. And just to make sure you do, here's something to help you remember." He reaches for the vials and holds them up to the class.

"Every time we do this class, the volunteers always taste it. *Always!* So, in the first two vials, we put substances that will be easy to recognize; salt and sugar. But in the third one, we wanted something different. Something easy to get, something white, something you'd remember for the rest of your career. And, people, sometimes when you're looking for something, the answer just drops out of the sky." With a snicker, he gestures toward the classroom windows which face the Academy courtyard, where pigeons swoop and flutter, dive-bombing the decorative statue.

"Oh, *shit*!" moans one of the volunteers, clutching her mouth.

"Exactly!" The instructor laughs, and gathers up his books. "Anyone who wants seconds can adjourn to the courtyard. The rest of you, have a nice day."

Firearms Training is the highlight of each day. There's a classroom segment that teaches you about the weapons you'll be using, how they work, how to use them, clean them, even what to do with them when you're on duty and nature calls. Which sounds ludicrous—until you think about it. Most cops working a beat car use public restrooms. In the interest of convenience, hygiene, and safety, what do you do with a thirty-pound equipment belt (holding weapon and holster, handcuffs, radio and speed loaders) while you're using the facilities? None of us have thought about that until our instructor mentions that an unfortunate number of cops have managed to shoot themselves in the leg—or worse—while indisposed.

After the classroom training, we hit the range for firing practice. We fire at paper targets in timed intervals and at variable distances. It's a standard combat-shooting course designed to teach us how to fire quickly, with accuracy and at a moving target. Holding a ten-pound piece of steel with the power to stop a bad guy cold—forever—is disconcerting, at first. Once we strap our gun belts on, our instructors tell us, we're armed and dangerous, and we should accord our weapons the proper respect. The gun feels foreign at first, a cold, heavy reminder of death hanging on your hip. But after a while, you realize that someday, the only thing standing between you and the grave will be your own instincts and Smith & Wesson. After that, you blast away at the man-shaped targets without batting an eye.

The firing range is the class that changes us. In Physical Training, we sweat through long-distance runs and endless calisthenics, laugh at the hokey judo positions our kung fu–wannabe instructor demonstrates in Defensive Tactics, and grab-ass during the simulated crime-scene reenactments. But on the range, we're dead serious. In the other classes, you can fudge on the answers. Here, one mistake could be the last. No one learns that quicker than Booker Dubois.

A former maintenance man with a thick, lumpish

body, Booker is a quiet guy who keeps to himself. He struggles through the classroom work, barely scraping by on the weekly tests. Applied academics never came easy for him, but what he lacks in scholarship, he makes up in heart. His dream is to move his wife and baby daughter out of the projects, away from the crime and violence, to a quiet residential neighborhood where his family can grow and his dreams can be realized. This job is just the ticket. So he swallows the taunts from gym instructors aggravated by his lumbering gait (*"Let's go, Fat-ass! Pick 'em up and put 'em down! You'd hold up a one-car funeral!"*) and the snipes of snotty classroom teachers (*"The next test will be on Monday. Hopefully, Dubois will have mastered his ABCs by then"*). He keeps to himself, doing the best he can do, and praying, like the rest of us, that he'll make it through these twenty-three weeks.

One day on the range, he comes close to blowing his dream.

We're lined up on the firing line, each in our own shooter's cubicle with weapons ready, earmuffs on, protective goggles in place. It's the usual drill. We hold six bullets in our hands which, on command, we will load in our weapon, assume the firing stance, and shoot at our moving targets. At the completion of the exercise, our targets will be collected and graded by the range instructors.

On this particular day, Booker is tired. Because of his size and limited coordination, he still hasn't made it over the wall, so he's the only male member of the Breakfast Club. Reporting for a daily 6:00 A.M. gym regimen is hard enough, but Booker's got other problems. His wife's recovering from an appendectomy, so Booker's doing the housework, the shopping and laundry, the child care. His daughter, who recently turned one, had a fever last night, which kept him up through most of it, administering cool compresses, soothing and rocking and worrying until dawn.

Now, on the range, he's completely exhausted, a mass of jittery nerves. In his cubicle near the end of the firing line, he steps into position, unholsters his weapon, and waits. When a piercing whistle sounds (the command to load weapons), he flinches, just enough to send the bullets in his trembling hand bouncing to the floor and downrange.

Booker doesn't think twice. If he doesn't load, he doesn't shoot, which means scoring a zero for today's work. He can't afford to fail any class, so he dives downrange after the bullets, making himself an open target for a few he hadn't planned on. Live rounds whistle all around his shambling body. At first, nobody can hear the instructor screaming—not with our earmuffs on and the deafening thunder of gunfire. But when the red emergency light flares on— never a good sign—we lower our weapons and wait to see who fucked up this time.

The range instructors—all five of them—are down at cubicle two, towering over Booker, who's sprawled on the floor. Even with our earmuffs, we can hear their screaming now, some top-notch swearing that would definitely qualify them as contenders in Obscenity Olympics. Suffice to say, they're not pleased. For Booker's part, his quaking would qualify for a six-pointer on the Richter scale, and the seeping puddle around him means he's taken an unscheduled restroom break.

But it's his shirt we're all gaping at. There are holes in it, singed-edged circles in the regulation khaki cotton courtesy of some .38 caliber slugs. Unceremoniously, the instructors rip Booker's shirt off. The Academy administration frowns on recruit execution. If Booker's dead, *somebody's* going to be writing paper for days.

"Oh, you rotten motherfucker! You miserable bucket of whale blubber!" The instructor's fervent moan bounces off the range walls. In copspeak, he's just conveyed his feelings of profound relief. Booker isn't dead. Miraculously, he isn't even injured, except for a few skid marks made by bullets that went through his voluminous shirt, skinned along the surface of his arms and back, and exited through another part of the shirt. And since Booker *isn't* dead, he'll be the one who's writing reports, about his stupidity, his incompetence, and anything else the instructors can think of.

"Don't worry about it," I whisper after the raging instructors have finally stomped off.

"I fucked up bad this time!" Booker groans, rolling his eyes. "They're *never* gonna let me forget this."

"Forget them!" I advise, with all the departmental wisdom these few weeks will allow. "You're alive— that's all that matters. It's a miracle you weren't killed. That means you're destined for big things on this job!" I help him collect his scattered ammo, give him some blank targets to hold over his soiled slacks while he goes to his locker. "Just wait and see, Booker. Someday these guys will be calling you 'Boss.'"

Booker is unconvinced. "It's what they're gonna call me *now* that worries me. Like maybe 'ex-recruit.'"

"Not a chance. What makes you think these guys are such rocket scientists? They had any brains, they'd be firemen!" It's a flimsy joke, given the circumstances. But it's enough to forge a friendship that lasts for the duration of our careers.

The weeks pass, and with them come changes in all of us. Almost without realizing it, our class develops a cohesiveness, a sense of camaraderie and fraternity that many of us have never experienced before. The Booker incident brings us all together, makes everyone realize that it could have happened to any of us. If Booker, or anyone, receives a punishment—ten extra laps around the Academy, an extra hour of calisthenics—we *all* do it. Some of the guys volunteer to work with the Breakfast Clubbers and one glorious morning, every one of them, Booker included, fly over the wall and through the rest of the obstacle course to the cheers of a couple hundred recruits. Our solidarity is unshakable, which surprises us and secretly satisfies our instructors. It was supposed to happen all along. Good practice, we're told, for when we're on the street, partnered with another uniform who's responsible for watching our backs. It's the beginning of the "us versus them" mentality, but we don't recognize it yet. At this point, it just feels like the closeness of shared trauma. Like any army vet who considers his platoon his family.

After the first week, we all learned why each other is here. Some Research and Development genius got the idea to have a class early in the program where each recruit stands up and recites why he wants to be the *po*-lice. Some of the answers are the expected drivel: to save lives, stop the bad guys, help people, blah, blah. Some are refreshingly honest: a good way to meet women, because their other job sucked, so they'll never have to get another traffic ticket again. And there's a core group with reasons, like mine, that don't even hint of a need for glamour, glory, or grit: families to support, a better way to pay the bills, get the benefits package. Not to mention job security. There will always be bad guys.

From some classmates, I learn a whole new meaning of "determination." Like Booker, they want this job and will allow no one—and nothing—to interfere with them getting it. One guy, who'd been gangbanging with the Latin Kings since before puberty, had all his gang tattoos laser-removed before his police physical. And, when filling out the job application form, covered his ass like a champ by listing his hobbies as community volunteer work and scripture study at the Moody Bible Institute.

One woman was told she was too fat to be admitted to the program. Weight must be proportionate to height and, while there are no minimum height requirements, you can be rejected for being overweight. But the doctor giving the physical was a wheezy old fossil, with rheumy eyes nearly invisible behind pop-bottle glasses, who wasn't overly concerned about details . . . none that he could *see,* anyway. During the physical, each recruit's height and weight were recorded by an equally ancient nurse and recited to Dr. Fossil, who then either approved or rejected the applicant.

The recruit in question was 5'3" tall and weighed 167 pounds. She also was a single parent with four kids to support, and she'd just given up an assembly-line factory job to be the police. She decided that no half-blind, befuddled insurance-risk of a doctor was going to stand between her and a new career. She rescheduled her physical and got a plan. And showed up in the doctor's office wearing a wig that put Dolly Parton's to shame. A wig that she'd stuffed with layers of folded paper towels, adding inches to her height. The nurse weighed her: 167 pounds. And then measured her height, and recorded her official Civil Service Physical Exam height as 5'7¾"— within acceptable limits for her weight. The recruit was admitted to the program—another fine example of "creative imagery" in action.

From our seasoned veteran instructors, we learn by example the importance of having a game face. The one that allows you to appear detached and impassive no matter what you're feeling inside. Useful to have when the district commander trips over his own lead feet while conducting a uniform inspection and tumbles ass-over-teacups at your feet. Or when the extremely pregnant woman who's flagged down your car decides, why wait for an ambulance? Have the baby on the hood of the squad. Or when you're handling a traffic accident where the injured passengers are screaming about their baby. Baby? There's no baby . . . just blood and carnage and the twisted remains of crumpled vehicles. And then you discover a tiny torso impaled on a fence post across the street, where, on impact, it flew like a projected missile because Mom and Dad never got around to getting an infant car seat.

In Crime Scene Investigation class, we're clustered in groups, examining sheaves of 8×10 glossies taken of suicides. Our instructor strolls from group to group, adding his comments, gauging our reactions. We're all horrified, and sickened, and perversely fascinated by the grisly photos. Some of them are so graphic, it's hard to fight back the nausea.

When the instructor reaches our group, we're examining a shotgun suicide. A headless corpse is sprawled in a chair, with lifeless hands still gripping the shotgun that rests on a bloody chest. In the background, gore and skull fragments are splattered across the wall like macabre modern art. Next to the corpse is a table holding a half-full liter bottle of Pepsi and a submarine sandwich with one bite missing.

"Anything you can figure out by looking at this picture?" the instructor asks.

We study it more intensely. Must have been a fairly young guy, someone says, judging by the clothes and shoes. A Caucasian male, another says, pointing to the hands.

"But what's the most important thing?" the instructor asks. We're clueless. There must be something here we're missing, something only seasoned cop eyes can see. A suicide note in some shadowed corner? Some nearly indiscernible sign of foul play?

The instructor huffs at our green ignorance.

"Jeez, you guys, it's obvious. See that sandwich there? One bite, right? The most important thing would be to find out where this sorry bastard bought it. Any place sells sandwiches bad enough to make somebody blow their brains out, I'd take a pass on it, wouldn't you?" He strolls off, whistling, to the next group. *Game face*.

In the classroom, the goal is to train our minds. In Defensive Tactics, they train our bodies. The instructors here are all buff, with rock-hard pecs and biceps straining against their CPD instructor T-shirts. They swagger around the gym like exaggerated superheroes just dropped in from the latest bodybuilding competition for a little light diversion, like crushing the bones of a bunch of pathetic recruits. Since we're a captive audience, there's nothing we can do but go along with the program, try to remain physically intact, and *never* volunteer for a demonstration. After the first week, you'd have to be blind or dead not to realize that these guys are sadists, and they're not satisfied until they've seen blood flow, definitely not their own.

Their specialty—"defensive training skills"—is a polite title used to include all variations of physical torture that feed their blood lust. They challenge the recruits to a little one-on-one combat, encourage them to fight back, insist that they do, but it's a fool's game. Who's willing to gamble a passing grade for a few seconds of salvaged pride? In other arenas, these guys would be called bullies, sadists, even felons. Here, their job description includes doing what they love most: hurting people, and making them hurt each other. It takes some of us longer than others to catch on.

For the most part, the women figure it out right away. Volunteer? Don't think so. Move to the back of the line, look as inconspicuous as possible. Allow the instructor to demonstrate a hold on you? Not today—maybe next millennium. All it took was one incident with Cassandra Rivera to put us wise.

Cassandra, a sinewy little Puerto Rican girl, spent hours in the gym and prided herself on her athleticism. So when the instructor asked for a volunteer to demonstrate a "come-along"—a type of pain-inducing hold on the hand used to get the assailant to move with you, without giving the *appearance* of exerting force—Cassandra rushed forward. She was strong, she figured, enough of an athlete to handle whatever the behemoth instructor dished out. But athleticism is different than brute force, a particular specialty of this instructor.

Sizing up her wiry 105-pound body, he nearly laughed. And decided to make things interesting by putting a different spin on the demonstration: a come-along coupled with a throw. Before Cassandra saw it coming, he snatched her arm in his meaty paws. The sickening snap of bones was followed almost immediately by a resounding *thwack*: Cassandra landing facedown, five feet away from her leering opponent.

In the months that followed, she tried to be philosophical about it. She'd always hated her nose anyway, she told us later, so when the doctors did the surgical reconstruction, she asked if they could make it different. And her arm and hand—once the pins were removed she was almost certain to have full usage again. It was only the nerve damage in the neck that was a problem. It made her *other* hand clench and spasm, twitching uncontrollably for no reason. She'd never be able to handle a weapon with a hand like that, so of course she had to leave the program. Which was just as well, she said, grinning bravely over her neck brace when we visited her in the hospital. Finding uniforms in a size two had been a real bitch! Which shows you what this job does. Not even a veteran cop, and the girl's already got her game face.

Even after Cassandra's accident, some of our male counterparts didn't get the message. Their instinct is to fight, jump in eagerly whenever called. Spar with an instructor? No problem. Let them demonstrate a choke hold? Why not? To them, the instructors are a force to be challenged. Call it macho posturing or testosterone overload, but not a day goes by without another cocky guy being carried, bloody or unconscious or both, off the floor.

When not breaking bones, the instructors content themselves with teaching us a lot of completely useless but very theatrical judo holds and stances that would look impressive if cameras were rolling (and which we discover, later, that nobody *ever* uses on the street). Who's got time to be Bruce Lee when bullets are flying?

We're taught how to approach the bad guy, and then, partnered in pairs, they teach us how to speed-cuff, how to take away the weapon of an armed man. I wisely team with Booker for these lessons. Neither of us has any macho showboating to work out, and we're both motivated by the same reason: to get out of the Academy, preferably alive. When the instructors leap around, all bulging muscles and flashing handcuffs, it looks impressive. It looks impossible. But then I think of the huge wall in the Police Headquarters lobby hung with the stars of officers slain in the line of duty, which is enough to keep my attention focused on the next demonstration.

My brain tells me what works for a bodybuilder-instructor in the Academy gym will translate differently for a female cop on the street. My instincts say even more. In a cop's life, survival is not a question of form over function—choreographed battle stances and fancy moves. It's about doing whatever it takes, whatever works. Lessons that can't begin until you're out there doing it.

3

Green in Blue

Dispatcher:	922? Beat 922?
922:	'22.
Dispatcher:	You workin' alone today, Manny?
922:	Negative, Squad. I got me a brand-new recruit to work with.
Dispatcher:	Better be on your best behavior, then. Don't teach him any bad habits.
922:	It's a *her,* Squad. I'm riding with a lady cop today.
Unidentified Unit:	Ask her if she does windows.

I hardly recognize myself. This can't be me reflected in the mirror, all trimmed out in spotless blues, with a star, a name tag, and a Smith & Wesson .357 Magnum hanging off my hip on a leather gun belt so new it squeaks. All my hair's been pinned up and hidden under the precisely angled uniform hat. No jewelry, very little makeup, and even my nails have been trimmed and stripped of their usual colored polish. It's definitely the unisex look, or maybe an asexual law-enforcer image, but as far as I'm concerned this is overkill on the "butch" look. Even my shoes—utilitarian black leather oxfords buffed to a dull sheen—look like they belong on a milkman. I feel like a pretender, like a kid playing dress-up, except that being the police was a fantasy that never occurred to me back in the days of hopscotch and Barbies. Somehow I managed to make it through the Academy, and now it's first-day jitters all over again: my first day on the street.

Along with five other recruits from my class, including Booker, I've been assigned to a South Side district, which will be my training district for the next six months. This begins the second half of our probationary period: the field experience. Only after the successful completion of six months on the street will we be allowed to graduate and become "real" cops. It's a political district known for its clout-wielding city workers, aldermen, and block captains who guard their turf, and their connections, like rabid rottweilers. The infamous Chicago Stockyards are located here, as is Comiskey Park, venerated bastion of South Side sports and home of the White Sox.

My stomach does a quick flip-flop when I walk into the squad room for roll call. I'm the first female recruit assigned here in over three years, and I know every jaundiced eye is on me as I take a seat. A quick glance tells me there's mostly old-timers here, guys who've been on the job longer than I've been alive. The type who still believe the department is one big boys' club and women are only good for one thing, and it *isn't* toting a gun. There's no game faces now. These veteran cops are staring openly at me, measuring. Thinking "new kid" because I'm a recruit, "fresh meat" because I'm female. The sea of faces is impassive, but the thoughts reflected in their hooded eyes are obvious.

"Greenhorn," says one pair.

"Snot-nosed kid," says another. And "Check out the tits." The first strike against me is beyond my control: I'm a female and, until I prove otherwise, I'm just here for decoration.

Prior to leaving the Academy, a female instructor was kind enough to gather up the women in her class and give us some idea of what to expect when we went out to our training districts. The younger male cops were more enlightened about women on the job, she said, and had no problems accepting us as coworkers and fellow officers. But there were still enough of the "old school" cops who didn't want to work with women, or whose wives didn't want them to work with women, or simply believed that female cops are groupies in uniform. A mind-set that allowed them to treat the women in the ranks with varying degrees of contempt, or disdain, or blatant and crude sexual overtures. We were cautioned to expect it all: the come-ons, the innuendos, even the interrogation by male partners about our sex lives. It happened all the time, the instructor told us, and was so prevalent that the guys accepted it as standard procedure. We were cops, but we were female, which made us sexual objects to be questioned, and explored. How far we allowed that to progress would be solely up to the individual.

Now, sitting among the probing male eyes, I try to be inconspicuous. No one offers a return smile, a word of welcome, so I sit and wait . . . and wonder what this day will be like. Just seconds before roll call begins, Booker comes lumbering in, perspiring openly as he awkwardly juggles his flashlight, report case, and citation book. His hat brim is pulled down so low I can't see his eyes, but his fumbling hands show a serious case of first-day nerves. I want to smile at him, send a silent signal to reassure him that we'll be okay; but he moves to the farthest corner chair, away from the clustered men, and sits ramrod stiff, staring straight ahead. It's a relief to know he's here. Even though we won't be working together, at least we're on the same watch, a quiet little cheering section for each other.

My assigned FTO (field training officer) is off today, so I'm paired with a short Mexican guy named Manny. He's amused by my brand-new blues and my greenhorn status and, although heightwise he hits me at nipple level, he's determined to take me under his protective wing and ease me through first-day jitters.

In the squad car, he proceeds to fill me in on "The District According to Manny." Flashing a gold tooth, he expounds on all the points of interest every cop should know. The best place for chili. Which Dunkin' Donuts has the freshest crullers, the freshest waitresses. ("Uh, sorry, hon. That's stuff the guys always want to know.") The ten-percent police discount they give at the corner drugstore. Avoid a certain watch commander who hates female coppers. Avoid another one who loves them. And if I plan to fool around with anyone in the district, I should be discreet about it. People talk. Just something he tells all the girls coming on the job, he says. The male cops can be dogs. Fool around with more than one of them, and you get a rep as the district punchboard. Oh, and just so I know, my name's already up on the district men's room wall. Not meant to be malicious, just the way things are. Something they do with all the broads.

I silently bless the female instructor for her warnings and predictions. Not twenty minutes into this first day, and already my partner is deep in the "boys' club" mentality. Even though he smiles often

and his conversation is deceptively friendly, I realize
that Manny is one of those who can't quite accept
females as cops. His comments over the next hour
carry a clear message: If you're a woman—
specifically a woman in uniform—then you're a
bimbo. Until the bullets start flying—and then you
damn well better turn into a cop. But once there's a
cease-fire, it's back to being a bimbo.

Manny's on a roll now. He don't like workin' with
women usually—'specially if they're short. Ankle
biters, he calls 'em. (Manny himself is vertically
challenged—only about 5'4", but apparently his
prejudice doesn't apply to men. The department's
height requirement was dropped years ago. Uncon-
stitutional, someone charged. Everyone should have
the right to get their asses blown to kingdom come,
regardless of how short they are.) Now, Manny's
eyes slide appraisingly across my lap, and the gold
tooth flashes again. Tall women are okay, he smiles.
I look like I can handle myself. The two of us, we're
gonna work out just fine.

The early-morning sun spills a pale wash of light
on commuters heading out for rush hour. Manny is
oblivious to the traffic, rolling along sedately as he
continues his running commentary. We glide down
the streets of our beat, a hardscrabble, blue-collar
neighborhood where tiny bungalows and two-flats
crowd cheek-by-jowl along narrow tree-lined streets.
It's a neighborhood with as much political infamy
as New York's Tammany Hall. Once the turf of Irish
stockyard workers, the area is now the home of Hispanics, Asians, and an assortment of gangs that fester in the close quarters like open wounds. Very
recently, enterprising developers attempted to gen-
trify the neighborhood by erecting rows of town

houses aimed at the upper-income yuppie consumer market. But because the Bridgeport natives refuse to be budged, the project has had only tepid results.

We cut over to Bridgeport, the home of the late Mayor Daley, whose family still lives here. The Daley bungalow on South Lowe Street is a tidy yellow brick that still has a twenty-four-hour police-guard detail assigned to protect his widow, Eleanor "Sis" Daley. It's a gravy detail, Manny informs me, pointing to the unmarked police cars parked in front of the house and in the alley. A uniformed officer in one of the cars nods to us as we pass. Manny snorts.

"Bunch of lazy slobs," he says. "All they do is sit through their tour of duty doin' crossword puzzles or catching some tube time on their mini-portable TVs. And all because they got the right Chinaman. Not a bad way to pull in a paycheck, huh, kid?" His voice carries just the slightest tinge of envy.

We head back to our beat. First rule of thumb, coming out on patrol, is to get your "mover," a traffic citation written for a moving violation. A "parker" is a citation written for illegally parked vehicles. A mover a day keeps the bosses away, my partner tells me. Bring in at least one mover and one parker a day, the bosses stay off your back. They like people who produce. Of course, you can write more than one a day, but why spoil 'em? Give the bosses too much work, they expect you to do it all the time. Manny nods wisely.

"On this job, kid, you give 'em just enough to keep 'em happy. That way, they stay outta your face, but you're not bustin' your ass. Know what I mean?"

He positions the squad behind a bread truck parked near a four-way stop-sign intersection. Within minutes, an aging Pontiac blows the sign and Manny pulls out after it.

"*Your* ticket," he smiles, generous with the new kid. I grab my hat—recruits are religious about being in full uniform—and approach the car.

"You ran the stop sign back there, sir. May I see your license, please?"

"No." The driver, a leathery old man with his face pruned in a scowl, barely spares me a glance.

"Pardon me?"

"No, you can't see my license. You must be new around here . . . I can tell by your uniform. You obviously don't know who I am." The man crosses his arms obstinately and turns to glare at me. I tell myself this is *not* going to be a problem. It's my first ticket, and I won't allow it to be. In my previous job as a therapist, I had to deal with angry and resistant clients all the time. Handling one disgruntled driver should be simple.

I glance at Manny, who's positioned on the other side of the car, to the rear. His face is unreadable. My call. *Calm*, I tell myself. *Remain calm, but be firm.*

"What I do know is you blew the stop sign. Give me your license."

The man huffs.

"Look, girlie, don't play police with me. I could have your job. You better think twice before you do anything stupid." He throws his license through the window.

"For your information, my brother-in-law, Lester, delivers doughnuts to the district desk crew every morning. He knows the desk sergeant, the commander, all those guys. You don't know who you're messing with." He looks smug. I can't believe the guy's serious. Or that he's acting like such a jackass over a simple ticket.

"I'm writing you a citation, sir. Remain seated in your vehicle until I come back."

In the squad, I write the ticket quickly.

"Can you believe this guy?" I ask Manny. "What kind of crap is that, 'My brother-in-law delivers the doughnuts'? Where do they come up with this stuff?"

Manny stares out the window, whistling through his teeth.

Ten minutes after Lester's brother-in-law peels away from us, we get a call on the radio.

"922? Beat 922?"

"'22."

"'22, go into your station. See the watch commander."

Now, what?

The commander is fuming when we get there. He slams his office door and whirls on me.

"How *dare* you fuck with my people? Do you think you can just waltz in, some wet-behind-the-ears goddamn recruit, and upset the order of things in *my* district?"

"No, sir."

"Didn't they teach you *anything* at the Academy?"

"Yes, sir."

"Then what the fuck gives you the right?"

"I thought I was doing my job, sir."

"Job? Your job is to fuck with the doughnut man's family? Are you some kind of moron? A man-hating dyke?"

"No, sir."

The commander snarls. "Another dumb broad. Figures. They don't teach these recruits shit anymore. Where's your ticket book, Officer?"

I hand it over.

Now the commander has to take the time to nonsuit the tickets. All because of me and my stupidity. He shoves his florid face in mine, so close I nearly gag on the Jim Beam he must have gargled with.

"I'll give you this break this time because you're new and don't know your ass from a hole in the ground. Don't ever let it happen again, or I'll bury you in the projects on foot patrol for the rest of your career!"

I wait until we're back in the car before I say anything.

"He gets that kind of attitude about the *doughnut guy*? What kind of district is this?"

Manny chuckles.

"A political one. This is the city clout built, remember? You don't fuck with the doughnut guy, the paper guy, anyone connected with the precinct captains and the aldermen. And, one other thing: Don't bother the whores working the south end of the district. Those are the ones who work the watch parties. Outside of that, you can pretty much do what you want."

The day grinds on—long stretches of driving punctuated by infrequent calls. It's because we're working the day shift, Manny tells me. Things don't start happening until nighttime.

A "disturbance at the bus stop" call turns out to be an old lady refusing to pay the bus driver because she doesn't know who he is.

"He's the bus driver," Manny tells her. "Who do you think he is?"

"How do I know that?" The old lady grimaces, never losing her white-knuckle death grip on her plastic-flowered shopping bag. "Could be an impostor, like those phony repairmen who wheedle their way into your house and then rape and murder you!"

She shivers, protectively tugging her raincoat tighter while the bus driver rolls his eyes. "I go to the seniors' meetings. I watch TV. I know what goes on!"

"Believe me, lady. This is a *real* bus driver. They gave him a bus and a uniform and, looky here—his driver's ID. A bus driver. Okay?"

Now the lady eyeballs Manny.

"And who are you?" she demands. "For all I know, you could be in cahoots with him. It's happened before, ya know. I read the papers." She backs away from us, our evil bus driver-police cabal. And gets a few yards away before she shouts, "I don't have to take this. I know my rights! I'm calling the police!"

We get a call to assist the inhalator at the car wash. Some guy keeled over while watching his Cadillac get the wax-n-buff. According to our dispatcher, paramedics are on the way. When we get there, the victim is laid out on the concrete apron, with a few semiclean wax rags bunched under his head. The car-wash crew is sudsing cars, oblivious, but the manager is standing by, concerned and dapper in his gray twill coveralls.

"How ya doin'?" he says to Manny, and nods politely to me. "Ain't seen ya in a while, man. Where ya been?"

Manny shrugs. "Here and there. Been busy around the house. The ol' lady decided she wanted to redecorate and you know how that is. So what's been up around here? You still got that goat for sale?"

I look from the victim's sweaty purple face to my partner. Goat? This poor guy's had a heart attack or a stroke, and they're discussing livestock?

"Uh, Manny, shouldn't we do something with this

man? CPR or something? Look at him!" The man has segued from labored gasps into some ominous-sounding gurgles. Forgive me for being conscientious, but he could be checking out here.

"Don't worry about it, kid. The paramedics are on the way. They're the experts."

"Yeah, but—"

"'Long as the guy's breathing, we're not s'posed to mess with him." But, in deference to my obvious recruit panic, he pauses to make a cursory inspection of the man. And pulls me off to the side for a whispered reminder.

"We're not certified for that stuff, remember? Do the wrong thing and the guy could die . . . and then what? So we'll just wait 'til the inhalator gets here, okay? And, listen, did I introduce you to my man, Rudy? You ever want your car done right, he's the guy. Won't gouge you on the price either. If he likes you."

They both laugh.

"He's got this car I've been trying to buy from him for months. A GTO—*real* cherry! Beautiful!" Manny's eyes are starting to glaze. "I practically bust a nut just thinkin' about it. Chrome wheels with wire spokes . . . ohhh, man!"

The man on the floor sounds like a clogged drain.

"Manny, listen, we should do something—"

The fire department paramedics' rig rumbles into the driveway. A male/female team hops out and brings the gurney and equipment.

"How long's he been like this?" the female asks. "Connelly," her name tag reads. She's already crouched besides the victim, checking vitals. Her calm efficiency impresses me.

"I don't know. We just got here." She checks his airway and slips an oxygen mask over his face.

"I wasn't sure if we should raise his head or—"

The male paramedic flips a blanket open. "'Face is red, raise the head. Face is pale, raise the tail,'" he recites.

"When in doubt, leave it out," Manny offers, and the three men laugh.

The paramedics work quickly, adjusting tubes, gauging vital signs. Neither of them seem overly concerned about the man's condition, which, I learn later, is a mild heart attack. But to a novice, it's as scary as a full-fledged cardiac arrest.

"Say, Rudy, you sell that goat yet?" The male paramedic turns. "I was telling a buddy about it— 389 engine, four-speed. . . ."

"How 'bout that paint job?" Manny asks. "Custom. Gold flake. Don't see too many like that anymore!"

"No shit!" the paramedic agrees. He adjusts his sunglasses, obviously blinded by the glow of reverence in Manny's eyes. "Reminds me of this Barracuda my brother used to have . . ."

They babble on while Connelly and I strap the man onto the gurney. She's quick and competent, adjusting cannulas, positioning his head, murmuring soothing words as she attaches the monitor leads.

"We'll get him in the rig and stabilize him," she tells me. "Has his family been notified yet? Did he have any ID?"

"Power like a motherfucker, too," Manny is saying. "Blow everybody else right off the goddamn road!"

"Don't forget the upholstery," Rudy boasts. "Black leather—soft as a baby's ass. That thing's a chariot, man!"

Connelly and I exchange glances over the gasping victim. *Boys' club,* we're both thinking. She shoots me a quick grin.

"You're new around here, right?"

"It's that obvious?"

"I can tell by your uniform. It's so *clean*!" She lowers her voice confidentially. "Don't mind those guys. They're always like that, yapping about some car or other. It's like a gearhead circle jerk. And if it's not cars, it's women."

"Listen, do you think he'll be okay?" I whisper, nodding to the man. Already the sweaty purple has faded to a moist pink.

"Think so. His vitals are starting to even out. Once we get him to the hospital, he should be alright." She shakes her head at the three men, now deeply engrossed in goatspeak. "But those guys—I wouldn't bet on it."

The call comes in mid-afternoon.

"See the woman, 46— South Emerald, second floor. Information for the police."

I look at Manny. "That's the South End. We're a North End car. How come we're getting it?"

Shifting his toothpick, Manny groans.

"That's Canaryville. This one's a regular. She must have radar or somethin'."

"What do you mean?"

"You'll see."

The second-floor apartment door is open when we get there. It's dim inside, with enough putrid odors to warrant a low-tide alewife-alert notice posted on the door. Before my eyes adjust, I nearly trip over the humongous dog sprawled on the stained carpet. It's enough to have me backing away as I reach for my gun. I've heard millions of war stories about cops and dogs, and I'm not about to be another statistic.

"Don't worry about the hound," my partner says. He's huffing from the two-story climb. "He's older than Moses and half-blind. He won't hurt you."

"Where's your regular partner today?" A voice like an abrasion grates through the gloom, harsh and raspy. "Where's Eddie?"

"Day off, Pearl. I'm working with a recruit today." I squint into the darkness. There's a tattered brocade sofa just ahead of us, the old-fashioned kind with ornate curving wood and claw-foot legs that Mae West might have reclined on. But the woman sprawled across it is definitely not Mae. Her hair—what there is of it—stands up in sparse maroon tufts, a color that does not occur in nature. Two clownish circles of rouge have been ground into her withered cheeks, which are split in a toothless smile. She's skinny, so bony that her crepey skin drapes down into the canyons of her collarbones. And she's absolutely naked.

I avert my eyes hastily. Manny looks bored.

"So . . . you got yourself a young girl to work with, huh? I'm jealous." Pearl's shriveled lips smack petulantly. "What's your name, sweetheart?"

I don't want to look at her. I can't avoid it. The sight of her is so unexpected, so disgusting, it's hard not to gawk. She's lounging, spread-eagle on the sofa, skinny legs flung wide to expose her musty core. Her cackling tells us she's delighted to have company, and an audience.

"Come a little closer, honey."

"Don't fuck with her, Pearl. She's still green." Manny turns to the door. "We're gonna take off now. You got your jollies for today."

"Don't go yet." Pearl's breath hitches. "I just wanna be friendly. Gets kinda lonely around here." She smiles and extends a bony hand.

"Come sit next to Pearl, honey. Come give me a little kiss."

"Nah. You know me, Pearl. Ain't my thing."

"Wasn't talking to you, Manny." Deliberately, she licks her lips and throws me a kiss. "You might like it, missy. Ever been with a woman before? Pearl will show ya what to do. Make Mama feel better."

My thoughts flash to my four-year-old son, and the question I know he'll ask when I get home. *How was your first day being the police, Mommy? What kind of stuff did you do?"*

Oh, not too much, son. Wrote a few tickets, talked to a few loonies and . . . oh, yeah, got a whole new slant on the diversity of senior citizens.

"Come right on over here, darlin'. Come and get friendly with ol' Pearl." She's beckoning now with a trembling finger.

Manny snickers. "I don't think she's up for any of what you got, Pearl. Besides, maybe she ain't had a tetanus shot lately. That's gotta be some rusty stuff there."

We're out the door before Pearl flings the first ashtray. Her shouts and curses follow us all the way down the stairs. I lean against the car, grateful for the fresh air, and suck in huge gulps of it to dispel the odor of funk and filth and Eau de Crotch. I order myself not to vomit. It's only my first day here; I refuse to humiliate myself.

Manny strolls up behind me.

"You did good, kid. Lotta guys lose it halfway down the stairs."

"How many people has she done that to?"

"Many as she can. 'Specially the new guys. She thinks she's the district's welcome wagon, I guess."

"So how come we went there if you knew what it was?"

He laughs.

"You never heard of the South End before? Folks that live in Canaryville are notorious for brawling and boozing and everything that goes along with it. You see people straight out of the backwoods around here. It's like Appalachia, Midwest. Old Pearl used to be one of the most, uh, active women around here. Like the poster girl for Canaryville, with four teeth in her head, skinny as a skeleton, but any guy could fit both fists up her—uh, never mind. Anyway, it's hard to say what hit her worse; the booze or the men. Either way, whatever's left ain't a pretty sight. The only way she can get a man within fifty feet of her is to call 911. Everybody in the district runs into her sooner or later. It's something you gotta see to believe."

"No kidding!" A few more breaths should do it. "She's really disgusting!"

"Yeah. It's kind of pathetic. But you'd be surprised." He looks back at the stairs. "Sometimes she gets takers."

"Stop it! You'll make me puke."

"I'm not kiddin'! Some guys actually take her up on it!" He sucks in his gut enough to slide behind the steering wheel. "But then again, those are the same guys who'd fuck a keyhole, so you can't judge by them." Ever the gentleman, he waits while I shallow-breathe, to make sure I don't lose my lunch all over the company car. And then he winks.

"Wouldn't worry about it if I were you. She doesn't get any takers, she goes to Plan B."

"Which is?"

"The dog. You never heard of 'man's best friend'?"

4

The End of Innocence

Dispatcher:	936? Beat 936?
936:	'36.
Dispatcher:	936, and all units in the Ninth District and on citywide, there's a battery in progress, a battery in progress at the liquor store, 49—South Halsted. Complainant's name is Watson, says there's two men beating up another man in front of the store. Units are advised to use caution—possible weapons involved. 936, did you copy?
936:	Uh, we didn't catch the last part of that transmission, Squad. Did you say 'weapons involved'?
Dispatcher:	Ten-four, '36. This one's your assignment.
936:	Uh, yeah, we'll get there as soon as we can. We're detained right now with an unavoidable traffic stop.
Dispatcher:	What've you got there, '36?
Unidentified Unit:	He's got to go hide somewhere until the cavalry arrives because he's chickenshit!

"Nobody tells the truth."

So says Vaughn, my field training officer, who assures me that this will be one of the most important things to remember on this job. In his years on the force, he's come to realize that no one tells the truth—not ever, not under *any* circumstance. Every one's out for themselves.

"Is that like 'covering your ass'?" I ask. It all sounds the same to me, but maybe there's some nuance I'm missing.

"Not like that at all," Vaughn corrects me. "Police have to cover their asses, and watch their partner's back, too. There's a lot of people out to get us, who would love to see us go down. You'll see. You go answer a call, the victim lies. Take an accident report, the drivers lie. Testify in court, the defendant lies, the plaintiff lies, the attorneys lie. Everybody lies. Something happens that's crime related, the press lies. Think about it. Every time some little slimeball gangbanger gets waxed, the papers have a field day. Suddenly little Willie was a saint. A model student, perfect son, neighborhood hero who went to church every Sunday. What a crock! This is the same kid who stabbed his mother, carved up grandma, and would turn his baby sister out if it meant he could get a fix. But once he's snuffed, he's an angel. Everybody *loved* little Willie. That's what the public wants to hear, I guess, just like they wanna believe we're the bad guys.

"Cops are the media's favorite scapegoats. Any major problem, blame it on the cops. If there's a riot or demonstration, they say we ain't doin' our job. When we go in there and try to maintain order, somebody screams 'police brutality.' Either way, we're fucked. Civilians lie to us all the time, and then try to screw us. So of course we gotta cover our asses. How else ya gonna make it out here?"

Sounds like pretzel logic to me, and a weird convolution of it at that. And it doesn't take a genius to figure out that it's fear talking, the same emotion that ripples through all of us out here on the street. It takes all forms, displays its symptoms in a variety of ways, but it all has the same bottom line. Cops are out here, on the line, dealing with human behaviors that run the gamut from mildly eccentric to clinically certifiable. The only thing we know that's an absolute is to expect the unexpected. And live with the knowledge that sometimes, however much we experience or think we're prepared for, there's going to be circumstances beyond our control, situations that we might not be able to handle. Injuries we won't be able to prevent. Fear of the unknown, fear of our own capabilities when it comes to the sticking point.

When Vaughn says that most people lie, I'm inclined to believe him. We're the cops, authority figures who have the power to arrest, incarcerate, or instill just the right amount of aggravation or paranoia to ruin the average citizen's day. More fear, this time from the public we serve. Fear of what *we* can do to *them*. Fear of not having control over your life when the police are involved. Lying would be one way to try and maintain some semblance of control.

I think back to my own civilian days, the times I was stopped by traffic cops. And how I lied, careful to use a combination of sincerity and charm that was just enough to get me out of a ticket. It was a lie, one which I'm sure the traffic cop was aware of, but it worked. Which was all it was meant to do—just to get a break on a ticket. No disrespect meant to the officer involved. It didn't make me bad, or the cop stupid. Just a way of trying to maintain a little bit of control in a threatening situation.

I haven't been the places Vaughn has, or encountered the same situations, so I have no idea what's contributed to his hard-line attitudes. And I can't ask him . . . not yet. I'm just a recruit, and Vaughn is the guy I'll be working with for the next twenty-nine weeks. Vaughn will be the one to guide me through my street training, my arrests and court appearances, all the real police stuff that recruits have to cut their teeth on before they can graduate to "rookie" status. Vaughn will also be the one who grades me, who has the power to flunk me out of the program. Do anything to piss off Vaughn, and I'm up shit creek without a star.

When I'm introduced to him after my second roll call, I'm surprised at how young he looks. This is his first year as a training officer, and I'm his first recruit. This is something to think about. I was hoping to be paired with a *real* street veteran, someone who'd seen and done just about everything. Someone like Charlie Sutton, who is Booker's training officer. Charlie's got twenty-four years on the job, and spent the better part of those in the war-zone districts, the Gang units and plainclothes covert operations. Word around the district campfire is that Charlie's so tough, he chews up coal and shits diamonds. He *looks* tough, with a Maytag-size chest and arms that could pump freight trains. By comparison, Vaughn is tall and skinny.

But appearances can be deceiving. Maybe Vaughn's a supercop in disguise and I just don't know it. He's got to be fairly good at what he does—otherwise, why would they make him a training officer?

I wait until we're in our squad car—Beat 936, the sector car for the south end of the district—and cruising before I try to pump him for more information. I'm ready to absorb any pearls of wisdom

Vaughn's learned through sweat and experience—anything that'll help me be a better cop.

I've already noticed that Vaughn has a certain ritual to begin the tour of duty. He produces a plastic sandwich bag full of premoistened diaper wipes and proceeds to wipe down the car seat, dash, and steering wheel. Pathogens, he says. Cops are a filthy bunch. Never know where they've been or with whom. God knows what kind of germs are smeared around, just waiting to infect us.

The next step is fastening his personal wooden-ball self-massaging car seat, presumably for the same reasons. You never know where the last ass has been.

Then he takes out his portable radio, tunes it to the oldies station, and rubber-bands it to the visor. Music makes the tour go by faster, he tells me. Takes your mind off the bullshit. He assures me that in no time at all I'll be just like a seasoned vet—able to carry on a conversation with my partner, monitor the police radio, *and* sing along to my favorite tunes.

After adjusting his "official badass" aviator sunglasses to just the right macho angle, checking the sparse tendrils of his blond mustache in the mirror, and baring yellowed teeth for a speedy plaque test, we're ready to roll.

"First thing you do leaving the station," he tells me, "You go to the 7-Eleven and get your coffee. If you're working days, you get a paper, too. After that, you make the most important decision of the day, which is, where you gonna eat lunch. Now I, myself, I'm a chili man. I love chili! There's a great place on 31st Street—the Chili Wagon—that I usually hit. Thought we could go today. You like chili?"

I've seen the place he's talking about, a seedy

graffiti-laden dive with the front window boarded up. I've never eaten there but I can imagine the blue plate special: Chili *con cockroach*.

"So, Vaughn, what made you want to become a training officer?" Tell me it was because of your three hundred department commendations, your medal of valor, your unwavering cool in the line of fire? Because you wanted to teach others to be as great a cop as you are?

"My old district sucked!"

"Your . . . what?"

Bopping to some vintage Chuck Berry, Vaughn noses the car down quiet side streets.

"Yeah, see, they came up with a new policy for the FTO program: if you sign up, you get sent to a designated training district. Before that, the training officers would stay in their old districts and train the recruits there. Now, if you're an FTO, you get shipped somewhere else, and usually, they let you pick the district. For the past three years, I been stuck in 'the Deuce.'" ("The Deuce" is the Second District, one of the most notoriously crime-ridden areas of the city. It covers an area comprised of high-rise projects and burned-out buildings, crack houses and heavy gang activity. The Deuce is known throughout the department as a punishment assignment or a dumping ground for the clout-free.)

"And I gotta tell ya, kid, that really sucked. Every day there was like a year. And a lot of the old training officers quit cuz they didn't wanna leave their old districts. Me, I couldn't wait. First day I came to this district, drove down the street, and saw *white people,* I thought I died and went to heaven!"

This is a lot to think about, harder to digest than the chili Vaughn raves about.

"So you decided to train people to get away from the Deuce? And you've been a cop for only three years?"

"Three years is the minimum requirement," Vaughn tells me, and segues from "Roll Over Beethoven" to "Satisfaction." He waits for the last haunting guitar riff to vibrate from the tinny radio before continuing.

"You have no idea what it's like to work in the projects. Absolutely *no* idea. They hate us there—white cops, black cops, doesn't matter. We're the enemy, long as we're in these uniforms. Almost every call—especially on the midnight watch—is a guaranteed fight." He pulls up to a stop sign and eyes me somberly.

"Thing is, it ain't the police that's the real enemy there, or the gangs, or the crime. It's the *life* . . . and everything else is the by-product. It's like being forced to live like that, in those conditions, just sucks the life out of people. First time I ever saw a dead baby was up in the projects. Baby'd been dead for two or three days, and everybody in the apartment was too high to notice. My first thought, going in, was, 'These people are animals—they don't deserve to have children.' Didn't find out 'til later that the Housing Authority had shut off the heat in that block of apartments. This was in January, mind you, and no heat. They said later it was because there was a wiring problem they were fixing, which may have been true. Except they never turned the heat back on. Two weeks in winter with no heat. And these people—the one with the baby had an apartment door with no lock—building maintenance never fixed it after the last burglary. No furniture, just some mattresses on the floor—that's all that was left. And didn't matter that they were getting welfare checks . . . those get stolen from the mailboxes same day they're delivered. All the mailboxes are on the ground level, near the street. No locks on most of 'em, just little rinky-dink latches anybody can pry open with a screwdriver. Perfect photo op for any junkie who needs some quick cash. And what happens when you live on the fifteenth floor—how you gonna get your mail before they do?"

He shakes his head slowly.

"That's the bite, kid. All the things that go on there—any *one* thing would be plenty to screw up a person's life, but this is ongoing, just constant problems. Which creates all the other problems; the drugs and the crime, and the hostility that gets dumped on us. Maybe it ain't their fault, but it ain't ours, either, y'know? Not any way I can see. So it's like two ends pushing against the middle. And there's no percentage going into situations where they want to kill you, for shit that ain't even your fault." Clearing his throat, he looks at me again. For emphasis, maybe, or just some need for understanding.

"It ain't worth dying over. That's what I think. We're there to protect, but we can't do jack about the environment. And that's what creates all the problems. Working a beat car in the projects is like trying to keep your thumb in the dam—a losing battle. No matter what you do, it ain't enough, and somebody's gonna take you down, anyway."

Silence while I try to digest all this. But then I have to ask, "And the baby . . . ? What happened?"

"Baby was dead. That's what happened." His tone is gruff, meant to be dismissive, but I can hear the emotion behind it. "Paramedics said pneumonia— who knows for how long. All I know is, I was standing in that apartment in full winter uniform, coat, sweater, the whole thing—and I was freezing. And these people were huddled on mattresses, with nothing. Passing around a bottle of cheap wine. Maybe that was the only thing that kept 'em warm. Or the only way they could forget where they were. No heat, no locks, no food in the place that we could see. And when we removed the baby's body, the mother just looked at us, just stared with these huge eyes, and didn't say a word. Not one single thing. First I was pissed, wanted to kill this unfeeling bitch. And then I realized, she probably knows the kid's in a better place. At least out of the shit that she still has to deal with. And maybe that's a good thing—who knows?"

This is the first of the many street philosophies I'll hear from Vaughn and countless other partners during the course of my career. All of them will be different, shaded by experience and personal beliefs. All of them will be a way of reaching out, a need to explain why and how cops become what they do. Now Vaughn offers me a wry smile and assumes his cocky tone.

"This district doesn't have any badass projects, so there's nothing to worry about. This is a piece of cake, kid. Just gotta learn a few basics. Stay out of shit, keep a low profile, and don't be a hero. Any moron can do it."

Teamed with Vaughn, the days pass while I wait for experience to rear its exciting head. A car chase, a street fight, an armed robbery in progress that we foil—*anything* that'll make me feel like I'm up to my gun belt in urban crime-stopping. Booker and Charlie have already snagged some car thieves, captured a rapist, and stopped a car containing enough marijuana to make the six-o'clock news. My other fellow recruits are in the thick of it too, but the only really bad thing I've encountered so far is Vaughn's chili, which *should* be a crime.

Vaughn tells me to relax. The bad stuff is out there, and I've got my whole career to find it. We're bound to run into it sooner or later. But not, I realize, if Vaughn can run away from it first. Whenever the dispatcher gives us a call that might turn out to be something, like "Check the open door at the warehouse—possible burglary in progress," Vaughn will ask if there's a backup car to ride with us. If there is, he'll take his time and let the other car get there first.

"No sense rushing into shit," he tells me. "Why put ourselves in danger?"

No backup car means that we'll take even longer to get there, and when we do, it'll be with the siren blaring from three blocks away, just to let the bad guys know the cavalry's approaching and they should exit stage left.

Any "street disturbance" means that Vaughn will circle the block and creep down the alleys first to make sure there's not a mob. Don't want to get into more than we can handle, he tells me. By this time I'm wondering if there's *anything* he's willing to handle.

He has no problem with the safe stuff, like writing parking tickets, say, or traffic accidents. He's pretty certain no one's going to blast him while they're slumped across the steering wheel, bleeding. And when we go on domestic disturbances, which often start out being fairly innocuous but have the potential to turn into a knock-down-drag-out, he defers to me.

"You gotta learn to talk to the people," he tells me, sucking his teeth. "Learn how to defuse a situation. Use a woman's touch."

In our time together, I learn that Vaughn still lives with his mother, who monitors the police scanner every night that he's on the street. And waits, no doubt, like my mother did, like all police spouses do, for their loved one to walk through the door. It occurs to me that Vaughn's reluctant attitude is fed by his family obligations, his role as provider. But images of my wounded father, attached to tubes and machines, cloud that logic, make me wonder what the balance is between good cop and bad. Or if such clear-cut distinctions can even be made when fear is thrown in the mix.

After a week of working days, all the recruits and their training officers are transferred to afternoons— the 4-to-12 shift. More crime happens at night, I'm told. More potential for trouble. Maybe now Vaughn will show a different side.

On afternoons the pace picks up. The jobs come more frequently now, of a more serious nature. Burglaries, disturbances, and all the in-progress calls start flying once the sun goes down. Jobs that you'd think Vaughn can't slide on, but he still manages. We're assigned an auto-theft-in-progress one night, and by the time we get there, Booker and Charlie are assisting three handcuffed prisoners into the squadrol. Booker shoots me a quick, sympathetic look before he slams the door shut. Charlie is less diplomatic. The sneer he aims at Vaughn is accompanied by a single caustic question.

"You plannin' on teaching this kid anything besides how to be a dog?"

Vaughn is furious.

"Can you beat that?" he asks me. "Lazy mother-fuckers get bent out of shape if they have to do a little work! Guess that old bastard's pissed cuz he had to break a sweat!"

"Vaughn, that was *our* assignment." I'm embarrassed and ashamed. Bad enough that we blew off our own job; worse that other cops noticed.

"Yeah, and we woulda handled it if that goddamn hot dog hadn't jumped in. What is he, fuckin' John Wayne?" He directs a sharp look at me. "And if I were you, I'd watch out for that nigger."

"Are you talking about Booker?"

"Who else? I seen you talking to him before roll call."

"Yeah, so?"

"So it's not a real smart idea—know what I mean?"

"I have no idea. Booker and I are friends."

"Friends!" He smirks. "Just don't get *too* friendly. Otherwise, word's gonna get around that you're fucking him."

"He's my friend, Vaughn, and I don't care what you or anyone else thinks."

"No need to cop an attitude. I'm just trying to save you some grief. Rumors start flyin', you can't stop 'em. You wouldn't want that, would ya? Nice girl like you fucking a nigger? It'd kill your reputation."

"As much as putting in eight hours every night of doing absolutely nothing?" I'm outraged enough to consider stuffing a few handfuls of his diaper wipes down his big mouth.

"Hey, I'm just tryin' to help you, kid. The bosses would go crazy if they heard about anything like that. This is a man's world, remember. And coppers talk. So don't give 'em anything to talk about." He climbs back in the squad and slams the door. "You only been on this job a couple *minutes,* kid—you're still a baby. You don't know how it is. These black cops—a lot of 'em come out of the projects. Now they wear the uniform, but they still got the attitude. Only now, they think they're better than the project dwellers. And you think, if push came to shove, they'd do anything for you? You're just some little white girl they'd like to jump. That's it. It ain't about being friends. This ain't the United Nations, kid. So just keep your nose clean, avoid the hassles, and do your job."

Do my job. Exactly what I've been trying to do. The only question is, when?

"Armed robbery in progress." We get the call one late afternoon, when rush-hour traffic has clotted the streets. On this particular day, we're assigned to the South End, an area populated primarily by lower-income blacks. But for the past hour or so, Vaughn's been meandering through the streets of Brighton Park, a tidy, mostly white enclave on the Northwest End. Our job location is a Southeast Side business, at least fifteen minutes away under normal circumstances, much more during rush hour.

"936? Beat 936?" It's the dispatcher paging us, wondering just what in the hell is taking so long.

"936."

" '36, be advised that 999 is in the field and riding on your job. Is that a ten-four?"

"999" is the watch commander, our illustrious captain, the Big Kahuna. From time to time he has a driver take him out tooling around the district to make sure the troops are doing what they're supposed to. Having the boss show up at one of your jobs is good only when you're where you're supposed to be, doing what you're supposed to do. Right now Vaughn and I aren't in that category.

"936, did you copy? Is that a ten-four?"

It's more than a ten-four, it's an *"Oh shit!"*

Even Vaughn knows it's going to hit the fan this time.

"Don't worry," he says. "Flip on the lights and siren. We'll blue-light it all the way."

We careen around corners, over curbs, down alleys, and finally make it to 47th Street, which will be a straight shot across the district to our job location. Vaughn swings over into the oncoming traffic lane and floors it.

I've always assumed, even before I was a cop, that when people—drivers or pedestrians—hear emergency sirens, they get out of the way. Just pull over to the side and let the vehicle pass. I assumed wrong. There's always at least one person who thinks he can beat it, no matter how close that siren is.

In this case, it's a lady parked at the curb, her spiffy new Grand Am pointed in the same direction we're heading. All other traffic has stopped or pulled over. She must think it's the perfect opportunity for her to pull out, cut across three lanes of stopped traffic, and go into the mall parking lot across the street. Barreling along in excess of 60 miles per hour, Vaughn never sees her.

But I do.

Our cars collide with so much impact that the effect is a slow-motion death dance. I'm sure I'm dead, but I won't close my eyes or I'll miss the details. I see the horror blooming on bystanders' faces, the fervent *Oh, my God!s* mouthed on strangers' lips. The squad-car bumper flies up, a gleaming, twisted saber that slashes through the Grand Am's windshield, severing the hand the woman has thrown up in last-minute defense. Slowly, slowly, the bloody hand arcs into the air with fingers trailing before it lands with a muffled splat on the hood of our car.

I can't stop myself moving—I shouldn't be, but the seat-belt mechanism snapped. That's what someone tells me later, but I don't know it then—only that I'm pitching forward, over the dash, through the windshield.

Memory random after that. Faces splash and fade before me, sounds rise and ebb. I drift in suspended time—seconds? Hours? Drops trickle onto my face, but it's not rain, rather, the sweat of the rescue team working with torches and pry bars. I don't remember them lifting me out of the wreckage, only the white circles of fear that freeze Vaughn's eyes as he stares at me. People around me are murmuring, asking questions. But I can only hear the screams of the maimed woman.

Finally, the hospital with smells as sharp as the needle they slide into my arm. Just before I drift off, my partner, with only a tiny bandage on his chin, leans over my gurney.

"Just remember, it wasn't our fault," he whispers urgently. "Anybody asks you, that's what you tell 'em. Cover your ass!"

5

First Blood

936:	936, EMERGENCY!
Dispatcher:	All units stand by. 936, go ahead with your emergency.
936:	I'm in foot pursuit of a male subject wanted for aggravated battery, northbound in the west alley of the 5000 block of Normal. Subject is a black male, approximately 6'3", 160 pounds, medium complexion, bald head, wearing a gray trench coat. Subject is possibly armed and—
	(The sound of shots fired, then static)
Dispatcher:	936? Come in, '36! '36, do you copy?
933:	933. Squad, we're right around the corner from that location. We're on the way. Sounds like shots fired.
Dispatcher:	Ten-four, '33. 936, come in. Unit 936, do you copy?
931:	931. We're gonna ride on this, too.
Dispatcher:	Okay, '31. Unit 936, come in. 936? . . . 936? Attention, all units in Nine and on citywide, we got a chase going on in the west alley of 50th and Normal, authority of Beat 936. First unit on the scene, let me know what's going on over there. We have no further transmission from 936.

Just two days out of the hospital, I'm back at work, back with Vaughn, patrolling the streets of the city. My partner had made a point of coming to the hospital, after the tubes and machines were removed and he was certain I could comprehend the message he had for me. During that visit, he warned me to keep my mouth shut in case I was interrogated by Internal Affairs, the Office of Professional Standards, or any of the brass from the Ninth District. What we did in our squad was our business, he warned, and it didn't pay to let the assholes from downtown dig around looking for dirt. If anyone asked, we'd had a job to do, and we were on the way to doing it. The accident was unavoidable. Period. At this point, Vaughn offered a big smile and reached over to squeeze a hand still swollen from various IV needles.

"Partners gotta look out for each other," he said. "That's what it's all about. You know I got your back, kid." A discreet silence when the nurse bustled in to check vital signs, and then, "Better not take too much time off on this thing—know what I'm sayin'? You're still a recruit, and you know what that means."

In case I didn't, he proceeded to spell it out. As a recruit, as a woman, I'm under scrutiny. Everybody's watching to see how I handle myself. A car accident's no big deal, not in a cop's life. If I want to be a cop, I have to roll with it. Take too much time off playing sick, and the bosses might think I'm a malingerer, or worse: a whiny, sissy broad who can't take it. Everybody gets banged up sooner or later—it's part of the job. Better take my lumps and get over it. Keep my mouth shut and our collective asses covered.

And anyway, people at work were starting to talk. Rumors about how Vaughn had nearly gotten his first recruit killed. The department is willing to tolerate a smashed-up company car now and then. A mangled recruit is a different story. That means there's a loss of manpower, and the possibility that the City of Chicago might have to shell out disability pay, which really pisses them off.

When I finally make it back to work, the people on my watch are acting differently. They're warmer now, going out of their way to talk to me, ask me how I am. Just happening to drive by our job locations, providing backup before we even ask for it. In short, looking out for the new kid. Which is a comforting thought—more backup means a better chance of beating the incredible odds cops face.

Sensing the change in our watch members' attitudes, Vaughn goes out of his way to be careful, if not more motivated. Maybe the fear, or the caution, is too much a part of his character now to really change, but he makes an effort. It would be a mistake to be labeled, in department jargon, a "dog-ass"; a malcontent who skates by doing as little as possible, not a team player. Which can be dangerous for everyone, since policing is the ultimate team effort. Not a healthy situation to be in, since cooperation—or lack of it—works both ways. If your watch members decide they don't like you, you're out there alone. Call for backup and nobody shows—or, if they do, take a *long* time coming. Get in a street fight, and you'll get the shit kicked out of you before anyone intervenes. But while my watch members remain undecided about Vaughn, there's a tacit understanding that they'll look out for me—the new kid who just happened to have a bit of bad luck.

It's nice to know the people on my watch are being supportive, but I'm still worried. So far, I haven't made a single arrest. I've never filled out an arrest report, never had to appear in court. Everything I learned in the Academy about report writing and arrest procedures is fading fast. It's not something you can learn strictly from a few lectures. You have to do it, be involved in it enough times so that it becomes second nature. A criminal isn't going to stand by while I'm deciding whether to read him his rights, get a complaint signed, or call for backup because my FTO never taught me how to do it during my probation.

It still seems to take forever to get to our assignments. Vaughn cites my "post-traumatic stress syndrome" as the reason he won't allow me to drive our squad car. I'm not sure about that, but if driving is so important to him (boys' club thinking again), he can do it. One thing that's definitely changed since the accident is that now he's careful to patrol within the boundaries of our assigned beat. The watch commander had a few words to say to him about the lag in our response time to that armed robbery. And wondered what kind of example that was to set for a recruit. And tossed out some other ideas, like stripping Vaughn of his training-officer status. Bouncing his worthless ass back to the Deuce. Maybe some suspension time thrown in for "conduct unbecoming. . . ." Vaughn understood. No more hiding out on the North End.

"936"

" '36."

" '36, take the disturbance, 51— South Normal. It's a house, complainant's name is Lomax. Says she'll meet you on the porch."

"Ten-four, Squad."

It's a chilly Tuesday, with rain sheeting down from the dull pewter skies of late afternoon. Just the thing to slicken the streets and complicate rush hour.

"Jesus, we just get out here, and they're hammerin' us already. Didn't even get my coffee yet." Vaughn hawks up a phlegmy rumble and spits out the car window.

"Think I'm comin' down with a cold or something. Didn't even feel like comin' in today. But then, what kind of example would that be for you?"

The arterial streets are gridlocked. Traffic lights are out, intersections clogged with beeping bumper-to-bumper vehicles. Enough to slow us down even more than Vaughn.

"936?" The dispatcher's voice cuts through the bleating traffic.

"Christ, give us a chance!" Vaughn mutters. "Don't they know it's a nuthouse out here?" He swerves the car to avoid a lumbering pickup truck hogging two lanes.

"'36."

"'36, use caution on that disturbance. We're getting information now that there's a possible weapon involved."

"Ten-four."

"Let us know what you got when you get over there, '36."

"Okay, Squad."

By the time we pull up in front of the two-story frame house, we've received four more messages from our dispatcher—all of them warning that the situation has escalated. The complainant's house is on a narrow, tree-lined block with foliage so heavy that it blocks the streetlights. Doesn't matter because, for most of the block, *there are no streetlights*. This is an area we call "the Creep Zone." It's a depressed neighborhood, with ramshackle buildings and residents more likely to make a living from carjacking and drug dealing than a daily 9-to-5. It's also the turf of a notorious gang which doesn't take kindly to anyone who invades their space—police or otherwise. They carry on their business, oblivious to patrolling squads, even inviting a confrontation that will give them the opportunity to take out a few cops. With the assurance of players with the home-court advantage, they make sure the odds are in their favor. Sentries are posted at various locations to signal when police approach. The streetlights are shot out so the street remains dark, the better to provide cover for drive-bys, robberies, and other assorted criminal activity. And when the cops show up, there are snipers ready in the second-story windows with night-sighted weapons trained on approaching squad cars. Shooting up a squad car ranks high on a gang member's list of accomplishments. Killing a cop is even higher. So whenever police are summoned to this block, they *creep* in, testing the war zone before getting out of the car.

But right now, there's still some daylight left, filtering through the clouds. The rain's slowed to a fine mist, so I can make out the woman standing on the porch. She's young, not more than mid-twenties, and her arms are folded tight across her chest, in anger, I think, or impatience. As I step out of the car, she starts to scream.

" 'Bout time y'all got here. There he is, right over there!" She thrusts her chin in the direction of a tall, thin man in a gray trench coat sauntering down the sidewalk.

"I *said,* go grab him, goddammit! That's the nigger who cut me!" She unfolds her left arm and extends it, enough for me to see the jagged wound that gapes, drooling blood. "He cut me, goddammit. Go on and get that muthafucka!"

The man in question is strolling, almost diddy-bopping. He doesn't appear to be concerned by the woman's screams, or the fact that he's now the object of police scrutiny. He's just bopping along, the soiled hem of his trench coat flapping behind him like a sodden banner. I reach for my gun as two thoughts hit me simultaneously. *Am I justified in using deadly force?* And *Where the hell is my training officer?* With my eyes on the suspect, I can't see Vaughn in my peripheral field, can't hear his voice or footsteps behind me. I'm not even sure I heard him get out of the squad, but there's no time to think about that now. This guy's going to get away.

"*Police!*" I shout. "Put your hands on your head and don't move!"

The man stops and turns, casually, it seems. Unconcerned. His head is completely shaved, and his eyes have the weird, unfocused glaze of the seriously deranged.

"Get your hands up," I shout again, and edge toward him, arms and gun fully extended in a combat-shooting stance. I hear voices around me, neighbors, coming out on their porches to see what the shouting's about. And adding some shouting of their own.

"What's that white bitch doin' with our homey?"

"Kill that fuckin' bitch—take her white ass out!"

"She thank she can come over here and fuck wid us?"

It's a rumble of voices that grows into a roar, shouting and threatening. Along with the voices come the sounds of screen doors slamming, footsteps slapping down stairs as a crowd gathers. And then I remember where I am. *The Creep Zone.* And realize I'm in one of those no-win situations that no amount of Academy training can prepare you for. If I shoot this guy, someone's going to shoot me. If I *don't* shoot him, he'll get away—and I can still get killed. It feels like all the air has gone out of my lungs, like time and sound have been frozen in this one critical moment. No sensation but the weight of the gun in my hand and the sweat trickling down my spine. No sound but deep, measured breathing— mine, or the man in the sights of my weapon?

Homey looks not the least bit concerned about the .357 that's pointed right at his chest. He raises his arms and lifts them out high, higher, fully extended in a T. Or the crucifix on which this white bitch is nailing him. He rolls his eyes heavenward and pronounces, "I am the Lord, Jesus Christ, and y'all done crucified me too many times!" And then folds his arms tight across his chest, like the woman on the porch, and pulls from beneath his trench coat a butcher knife in each hand, which he thrusts toward me.

"Y'all better shoot me, bitch, cuz I'm about to cut your fuckin' heart out!"

Shock and fear spurt through me in equal measure. From a simple disturbance call to a duel to the death? Raised high, the knife blades sparkle with beaded mist like glinting fangs about to devour me. Shoot? Don't shoot? Hypnotized by the fearsome blades, I'm paralyzed. No sounds now but the blood roaring in my head. They're coming closer. *Shoot him! Pull the damn trigger and kill him! And how many other homeys have guns pointed at my back this very instant?*

Finally, instinct kicks in.

"Drop the knives, you son of a bitch. I may die, but you're coming with me!" I'm growling now, an animal as frenzied as the one I face. No more hesitation. Just do it.

The glazed eyes snap, the knives clatter, and the man is running, sprinting around the corner, with me on his trail. I chase after him, weapon drawn, and send a ten-one (the most urgent distress call: cop-speak for "Send in the cavalry!") on the radio, giving a description of the fleeing felon.

He cuts down an alley and I'm right behind him, close enough to see the gun in his hand when he whips around and drops to a crouch. The clatter of the trash cans I hit when I dive for cover is nothing compared to the roar of his gun. He fires off two more rounds and then streaks off again. Panting, garbage-strewn, I follow behind him, through the alleys, across an empty lot, over the railroad tracks.

Finally, I hear sirens, see the squads tearing around corners. And slow to a stagger, trying to catch my breath. Eight blocks? Ten? Just over a mile—nothing compared to the long runs we did in the Academy. But a huge difference on the stress scale. I've lost him.

He ducked down a gangway somewhere, slipped through someone's backyard—and vanished. But the radio is crackling now with the messages of units now in pursuit, so I can relax. Peel off some of the garbage that still clings to my wet, filthy uniform, and try to figure out how to get back to Vaughn, and my assigned car.

There are blue police lights flashing on the next block. I can see them from the alley, through the empty yards. I'll ask one of the squads to take me back to the Lomax house, see if Vaughn's still there. Turning down a random gangway, I cut through the yard, brushing at the clumped mud and cinders on my slacks, and get almost to the front of the building when he leaps out of the doorway he'd been crouched in. Hiding or waiting? I don't see the trench coat now, or his crazy eyes—only the bore of the gun he's pointing at me.

I don't remember doing it. Instinct, survival mode, whatever it is, I don't remember raising my gun. He's close to me, less than three feet away, and when my gun discharges, it looks like a splat of ketchup lands on his cheek—the entry wound from a bullet that carries enough force to knock him out into the front of the building and take off the back of his head.

That slow-motion sensation again. And the roar in my head that blocks out the sound of more police arriving on the scene, staring at me, at the corpse. Blockading the street from the gathering crowds whose mouths move in outraged pantomime. Uniforms move along the sidewalk, stretching the yellow tape that marks off an official police crime scene. And keeping the surge of shouting citizens a safe distance from the teams of workers who must process the crime scene.

The paramedics arrive, and are dispatched quickly. Resuscitation won't be necessary in this case. The mobile crime lab unit arrives to take pictures of the body, collect my gun for analysis. I see Booker and Charlie across the street, stationed there to prevent anyone from crossing the police line. Charlie catches my eye, nods almost imperceptibly. His message is as clear as a hundred blaring sirens: *You did good, kid. Stay strong.*

The expression on Booker's face tells a different story. There's fear, awe, disbelief . . . mixed with slap-in-the-face shock at the reality of the situation. This is the first shooting either one of us has witnessed. As the shooter—the *killer*—I'm the first of our class, a grisly distinction. Now Booker's watching his friend stand over the body of the man she just took out. His eyes sweep the area, looking for Vaughn, who still hasn't shown up, and then another look at me, another message: *Hang in there. You'll get through this.*

More arrivals. The detectives, the watch commander, investigators from the Office of Professional Standards. They stand in somber clusters, pointing and talking. I can't hear any of them.

The body lies sprawled on the sidewalk for an obscenely long time, what seems like forever. Blood flows down the sidewalk, diluted by the rain to a pastel wash. It reminds me of watercolors, of the paint box I had in first grade at Our Lady of Good Counsel School. Where I learned how to read, and write, and obey the Ten Commandments. *Thou shalt not kill.*

I stare down at the shaved head, what's left of it, and the unseeing eyes. *I am the reason this man is dead. I ended his life.* And I wait for the guilt, the horror, some emotion equal to the deed. And am surprised when I feel nothing. There's a void there, some blank slate waiting for instructions on what I'm supposed to feel. But right now, there's nothing.

A jack-o'-lantern grins from a porch across the street. Halloween is coming and my kids are waiting to carve our own pumpkin. My sons, who wait for me every night and ask what exciting things I did. Tonight, I'll say, "I got to come home to you."

Someone touches my arm. It's my field lieutenant, who's searching my face for signs of—what? Shock, or remorse, or the expected recruit hysteria? I have none of that to give him. A line's been crossed, a chasm that many cops never encounter in the whole of their careers. In milliseconds, I've become someone else, lost something I can never regain. I just killed a man. And the only thing I'm thinking is that I get to see my kids again.

Someone else approaches me. It's Vaughn, face pale and pinched and more than a little nervous in the presence of so many supervisors. He draws me aside.

"I was looking for you!" he begins. "I was back there, trying to take the report from the victim, and you just vanished! I. . . ."

I stare at him, at my trembling hands streaked with sweat and cordite. And just glimpse the specter that hovers at the edges of this scene, of any ground cops dare to tread. It's fear again, the nemesis that can make men freeze, paralyze what should be instinctive survival skills. This time, my first time, I wasn't one of the victims.

Looking at Vaughn, I can't distinguish truth from lies, fear from shock. The only truth now is that I'm still alive.

"I killed him," I whisper, holding up my hands as though they tell the whole story. And I allow my partner to lead me away.

6

Street Protocol

Dispatcher:	1231? Beat 1231?
1231:	'31.
Dispatcher:	'31, check this one out. A citizen called in to report two men selling guns and sides of beef out of the trunk of the car at 16th and Blue Island.
1231:	Nothing for me, thanks. I had a cupcake on the train.
Dispatcher:	Says here it's two male Hispanics with a green Pontiac, plate number unknown, parked on the southwest corner.
1231:	Anything I can get for you? Rib roast? A steak? An Uzi?
Dispatcher:	Sounds good. Make it an Uzi, medium rare, mushrooms on side.

Graduation day. The event many of us thought we'd never see—the department's rite of passage that takes us from lowly recruits to rookies—the *real* police at last. We're all back in the Training Academy gym, decked out in white gloves and dress blues, marching snappily in formation past the official gaggle of assembled stiffs, which includes the mayor, the police superintendent, and the hierarchy of department brass. Also on hand are assembled family and friends, who provided the mental and emotional support that got us through this challenging year. And who wouldn't miss this photo op to watch us trot along like trained monkeys in formal uniform attire, looking like a recruitment ad: sharp-pressed, sharp-eyed, with just the faintest hint of menace in our eyes. Or maybe it's the agony of being swathed in these itchy wool suits on such a sweltering day. All of this so we can usher past the suits, shake hands, receive our diplomas, and, later, trade a few fledgling war stories of our own.

As each recruit is called up to the podium, the number of honorable mentions and other awards he or she has received this first year are also announced. The audience murmurs, applauds, sometimes gasps in admiration as the awards are recited. *"Janice Albright, three honorable mentions. Clyde Axelrod, two honorable mentions, one lifesaving award. Luis Benitez, five honorable mentions, one Mayor's Citation for outstanding citizenship. . . ."*

Everyone's already heard about my shooting (word travels fast within the ranks), and the remarks I hear are an odd combination of awe and envy. I've killed someone; I'm *really* "the Man" now. I exchanged one bullet and one person's life for a career-long reputation of "having brass balls." Everyone congratulates me, smiling and patting my arm as if I'm a hero. The police department is the only organization I've encountered (outside of street gangs and organized crime) where killing earns you a pat on the back.

By now, our graduating class is seasoned just enough to gripe about having to wear the monkey suit—the wool dress slacks and formal jacket—but we strut past the incoming recruit classes like conquering heroes. It's been a year since we first assembled in this building, and we've all changed since then. Eyes that once shone with idealistic dreams are now washed by reality. On this job, the only truth is reality, and that reality changes from place to place, minute to minute. Dreams of glory have been tempered by the law of the street: survival of the fittest. Sergeant Woods wasn't kidding when he told us to keep our eyes open and our mouths closed. If we hadn't been so green, we would have heard the real message: Be smart, stay sharp, and stay alive.

After the diplomas have been collected and the last group photos snapped, it's official. We're the real police now, no longer callow recruits, and are vested with the authority to uphold the law and preserve the peace. How that authority will be interpreted is anybody's guess.

After graduation, we're all assigned to our permanent districts. I discover that whatever dream I'd harbored of being assigned to the department's Counseling Center is just that: strictly a dream. Despite my background and qualifications, I, like everyone else in my class, will be shipped out to a district to work the streets as a beat cop. Which means saying goodbye to Vaughn, to the Ninth District and all its members who helped me through that first grueling six months. I'm assigned to a West Side district that's comprised mostly of gangs, projects, gangs, whores, hustlers, and . . . did I mention gangs? After working with Vaughn, this may be a baptism by fire. I find out that Booker and four other recruits are assigned to the same district. A relief—although departmental policy prohibits two recruits from working a car together, at least we'll be on hand to back each other.

My reception in the new district is friendlier than day one had been at my training district. A number of the people on my watch are fairly young, with less than fifteen years on the job, and they're very supportive of the six new rookies. They're young enough to remember the terror of being green, eager to pass along helpful tips and clues about working the streets. We're all assigned to the day watch, all partnered with someone for the first day. After that, we're on our own.

On my first day as a ten-ninety-nine unit (officer working alone), I'm assigned a project beat. Fifteen-floor high-rises filled with guns and drugs and more potential for ambush than the Creep Zone ever imagined. I'm scared right down to my socks. Other, more experienced cops have told me that the most important thing about working in the projects, or any high-crime area, is attitude. In copspeak, that means you have to walk the walk, display an equal mix of confidence and authority. For male officers, that's usually backed up by the promise that they will not hesitate to jump in if things become physical, in most cases using muscles that could easily hoist a large appliance. For a female, it's different.

The job teaches us early on that, for any cop, your brain is your most powerful weapon. Strategy, diplomacy, and common sense can go as far or farther than any muscle-rippling goon squad. In lieu of a female cop's body mass, her strength lies in her ability to communicate. The people we encounter on the street are more likely to talk to a female cop, and expect a higher level of understanding or compassion than might come from a male officer. We're the ones who soothe the children, calm the combatants during domestic disturbances, comfort senior citizens. The brute strength—the upper hand in physical confrontations—is traditionally left to our male counterparts.

On this first day in my new district, I stare at the monolith project buildings I'm assigned to, and consider my game plan. For me, walking the walk will be less about implied threat and more about a willingness to listen. In my brief field experience, I've learned that many of the altercations between police and the public occur due to frustration—people want to be heard, and feel that no one is listening. Someone is angry, or upset, or outraged over a neighbor, a woman, a job—but there's no one to listen, no place to vent. For me, it will be easier to listen, to assess the situation, and defuse it by talking. In theory it sounds like a plan. But since nothing is absolute on this job, the reality may be another story entirely.

My first job is a domestic.

"See the woman, apartment 1502, name of Boyd. Offender is on the scene."

Of course he is. And I'm wondering if this is going to be a replay: Homey Part II. But when I pull up to the building, where lizard-eyed junkies nod in the grimy vestibule, another squad car is waiting. It's Lundegaard, a beefy blond Swede assigned to the neighboring beat. My backup, he tells me. Domestics can be tricky until you get the hang of them, so he thought he'd mosey over, give me a hand. Besides, it's not a good idea to go in the jets alone.

"Jets?"

"Jets. Y'know, pro-jets. You're in the 'hood now, kid. When in Rome, right?"

We enter the building, squinting in the sudden dimness. No windows on the first level, no lights. The stench is unbelievable.

"Winos," Lundegaard says, skirting a puddle. "They think the whole place is their bathroom."

When I move toward the elevator, he directs me to the stairs.

"But it's on the fifteenth floor!"

"Yeah, and if you wanna make it up there, you'll walk."

The stairwell is worse than the lobby. No lights, worse stench, the scurrying sounds of assorted vermin.

On the way up, Lundegaard offers some pearls of wisdom.

"It's not a good idea to take elevators in the jets," he tells me. "Half the time, they don't work, and the other half, well . . . anything could happen. The elevators are a 'dead zone.' That means our radios don't transmit in there. If we're in trouble, there's no way we can call for help. Lotta times someone will call the cops on something hot—like a battery in progress, say, and it's always on one of the higher floors. So the squads come flying in, and some guys, trying to get there quicker, will take the elevator. Which is just what *they* want—whoever called in the first place—because it was a phony call. And now it's an ambush, with two or three or four cops stuck in the elevator. So then the little gangbangers—or the bad guys, whoever it is—jam the elevator mechanism and you're stuck in this dark reeking little box and you can't radio for help. Other times, they've been known to pour gas or alcohol down the elevator shaft, set the cables on fire. 'Roast pig,' they call it. Real funny, huh? So the stairs are a better bet."

By the time we make it up to the fifteenth floor, I'm ready to pass out. Between the stench, the stairs, and no ventilation, it's the StairMaster from hell. Lundegaard is sympathetic. And tells me I'll get used to it. The trick is pacing yourself . . . and breathing through your mouth.

In apartment 1502 the complainant, a woman in her early twenties, ushers us in.

". . . and I'm just tired of all this, Office! Tired of this raggedy muthafucka thankin' he can come up in here, eat up all my food, get him some pussy, and then don't give me no money?" She chicken-necks at me, her eyes wide. "*I don' thank so!* Y'all know how it is, don't you, Miss Lady?" Before I can say anything she points to a tattered yellow couch, where the raggedy muthafucka in question is stretched out in cutoff sweatpants, balancing a can of malt liquor on his bare chest, deeply engrossed in *The Flintstones* on the portable TV.

"This man call hisself lookin' for a job, but I thank he be hangin' with some other bitch. Stay gone two, three nights at a time, then come back up in here startin' shit. Go upside my head, call me all kinds of bitches and hos! In my own house? Y'all better lock his black ass up!" She wheezes a little, pausing for breath. Caught up in the adventures of Fred and Barney, the man on the couch makes no comment.

I'm ready to pull out a set of complaint forms, have her sign, and escort the man off to jail. He smacked her around, she's pissed. Why prolong the inevitable? And besides, I can't do the ghetto shuffle—that fidgety little sidestep so the roaches don't crawl up your pants leg—all day.

But Lundegaard—the voice of experience—intervenes. "You say you've been together for a while?" Did she say that? That's not what *I* heard. "Smart young lady like yourself, you must know a thing or two about keeping your thing together, if it's a good thing. Must be, if you and your man are still together."

I eye Lundegaard in amazement. Where did he get this rap from? Either he's a student of Motown 101, or he's a New Age therapist in cop's clothing. In any case, it's effective, because the woman is staring at him, completely nonplused.

"Yeah, well, you know. . . ." she mutters finally. "Ain't much of a woman if you don't know how to treat your man."

Lundegaard nods. "And he looks like a happy man, to have an understanding woman like you. Ain't that right, friend?" He harrumphs in the direction of the inert Flintstone fan.

"Huh? Oh . . . yeah. Uh-huh." The man sets his can down and belches loudly. "Baby, y'all gonna make me a sandwich or what? How long I got to wait?"

"See there?" Lundegaard smiles like a benign uncle. "He knows he's got a good woman. A woman who can see to all his needs." And to me. "Let's go, Office. Leave these good people to their business."

Back in the stairwell, I'm laughing.

"I have to hand it to you—that was pretty slick."

"Slick? That was a no-brainer. She just wanted some attention. Had to call the *po*-lice to get it. Happens all the time. If we'd have tried to arrest him, she'd go ballistic, fighting us for taking her man. This way, everybody's happy. They're probably knockin' boots right now."

"You're pretty adept at the ghetto slang, Blondie."

"You will be, too, when you've been here a little while. You pick it up without even thinking about it."

"Speaking of which, what's with this 'Office' thing? She kept calling me 'Office.'"

Lundegaard neatly sidesteps a pile of vomit.

"'Office.' Instead of 'Officer.' You're in the ghetto now, kid. Don't expect any formal salutations. When in Rome, remember?"

In my new district, I learn more in one month than Vaughn taught me in half a year. I learn that it's more about teamwork and attitude than self-promotion and glory. On my assigned watch, it doesn't matter if you're a female or a rookie. What counts is that you're there, another body for backup and support.

When my workday starts, I become a uniform and an attitude. That's what the citizens see: another uniform, a necessary evil that they tolerate like all the other uniforms that prevent society from running amok. My attitude represents 16,000 other uniforms. If citizens have a positive encounter with me, they might say, "Wow! A nice cop! That's a surprise. Finally, someone who was willing to help me!" A not-so-pleasant encounter, and they're saying, "Typical police bullshit. They're all assholes!"

I learn that respect is what holds it together on the street. Everyone wants it; not enough are getting or giving it. Lack of it can cause a minor situation to blow up; enough of it can defuse something really nasty.

On a typical West Side Saturday night, we receive more domestic calls than any other night. It's the woman who usually calls, shouting that she's been beaten, they're fighting, come and lock this motherfucker up. When we get there, she's hysterical, he's fed up. He's had a rough week and he's tired. It's Saturday night. Time to chill, maybe party a little, go out and have a few drinks. When he gets home, it hits the fan. She's pissed. Who's cleaning the house, taking care of the kids, cooking the food while he's out fooling around?

He's too tired to argue. Just once he'd like to come home to some peace; maybe if that happened, he'd stay around more often. But she's not letting it go, so they go a few rounds. Some name-calling, a few threats—and then they really get into it. When we get there, she's nursing a swollen lip, he's bleeding from the bottle she cut him with, and everyone's miserable. Invariably, she'll look at me, that woman-to-woman look, and say, "You understand, Office. You know how it is."

And he'll say to me, "Baby, I'm just tired of this woman's shit."

To him, I'm "Baby." It's not a come-on, just a plea for recognition: *I'm a man, trying to do a man's job, and this woman of mine doesn't see it. How about giving me my propers?*

Some female cops hate when that happens. They'll snap, "Don't call me that! I'm not your baby!"

They don't realize that it's a cry for respect. But I'll be "Office," or "Baby," or whatever, and I'll let them talk, both of them. Many times, that's all it takes. They just need to be heard, to hear each other. Sometimes they work it out, sometimes I have to lock him up. But when that happens, he'll come with me, like a gentleman, without a fight. Because I gave him his respect.

Sometimes a situation is too far gone for diplomacy. The police are called to referee a fight that's already raging when we get there. She wants him locked up, she'll sign the complaints. But once we put the cuffs on him, she becomes a maniac. And jumps on the closest uniformed back, kicking and screaming.

"Where you motherfuckers think you takin' my man?"

And then it becomes a free-for-all. It's during one of these encounters, when my shirt's ripped off my back, that I learn the importance of wearing an undershirt.

There are cultural differences to consider in encounters with the public. In the Hispanic and Asian cultures, the man will usually speak to the male officer instead of his female partner. Women, who are expected to be subservient, are beneath consideration. So it's always interesting when he has to deal with a female officer alone or, even better, a two-woman team.

In the projects, a situation can develop depending on who's assigned to answer the call. An African-American male cop walks in, the man of the house thinks he's a sellout. "We're brothers, man. Don't gimme any of that *po*-lice shit!"

An African-American female cop might get the same attitude and be accused of siding with his woman. "You bitches are all the same."

A Caucasian male cop could be considered an outright threat, an invader on his turf. One of these guys shows up, and he's ready to fight. But a female Caucasian or Hispanic might be viewed simply as a woman—not a threat, not a violation of the brotherhood/sisterhood, who just might be willing to listen.

From my street stops, the hustlers and cons, dealers and thieves who are out there every night, trying to get over, I learn that there's a language of the streets, a dialect of nuance. It's communication with attitude more than words, an understanding that we're all out here together doing our thing. My thing just happens to be preventing them from doing theirs. The surprise is that they respect that, as long as you're doing your job the right way. It's a *job* out here, for us and for them, and nobody's served if we start taking things personally.

Six months after I lock up a small-time dealer for possession and intent to sell, I meet him on the streets—and he tips me off to the whereabouts of a child molester.

"You was just doin' your gig," he grins, with light flashing off his diamond-studded tooth. "I know it ain't nothin' personal—just what you got to do. I can dig it. But go get this nasty mother. He's messin' with our kids."

I learn that everybody's got a story; a lot of people have scams. Reality is not necessarily what you hear, or even what you see. One thing's for sure. Everyone is trying to get over, to bend that reality in their favor, with results that are sometimes so preposterous there's nothing to do but laugh.

I get a call one day to check out two men selling guns and meat from the trunk of their car. It sounds strange, but just a few short months have taught me to expect the unexpected, that the improbable is the norm. When I arrive on the scene, two Hispanic men are slouched in the front seat of a rusty green Pontiac, with broad-brimmed cowboy hats pulled low over their faces. Because this is a call involving weapons, I wait for my backup before approaching the car. One of these *caballeros* could be cradling a sawed-off shotgun in his lap, not happy about the police interfering with what he thinks is fair commerce.

My backup arrives—Beat 1230, my sector sergeant, a youngish guy who keeps everyone laughing, and doesn't take much seriously except for baseball and his ever-present Marlboros. With guns drawn, we get the occupants out of the car, and draped, facedown, over the hood before the sergeant steps back to the trunk. There are no plates on the car, and the trunk lock's punched, indicating that the car either is or once was stolen.

"Don't bother running this piece of shit for a hot check," he advises when I reach for my radio. "Got so much rust on it, that's the only thing holding it together. Whoever stole it did the owner a favor."

With his nightstick, he lifts up the hood. The smell of rotted flesh is like a punch in the gut. There's definitely meat in there—what looks like a side of beef hastily hacked into random shapes the size of seat cushions. Meat that's progressed from merely rancid to serious putrefaction. Some of the hunks are edged in green, others are covered with a weird rainbow slime. It's all heaped and dripping on an old shower curtain, which barely covers a display of handguns. There's nothing impressive among the weapons— just a pile of cheap Saturday-night specials that look to be as rusty as the car. Or maybe it's the blood and juices trickling down from the fetid meat.

"Yo, partner, what's up with the arsenal?" The sergeant strolls back to the suspects, rubbing his eyes. The smell is rank enough to give him contact conjunctivitis.

Still bent over the hood of the Pontiac, one of the men merely shrugs. The other peers up, smiles his best "we're all brothers-in-arms" smile and, ever the entrepreneur, says, "You know, Boss, I could really make you a deal."

"Not me, man. Just smelling that shit's enough to make me a vegetarian for life." But the sergeant winks at me. He's one of the rare few willing to be entertained when the situation presents itself.

"Not just the meat, Boss. The guns. I could take care of you, you know? We could work out a deal!" The man smiles hopefully. "Just gimme a chance, man."

By now, I've searched both men—no weapons—so the sergeant is willing to allow them to stand and face him. Both of them barely reach our shoulders.

With great gravity, he considers the man's offer. "So, what kind of deal are we talking here?"

The two cowboys exchange a hasty look. A mumbled consultation in Spanish and then. "We could make you partners, Boss. You could sell the guns to the other *policía,* we split the money. *And,* I'll even throw in the meat for free."

"Hmmmm. That's quite a deal." Rocking back on his heels, the sergeant lights another cigarette. And peruses the jittery men through a veil of smoke for a few minutes—long enough to raise their anxiety level nearly as high as the stench.

The nervous cowboy decides to try a different approach.

"No need to get all *serious* about this. We ain't criminals. Just trying to do a little business, Boss. Be glad to take care of you here, so everybody's happy. . . ." His voice trails off as the sergeant strolls around the car. It really is a disaster on wheels. The tires are bald, the backseat is shredded down to the springs, and one of the doors is held on with a wire coat hanger. On the front passenger side is a large hole in the floor, giving the concept of foot brakes a whole new meaning. The sergeant is nodding, his face impassive, eyes shielded by his wraparound shades.

Finally he returns to the squirming men.

"That's something to think about," he says. "I've never been one to pass up an opportunity. But what's the *rest* of it?"

"Rest of it?" More mumbled Spanish. "That's all, Boss. You sell the guns, we split the money. Nothing else."

"And I guess, as business partners, we wouldn't arrest you, right?"

"*Es verdad,* Boss. Right, right. We're all gentlemen here." A fractional nod to me. "Uh, and you, *señorita.*"

The sergeant flicks away his butt and smiles. From his years of experience, he knows that it would be a waste of time to arrest the two men. Their car is one rust spot away from the junkyard, and no one in their right mind would bother to report it as a stolen vehicle. As for the cache of guns, it would take longer for us to inventory them that the amount of time these two would spend in gun court. There, a harried judge would consider the inventory of old and malfunctioning weapons, defer to his crowded court docket, and dismiss the men with only three months' 'suspended supervision'—a legal slap on the wrist which translates to "Gotcha! Don't do it again—now get out of my courtroom."

So the sergeant has already decided that these two won't be taking the ride to Men's Central Detention. But his twinkling eyes indicate he's going to have a little fun before he lets them go, and his definition of "fun" is anybody's guess.

"But, see, *I am* the Boss here, so I should get more,"

the sergeant drawls. "If your asses don't go to jail, I should get a sweeter deal."

The cowboy looks close to apoplexy. Just when he thought he'd finessed his way out of jail, this crazy *gringo* gets greedy.

"You talkin' money, Boss? Cuz you know, we ain't got none. That's why we're selling the guns—"

"I'm talking shoes," the sergeant says decisively, and points to their battered cowboy boots. "Or, as you say, *zapatos*. I want 'em. Give 'em up."

"*Que?*"

"The shoes, man. I like 'em, I want 'em. You want this deal to fly, give 'em up. Both of you." And to me. "I've always wanted cowboy boots. Maybe it'll be part of my new look. What d'ya think?"

I choke back a laugh. The dusty little boots are half the size of his feet, but the cowboys hand them over, goggle-eyed. Neither is willing to argue with the man with the gun. Next, the sergeant decides he wants their pants, their shirts, and finally their cowboy hats. When they're huddled, shivering in the brisk breeze, he eyes their underwear.

"You know, maybe there's something else I want. My dear old father, bless his heart, had prostate surgery a while back. Word is, he can't get it up anymore. Needless to say, my mother's not a happy camper. But I hear they can do wonders with dick replacements . . ."

The smaller cowboy is whispering urgently. "Your *dick*!" his partner hisses frantically. It's impossible not to laugh. I have to walk away or I'll wet my pants. Tiring of his cat-and-mouse game, the sergeant tells the cowboys to take off, without their shoes, without their clothes, without the miserable car and its strange cargo. And promises to lock them up for sure if he even sees them again.

"Oh, sure, you get the good stuff. What do I get?" I ask, when I finally stop laughing.

The sergeant spares me a pained expression.

"When you make rank, kid, then we'll talk. For now be satisfied with the crumbs I toss you." He points inside the car. "There's an air freshener with your name on it. A refreshing new fragrance: Eau de Stench."

The car is towed to the police auto pound, where the weapons are confiscated and destroyed.

The meat is another story. Thinking he's struck pay dirt when he discovers the load of beef, one of the pound attendants, whose sense of smell is nearly obliterated by a sinus infection, donates the meat to a beach barbecue held by the police in the First District. After the first three or four or nine beers, they say it's fine, especially with some barbecue sauce slapped on it. Of course, no one knows the meat's origins, so when most of the district members go to the emergency room with severe gastrointestinal complaints, no one makes the connection. And writes it off as just another variation of the Blue Flu.

7

Love Hurts

Dispatcher: 1233?
1233: '33.
Dispatcher: 1233, all units in Twelve and on citywide, we have a man shot, a man shot at 14— West Grenshaw in the house. A neighbor's calling it in, says the offender is still on the scene.
1233: Ten-four, Squad. On the way.
Dispatcher: Other units to ride with '33?
1237: '37, we're rollin'.
1231: '31's on the way.
1213: 1213. I'm not far from there—I'll slide by.
Dispatcher: Okay, we're getting more calls on this now. They say there's still a lot of screaming going on over there, so all responding units use caution.

From songs and movies, I've heard that love can move mountains, keep us together, and light up our lives. Love conquers all. But this job shows me that it also breaks bones, maims, and kills. Anytime there's a man and a woman, woman and a woman, man and a man, whatever the mix, and you toss in the "L" word, things get interesting and sometimes explosive. To some people, love goes beyond the usual concepts of caring and sharing. It plumbs the depths of possessiveness, obsession, and jealousy,

creating a whole new postscript to the Seven Dead-
lies that means if love flies out the window, pain
crawls through the door.

The crimes committed in the name of love are
legion—and more grisly than anyone would believe. It's an eye-opener for me, for anyone who still
believes in the "do unto others" part of the Golden
Rule. Out here on the streets, I learn that there are
no rules—only degrees of passion and rage which
are acted upon without thought of consequences,
and with sometimes disastrous results.

Tremaine Spraggins learns the hard way. He comes
home late one night whistling, more than a little
buzzed after tossing back a sixer of beer. When his
girlfriend asks where he's been, he's vague at first,
mumbling something about stopping for something
to eat. Thought he'd pick up a bucket of chicken to
bring home. But since Tremaine is standing in front
of her, chickenless and reeking of beer, she doesn't
buy it.

Drinking? No, ain't been drinking, he says, but
guess who he ran into in the chicken joint's parking
lot? Rodney—remember him? His homey from Far-
ragut High? Yeah, ol' Rodney—ain't seen him in a
dog's age! So they hung out for a while, catching up
on old times.

Three hours? She asks. With Rodney for three
hours in a parking lot?

'Course not, Tremaine says. He rode with Rodney
to pick up his girlfriend, Capri. The one workin'
over at the liquor store. Remember Capri?

The girlfriend remembers. How can she forget?
Capri is every woman's nightmare. Breasts that look
like she's smuggling cantaloupes, and legs that start
at her neck. Now the girlfriend is really mad. And

wants to know just what took so long picking up another man's woman at the liquor store.

Tremaine suppresses a belch and tries to look innocent.

"Ain't nothin' happenin', baby. I was just runnin' with my partner. You know I'm your man."

Not very convincing, but the girlfriend's willing to let it slide. And walks into another room, at which time Tremaine, thinking she's out of earshot, lets out a heartfelt moan. And his eyes glaze just slightly as he mutters to himself about his recent exploits.

"That Capri, mmmm, mmmm, mmmmm! Girl's wilder than a mustang! Just about broke my back!" Deep in his beer-fueled reverie, Tremaine never notices his girlfriend standing in the doorway.

When we arrive on the scene, there is no fighting. No shouting, not even a random scream or two. What there *is* is an ax embedded in the side of Tremaine's head, just behind his ear. He's calm, sitting in the chair, talking to us like it's just another day. And while we're waiting for the ambulance, he refuses to sign complaints. His woman loves him, he tells us; otherwise, she wouldn't have done this. It's a love thang.

The girlfriend looks smug when she announces that no bitch, not Capri, not *anyone* is gonna front her off. This is her man, her thing. Ain't nobody takin' it away.

At the hospital, the doctors tell Tremaine they can't remove the ax, or half his brain will come with it. It's lodged there, tight enough to prevent hemorrhaging, but it's in there for good. The best they can do is trim off the handle and excess blade, make it flush with his skull.

"Unbelievable!" I say to my partner as we're riding away. "He has to walk around with that for the rest of his life." Another victim of domestic violence, one of the thousands I'll see in this job. Acts of unspeakable violence that become commonplace to those who witness them. Somewhere along the way I'll learn that the only way to handle it is with emotional distance. Game face again. This is where the gallows humor comes in, perfected by cops and medical personnel and anyone else in a position to witness firsthand the fallout of human decency. My partner glances at me and responds in kind.

"Yeah, well, he should have covered his ass a little better." He looks at me impishly, barely able to suppress a grin. "Never should have tipped his hand around his girlfriend, especially with weapons in the house. Sounds to me like he *axed* for it!"

One night I'm working with Angie, a petite Latina with eleven years on the job. We're given a disturbance call: "Something screaming for help." *Something?* Ten-four, says the dispatcher. Neighbor's calling it in. Says whatever it is doesn't sound human.

The town house's front door is open when we get there, and the rooms inside are trashed. Some very pricey furniture has been smashed, pictures broken, tables overturned. It's obvious that someone took a lot of time to destroy what was once an elegant living room. We step over the wreckage in the dining room and, with weapons drawn, move cautiously up the stairs toward the bedroom, and a strange lowing noise that sounds like cattle in distress.

"It hurts!"

A moan, a muffled sob. I hear it before I know where it's coming from. Inside the bedroom, equally trashed, is an ornate king-size bed, laden with a huge mound of bedclothes. Bedclothes now twitching and shuddering as we move closer.

There's a person under there, somewhere, or maybe several, judging by the size of the mound.

"There's blood everywhere, Officer! It's ruined! You can't get blood out of silk."

A sheet twitches back and we see him. He's humongous, lying there shuddering like a beached whale, but a whale with exotic taste. His caftan is floor-length lavender silk covered with exquisite embroidery. Hand-stitched herons, cranes, flowering trees cover the cuffs and flowing sleeves. I've seen such caftans in import stores and know they cost a fortune. What I didn't know is that they'd come in such a huge size.

Another moan, and the weeping victim clutches my hand, gasping in pain.

I take a closer look. There *is* some blood, tiny spatters that look more like menstrual stains than heinous injury.

"It doesn't look bad," Angie tells him. "Just relax. We'll get the paramedics right away."

"Relax? How can I relax? My lover is a maniac! Who in their right mind would do this? I'm going to bleed to death before they get here."

"No, you're not. Just lie still."

"What got into that man, I don't know. He's always been jealous, but I never thought he'd do this." More sobs. "Just freaked out, went crazy. Doesn't he know how much I love him?" Another gasp. "It hurts, Officer! I can't stand it! How much longer?"

"They're on the way. Try to relax."

"Tell us what happened." Angie is the voice of calm. "And try to stop gasping like that, sir. You're starting to hyperventilate."

"I can't help it." A meaty paw dabs at tear-smudged mascara. The weeping man is a behemoth, roughly the size and shape of a sumo wrestler. And he seems to have a penchant for cosmetics. Tearstains track through several flaking layers of pancake makeup and rouge. The voluminous caftan drapes across his girth, with the golden embroidery complimenting the two earrings that glint in his left lobe. He notices me noticing his earrings.

"Yin and Yang," he sniffles, pointing to the Chinese symbols. "For Eldon and me. He's Yang, of course. A testosterone overload, I think. He has a hard time with impulse control." The weeping victim tries, unsuccessfully, to firm trembling lips, but another sob escapes.

"All I ever wanted to do is love him, but the man's an animal!"

Angie glances around the ruined bedroom. The gold-leaf bureau mirror is shattered, the elegant silk-upholstered slipper chairs slashed open.

"I'd say so!" She mutters. I know what she means. Anytime someone shoves a gourd up your butt, I'd say he has a hell of a time with impulse control!

The man swipes at his eyes again. His lids are done in purple shadow, to match the caftan.

"We've had some problems before—what couple doesn't? Like I said, Eldon is very jealous. But I thought we'd worked everything out. Last month we spent two weeks in Mexico"—the purple lids flutter—". . . the Mexican Riviera, actually. It was fabulous! Until Eldon started getting suspicious of the cabana boys, and—"

"What happened tonight, sir? Just stick with what happened this time." Angie is insistent. The female version of Joe Friday: "Just the facts, ma'am."

"Well, I have this friend who's an aroma therapist at the Inner Vision—that's that health spa and acupressure center on Broadway? Anyway, he stopped by this evening to drop off some of their special astringent. I have very large pores, you know, and he was just doing me a favor. And then Eldon came home and went crazy. My friend was gone by then, but Eldon saw the astringent. Accused me of doing the nasty with someone else!" The fleshy face crumples. "One thing led to another, and then. . . ." The man is too devastated to continue.

I leave the questioning to Angie. Despite the unusual circumstances, the man's story is familiar: love, jealousy, and violence. The three major contributors to most of the domestic violence we witness. I can understand his pain; but, at this point in my career, I'm not sure how you inquire diplomatically how a four-hundred-pound man gets sodomized by a gourd.

The clatter in the hallway tells us the paramedics have arrived. They troop in with the collapsible gurney, step over the upended vanity table, and eye the victim.

"What've we got here?" the shorter one asks. His voice is neutral, but his face has taken on that "Oh, shit!" look, as in, "Oh, shit! How are we gonna haul this elephant down all those stairs?"

Angie moves a discreet distance from the victim.

"Domestic," she murmurs. "Lovers' spat. The other guy went crazy and shoved a gourd up his rectum. A big one, from what he says."

"Not a gourd!" the man calls from the bed. "A *guiro*. Like they play in mariachi bands. A souvenir from our trip." He plucks fretfully at the back of his caftan.

"Christ!" The paramedic shakes his head. "So where's the other guy now?"

"Gone before we got here. Doesn't matter, though. Thor, here, says he doesn't want to sign a complaint. Just wants to get the gourd removed. So where are you guys taking him—to County?"

"Yeah. They have the best triage unit."

The other paramedic speaks in a whisper.

"Is this guy Chinese, or what?"

"Japanese, he says, and something else."

"Norwegian!" Thor calls. Intrusive trauma has sharpened his hearing. "On my mother's side. That's why I'm large-boned."

The paramedics busy themselves setting up the gurney, which will, for Thor, be like bodysurfing on a Popsicle stick. Like any professionals, their faces remain neutral, displaying no judgment, no surprise.

The shorter one smiles politely at the nervous victim. "Now that I think of it, I haven't seen too many Asians with platinum hair."

In spite of his agony, Thor giggles. And smiles coquettishly when he says, "Oh, I help it along a little, you know. Me and my hairstylist. I look better as a blond."

He shrieks as the four of us struggle to heft him onto the gurney. "I'm bleeding to death!" he cries, clutching at his lavender ass. "A beautiful caftan, ruined!" He knuckles away the leaking tears and blinks up owlishly at the shorter paramedic.

"Do you like it? The color, I mean?"

Grunting and huffing, the paramedics maneuver the overflowing gurney toward the door.

"Huh? You say something, mister?"

"I said, do you like my caftan? The color?"

"Oh. Uh, yeah, sure."

"Thank you." Thor smiles modestly. "I look best in orchids and grapes. I'm a summer, you know."

For some people, failed love can push them beyond the bounds of simple jealousy or bitterness into a whole new realm of behavior. It's the dog-in-the-manger syndrome: Don't want them, don't want anyone else to have them either.

In Demetrius Austin's case, he thought it made perfect sense. He'd invested a lot of time in his woman, whom he'd met in high school. Darcelle had been so fine, guys from four different schools were after her. But she'd chosen him. Or, more precisely, she was the chosen. Demetrius saw her and knew he had to have her. At seventeen, he was 6'3" and 270 pounds, a solid tower of muscle and mean. Known as "the Annihilator," he was a starring offensive football tackle at his high school, feared and respected by all who went up against him. Demetrius was used to getting what he wanted, and he wanted Darcelle.

After their first date, he had "D & D Forever" tattooed on his massive biceps. After that, no man who wanted to live dared to approach Darcelle. She was thrilled, at first, flattered by his devotion for the first month or two. But soon she realized she was just another possession, an ornament worn on his arm like his gold bracelets. And being Demetrius's possession meant he'd shove her aside when something—or someone else—captured his attention, which was often and easily. When she tried to leave him, it was too late. She was pregnant, a vessel carrying another of his possessions. He told her if she tried to go, he'd kill her—or anyone else who came between them.

Six years and five kids later, Darcelle had had enough. Demetrius was usually unemployed—a job would cut into his leisure time. It should be enough that she was getting welfare checks, and quick, brutal sex whenever he was in the mood.

"Lotta bitches want to be ridin' this dick," he told her, backhanding her across the room. "You don't know how lucky you is! Don't get up in my face 'bout no money. I look like a bank to you?"

Darcelle was desperate. The kids were always hungry, the rent was way behind, and bill collectors never stopped calling. Her friends were afraid to come around the combative Demetrius, who, after a beer or two, was likely to take a swing at anyone. There was nothing to do but bring her problems to God.

She started attending the Missionary Baptist Church each Sunday, praying for deliverance. Eventually, she found it, in the form of Avery Gerrard. Avery was the choir director, a thoughtful man as gentle as Demetrius was rough. He and Darcelle talked a little, then a lot, lingering after each service to savor each other's company. Avery gave her food, money sometimes, and boxes of donated clothing for the kids. It was innocent at first, a friend helping a friend. One day, it became more.

Demetrius was gone that day, out boozing with one of his whores. It was easy to leave the kids with a neighbor.

"I'm just going down to the church," Darcelle said. "Just for a little while. They're having auditions for the choir today."

"Praise Jesus!" The neighbor smiled. "Who better to sing for than the Lord?"

The first time with Avery opened a whole new

world for Darcelle. She discovered tenderness and feelings so profound that she wept. And knew she had to find a way—some way—to leave Demetrius.

Avery opted for a simple plan. Why not just tell him the truth?

"He'll kill me," Darcelle said. "He'll never let me go."

"We'll tell him together," Avery said. "If there's two of us, he might listen to reason. He's always laying up with some other woman, anyway. Maybe this is the right time."

Darcelle knew better, but she was a woman in love. And reality is no match for love.

"We'll pray on it," Avery promised. "The Lord will find a way."

That way came the following week. Demetrius had been home for two days, recovering from a bout of the flu. Weakened, almost passive as he sprawled on the couch watching television. It was the right time, Avery decided.

He came to the Austins' home bearing a bag of oranges and a jug of lemonade—a delivery from the pastor, he said. Something to help heal Mr. Austin. The congregation was praying for his recovery.

Other than a muttered "Who the hell is this faggot?" Demetrius ignored Avery and his offerings. And remained silent while Darcelle chatted nervously about church matters, attempting to fill the brittle void.

Finally, Avery made his move. He told Demetrius an amended version of the truth; that Darcelle had asked for guidance from the Lord, and peace from the burden of her hardships. Her relationship was wearing her out, the choirmaster said. She needed to be released. A man like Demetrius could find happiness in many places.

Lying on the couch, Demetrius was deceptively calm. His eyes slid from Avery to the tense Darcelle. He was so quiet that they never saw it coming, not the murderous rage kindling in his eyes or the fists that seemed to fly up out of nowhere.

When the police arrived, Demetrius was sprawled on the couch again, sweaty and smug after his bout with Avery and the whoring Darcelle. Just one punch had been enough to send the slender churchman flying across the room and start Darcelle screaming. But it hadn't been enough for him. They'd fronted him, this bitch and her faggoty man, disrespected him in his own home. Something he wasn't likely to forget, so now they had to pay.

Avery had been the easy part. Demetrius got his pistol and ordered Darcelle to strip off his pants. While the terrified woman watched, and screamed, he fired a single shot to the groin.

"Guess he'll be singin' soprano for the rest of his days!" Demetrius chortled.

For Darcelle, he wanted something more. He could shoot her, but death was too easy. He wanted her to suffer, to remember what he'd done for a long time. One punch was all it took to knock her unconscious. What he did next took a little more effort. Snatching off her underwear, he spread her legs and began to brutalize her with the fruit Avery had offered. Let the bitch take what her punk-ass boyfriend had brought. When he tired of that, Demetrius resorted to a broomstick. Finally, he simply got up and stomped her, the full weight of his body mashing her lower torso to pulp. Afterward, he stood sweating over the bleeding bodies as he poured himself a glass of lemonade.

Drinking deeply, he toasted them, and then hunkered down on the sofa to view his handiwork.

It took almost no time at all for Avery to die from a severed inguinal artery, and just an hour longer for Darcelle to be pronounced dead at the hospital ER. Doctors there said it was impossible to determine how much she'd felt after the knockout punch, but at least now her suffering was over. Maybe Avery had been right. Maybe the Lord had found a way.

It's impossible for me—for any of us on the street—to witness something like this without being changed. We view firsthand the depths of depravity, the seamiest side of the human condition, and are expected to remain professional and untouched. That's what cops are supposed to do; protect and serve, but not to process the horror that's all around us. To save ourselves from going insane, we have to change, but it's a gradual transition. After the first domestic call, or the thirtieth, the first child-abuse case we handle . . . at some point, we retreat. We have no place to shed our tears, nowhere to scream over all we witness and can't prevent. No one to listen when we need to talk. Our families won't understand—can't, unless they've experienced it, seen firsthand what other sick and twisted versions of life exist beyond the safety of their own homes. The only ones who understand are other cops. Cops who learn early that the only way to cope is to hide what's left of their hearts, and their emotions. And seek protection, through detachment or humor, or a careful callousness that gets them through the next call, the next tour of duty, the next pair of sightless eyes in a victim we were too late to help.

That's part of the way that cops change. In spite of how we struggle against it, the aftershock of sins and unspeakable acts we handle at work invades our personal lives. We begin to doubt what once was accepted, question anything beyond the concrete. Suspicion replaces trust as our circles of intimacy grow smaller. We see on the job what love does, how it hurts and kills, and begin to question it in our own lives. Any relationship becomes subject to scrutiny. In our eyes, anyone could become another Demetrius, another ax-wielding girlfriend—another *anyone* out to do us harm. It becomes riskier to share feelings, develop the intimacy we need but can't quite trust anymore. We've seen what happens out there. Allowing ourselves to be open and trusting—and thereby vulnerable to potential harm—might make us the next victim, and is a luxury few of us are willing to gamble on. And so the changes continue. And will continue, as long as we remain cops, protectors, and eyewitnesses.

Sometimes we witness true evil masquerading as love, like the call that takes us to the house of Clement Lee Gamble. A pale, disheveled young boy huddles on the steps, watching us come up the walk. He shivers, glancing fearfully at the broken screen door behind him.

"It's about Mama," he whispers. "Mama and Granddaddy." His eyes dart away from us and back to the door. Heavy footsteps from inside the house, and then—

"What the hell you waitin' on, Arthur? I told you, get on back to the kitchen."

The boy is up and running, a frightened, fearful mouse, past the towering man who looms in the doorway. Clement Lee Gamble eyes us, packing contempt, distrust, and loathing in his steely blue glare. He's a big man, 6'4" at least, and easily 300 pounds. Despite the sagging paunch and white hair that betray his sixty-two years, his arms are rock hard, thickly muscled. Not someone you'd want to mess with. Which, once we hear Clement's tale of love, is exactly what we have to do.

Clement Lee, by his own description, is a good man. A God-fearing man. Never was much on school-learnin', but he knows the Bible backward and forward. And knows the value of hard work. Picked cotton down home when he was just knee-high, and been workin' ever since. A body works that hard, he knows the value of a dollar. Couldn't have raised up his family if he didn't.

Clement tells us he's been married to Loretta near to forty-five years. Just a country gal when he met her, from the backwoods of Alabama. He brought her up here, to the big city, after their fifth, sixth child—he can't recall for sure—but she never did take to it. Felt like she didn't fit in, couldn't get with the city ways.

But she *did* know how to churn out them babies, and that's what she did, thirteen of 'em. The first nine, they was all boys, and then—finally—Raylene. She was a pretty little thing, delicate and blonde, pale like her mama. Sickly at first. Loretta took to fussing over her so much, she forgot her chores, forgot the other kids.

To his mind, Clement Lee tells us, she needed to have another child, take her mind off the runt. So he took it upon himself to make sure she did. But he kept his eye out for Raylene. She was his child, after all, his only daughter. And, gradually, he took her under his wing. A little extra attention, to make sure she knew her daddy loved her. Clement Lee looks away from us, sucking on his cheek. That's the main thing, he tells us. How much her daddy loved her.

Inside the house, we find out just how much her daddy loved her. The weeping Loretta tells us that by the time Raylene was four, Clement Lee was forcing himself on her in any way her tiny body could accommodate him. By the time she was eight, she was well beyond the nightmares, the screaming, the horror. A certain look from Daddy meant she should follow him, remove her clothes, and mutely endure each sexual assault. There was hell to pay if she didn't.

Loretta never intervened. She couldn't stop it. Nothing anybody could do would stop Clement Lee. He'd have killed anyone who tried. He was a man used to getting his own way, and he was strong as three mules. And anyway, it took some of it off her. Once he started on Raylene, he didn't come sniffing around her near as much. Besides, Raylene was a woman, and that was a woman's lot in life. You just had to take it. If it wasn't her Daddy, it would've been her brothers. That was just the way of things. And her boys, why, she was certain Clement Lee had messed with them from time to time. Made 'em tough, taught 'em to be strong. It was true, she told us. Ever' one of her boys was as big and strapping as their daddy.

Raylene was a mother by the time she turned twelve. Her father's child, of course. A child giving birth to her sister. By the time she was sixteen, she had four babies, all her daddy's.

And that's when Raylene changed. Some said she was simple from the get-go, always quiet, white-faced, empty-eyed. But she was different now, rocking for hours, babbling to herself, twitching and flinching like she had a demon inside her.

The God-fearing Clement Lee didn't want to tangle with a demon. Besides, Raylene was starting to look a touch raggedy—worn out and tired. Not ripe and firm-fleshed like before. So he started on Raylene's daughters, his babies, his grandchildren. There were three of them, each prettier than the one before. Raylene didn't catch on at first. She wasn't right in the mind, Loretta tells us. Didn't notice too much of anything. But she did notice when her thirteen-year-old daughter's belly began to swell. Which was all she needed to set her into action.

She waited until her daughter was asleep and took the cross, the one that stood next to the family Bible, and laid it over the sleeping child. Kneeling next to the bed, she asked Jesus to take her daughter into heaven, welcome her home, and protect her in the next world. She also asked forgiveness for what she had to do, but she was sure Jesus understood. Good must conquer evil. It said so in the Bible.

After that, she took Mama's butcher knife and slit her daughter's throat. One quick swipe, just enough to still that young body, free it from the devil growing inside it.

And then it was time to take on Clement Lee.

With the knife still clenched in her hand, she moved quickly through the darkened house, into her parents' bedroom. Her father lay sprawled on the bed, musty and sour-smelling, snoring like an old hog. Like the rutting hog that he was. She intended to be quick about it, and would have been. But it was dark, too dark for her to notice the teeth Daddy kept in a water glass on the nightstand. When she raised up her arm, she knocked the glass to the floor, shattering it and the dentures. Clement Lee was up in a flash, and on Raylene, Loretta says, like white on rice. Must've thought she was a burglar. It was really too dark to tell. He snatched her up and threw her clear across the room.

We find Raylene's body, still slumped against the wall like an old rag doll. Her pale blue eyes are open, glazed, her head tilted crazily from a broken neck. Worn beyond its young years, her frail body is still dressed in a threadbare nightgown. *A burglar in a nightgown?*

The body of Raylene's daughter has not been touched. Although the bedclothes are sodden with blood, the little girl looks peaceful, an angel as pretty as Raylene must have been. Her eyes are closed, as if in dreams. Or the safety of death.

Clement Lee sits quietly while we radio for a squadrol (paddy wagon), the crime lab, the Homicide detectives. And waits until everyone arrives before he decides to fight. It takes five men—five big men—to take him down. After he's cuffed, he's carried, struggling and screaming, to the back of the paddy wagon. And, once he's in there, spews out the Word According to Clement Lee.

It was self-defense. A burglar, he figured. A man has the right to protect what's his. Never on God's green earth would he hurt Raylene. She was his only daughter, his precious lamb. The one her daddy loved most.

8

Another Day at the Salt Mine

Dispatcher:	1225?
1225:	'25.
Dispatcher:	Listen, '25, I know you've handled this before, but that woman with the plumbing's calling again.
Unidentified Unit:	Don't all women have plumbing?
1225:	What's she want this time?
Dispatcher:	Something about bodies in her pipes.
Unidentified Unit:	Maybe she wants a pipe in her body.
Second Unidentified Unit:	Pipe dreams!

For some people, a typical workday means the same boring routine, the same tasks and projects you did the day before and will probably do tomorrow. For a cop, no two days are ever the same. There's a basic structure that frames the workday, but how it's filled is anyone's guess, depending on fate, misfortune, or the whims of the citizens we serve. The unpredictable nature of a cop's job is one of its greatest draws— and its greatest source of stress. Not knowing what comes next, or when, makes reporting to work each day a challenge. It also requires a constant vigilance, a wary eye. Experience tells us that even the most peaceable situations can become incendiary, a simple encounter can escalate to a bloody standoff at warp speed. Maintaining that hyperawareness, keeping your guard up constantly can be draining. It's also the primary reason why cops seem to be looking at you, around you, and past you, all at the same time. Because no one knows what's coming next . . . only that we have to be ready for it.

On any given day, there are two roll calls at the beginning of each shift of tour of duty. The watch personnel are divided into two groups: early and late cars. That's so there will always be police patrolling the streets. On the afternoon watch, the early cars work from 3:00 P.M. to 11:00 P.M. Late cars go from 4:00 P.M. to midnight. Seasoned veterans refer to the afternoon watch as "working the four to fours." That's because the afternoon watch is often the busiest, and some people, after getting off work, retire to the local cop ginmill until closing time. Four to four.

At roll call, a supervisor—usually a sergeant— reads the car assignments, passes along beat reports from the previous watch, and discusses any other miscellaneous information. Unless you're a permanent fixture on a beat car, the person you're partnered with can change from day to day. One day you might be assigned to work alone in a traffic car, the next night you're on the squadrol hauling stiffs and transporting prisoners.

After roll call, you sign out your squad-car keys and radios at the front desk and head out of the CDP corral. Some guys have a problem letting their female partners drive. Maybe it's a residual from that "Men are the masters of all things mechanical" mind-set. Other guys think it's a novelty to be chauffeured around by a woman. The rest of them, especially the younger guys, don't have a problem either way.

After cleaning out the previous watch's residue (newspapers, coffee cups, food wrappers) from the cars and gassing up, we hit the streets. For some, that means heading to the nearest convenience store and the first of many coffees. For others, it's an opportunity to get your required writing activity out of the way—the issuance of traffic tickets: movers and parkers. On afternoons, we're strongly encouraged to write rush-hour parkers—all those vehicles parked on the main thoroughfares in violation of the posted rush-hour times. After that, it's time to begin patrolling the beat, waiting for the jobs that are sure to come.

"1225?" The dispatcher's not wasting any time today. "'25, got a few to start you off. First, see the woman, 23—West Taylor, on a disturbance. Name is Fontana. Then you got a dog bite, U. of I. Hospital, Aguirre will be in the ER. After that, information for the police, 17—South Ashland, Espinosa on the second floor."

"Okay, Squad. We're about a block from the hospital. We'll take that one first."

"Ten-four."

My partner today is Ronnie Payton, a weightlifter nearly as wide as he is tall. His arms are massive, and he walks with the confidence of someone who knows he can handle himself in any situation. He grew up in the projects of our district and knows the people, the hustlers, the scams. On the street they call him "Mr. Payton," not "Ronnie," not "Office." And they say it with respect.

At the hospital, the job is routine. Take the information, consult with the hospital staff. It's a thirteen-year-old boy, bitten by a neighbor's cocker spaniel. He was late coming home from school, the mother relates anxiously in Spanish. That's when he was attacked by the dog. But there are no puncture wounds, only a trail of scratches from his shoulder down across his back. The silent boy sits staring at the floor, his head tilted toward his left shoulder. His worried mother hovers nearby.

After speaking with the nurse, Ronnie goes to the victim.

"Freddie—may I call you Freddie?—you're pretty tall for thirteen. Bet you shoot some hoops, huh?"

"Yeah."

"I know if I was playin' in a pickup game, you'd be my man."

The boy ducks his head, bashful but pleased.

" 'Cause you know, Freddie, that's what the girls like, am I right? They love them some athletes."

Freddie grins, but not before his mother shoots him a murderous look.

"Now, Freddie, I been lookin' at this 'bite' of yours. You sure that dog was a cocker spaniel?" Ronnie pretends to consult his notes. " 'Cause, see, far as I know, a cocker spaniel's a small dog. Small to be jumpin' that high to bite you. You're what, 5 feet 9, 10?"

The boy reddens. "Yeah, well maybe it was a big one. Or a mix." He ignores his mother's questioning look. "It was a red dog. A *big* red dog."

Ronnie looks at his notes again.

"You said before it was yellow. A little yellow dog."

"Maybe it was yellow. I don't remember. But it was big."

"Okay." Ronnie points to the Bulls jacket draped over a chair.

"That your coat, man?"

"Yeah."

"It's real nice."

"Thanks."

"You wear it today?"

" 'Course I wore it. It's cold outside."

"Yeah." Ronnie smiles at mother and son. "Funny how that dog, a big-little, red-yellow dog, can scratch up your shoulder and back without tearing your clothes or your jacket. And even leave that big ol' mark on your neck to boot."

He points to the hickey blooming on the underside of Freddie's tilted neck.

"*Que? Que?*" Mrs. Aguirre hisses, and snatches her son's face for a better look. A stream of heated Spanish, followed by a resounding smack to the embarrassed boy's head.

"If this is a dog bite, it's from the two-legged variety," Ronnie laughs. "Better be careful the dogs you run with, my man. Might get you more than just fleas."

We answer the disturbance call next. Mrs. Fontana, an elderly widow, is the only one there, but she's definitely disturbed. Her sink is messed up, she tells us. Water won't drain. Not in the kitchen, not in the bathroom.

And not a police matter, we say. She'll have to call a plumber.

She *did* call a plumber, she tells us. He said it was roots, that she'd have to get somebody to rod out the sewer.

"Sounds like a plan to me," Ronnie says politely.

No, she says. There's no roots. No trees or bushes on her property. Can't we get somebody over from Streets and San? We're all city workers. We have more clout than she does.

"Not really," Ronnie tells her. "Can't get 'em to pick up the garbage half the time. And anyway, that's the wrong department. You need Sewers." He gives her the phone number.

"This isn't the last of it," she calls after us. "My toilet overflows, I'm calling 911 again."

Over on Ashland, Mr. Espinosa is waiting for us. It's the vendors on 18th Street, he tells us. We should lock them up.

In this district, 18th Street runs through Pilsen, a Hispanic community with a population that mixes colonies of artists, writers, and enterprising yuppies with basically blue-collar Mexican families. As a result, there are galleries, lofts, and studios right alongside the fragrant *panaderías,* the *barbacoa* storefronts where succulent roast pigs glisten on the spit. An Old World atmosphere slowly being infiltrated by the young and trendy.

Spanish is still the primary language in this community, and its residents cling to their Old World ways. Mexican vendors push their wooden carts along 18th Street, selling everything from flavored ices to mango slices to delicate cream-filled churros. All of which is perfectly legal, as long as they have a vendor's license. Mr. Espinosa doesn't think so.

"What they sell, it's against the law!" he says. "Look what my daughter brought home. She said she got it from a vendor."

At first glance, it's a scrap of fur. A rabbit skin, maybe.

"*Es un gato!*" he snaps. "A cat!" A cat that didn't go without a fight. The head is still attached, with the face drawn into a snarl. The body is gutted and the skin scraped nearly clean. Some very disturbed and enterprising person has created a kitty-skin rug.

"My daughter, she says there were lots of them. All sizes, all colors. Who would do such a thing?" Mr. Espinosa tells us the kitty vendor was last seen in the vicinity of 18th and Bishop. We promise to check it out.

But before we can cruise for cats, there's a ten-one call broadcast over the radio. Gang fight in the alley at Cullerton and Hoyne.

All available squads, including the unmarked cars of tactical officers, rush to the scene. The unit that called the ten-one had their windshield shot out, but luckily, neither man was injured. Gang members are collared, cuffed, patted down. Enough weapons are confiscated, enough arrestees loaded into the wagon to mean the first assigned unit will be in the station doing paperwork and inventory for a very long time. When the last prisoner is placed in the squadrol, the other cars disperse.

"How 'bout some coffee?" Ronnie asks. "Still didn't get my caffeine fix yet."

But there's no time now. The pace has picked up, with multiple jobs handed out, more jobs waiting. Handle an accident. Disturbance at the laundromat. Another call from Mrs. Fontana. (Apparently, her toilet has overflowed.) It's starting to snow, a few tentative flakes that swell to a full-fledged storm. Take a burglary report; victim will be waiting in the garage.

When we get there, a middle-aged man shows us the pry marks on the service door.

"Must've used a crowbar or something," he says. "But look, there's more." He points to an overturned oil can, greasy footprints on the concrete apron. And offers a single cigarette butt which he holds with a tissue.

"I don't smoke, so this is from the burglar," he says triumphantly. "You can do DNA testing, maybe a saliva test, find out who the guy is."

"Uh, sir, we don't do that in this situation."

"Whattaya mean? They do it on TV all the time! Christ, I'm a taxpayer. I pay your salary. Least you could do is work for it!" He's still muttering indignantly, clenching his new burglary report in his hand, when we leave.

The storm worsens to a driving sleet. We go to the local grocery store to pick up a shoplifter. A guy who had the brilliant idea of putting a stack of plastic-wrapped T-bone steaks under his ten-gallon hat. Not a bad plan, except he made the mistake of lingering near the checkout, waiting to see if his girlfriend made it through with the baking potatoes she'd stuffed in her bra. When one of the cashiers noticed the hat man was bleeding—streams of it that poured down his face—she thought he was injured, blew out a cerebral aneurysm or worse, and called the manager. Who, upon attempting to assist the young man, discovered dinner for six dripping on his head.

Leaving the station after that arrest, we pass Booker and his partner handling an accident. It looks ugly—a crumpled compact car overturned on the sidewalk, a city snowplow rammed into the light pole. Paramedics are on the scene and one of them flags us down.

They need help, we're told. The car's passenger is dead, but the driver's still alive. They're taking him to the hospital now.

"So what do you need us for? Traffic control?"

Booker looks up from the snowbank he's wading through.

"Search party," he says. "The guy's thumb was amputated in the crash. If we find it, they might be able to reattach it."

Ronnie and I look at each other, at the driving sleet, the mounds of snow. Traffic is backed up, furiously honking, and visibility is so poor we can barely see a foot in front of us.

Ronnie is the first to say what we're both thinking. "Does 'needle in a haystack' have any meaning to you?"

"Hey, man, if it was *my* thumb, I'd want it back."

We tromp around, searching for the lost digit. Twenty minutes later, Booker's partner finds the thumb, but it's too late. The thumb is in the middle of the street, crushed to pulp by passing cars.

The jobs come fast and furious. A stolen credit card. Disturbance with the taxi driver. A domestic. Mrs. Fontana and her plumbing from hell.

We're called to assist a citizen at his town house. It's an exclusive address at a posh new development near the medical complex. We're admitted by a silent man in a silk robe who ushers us into an elegant dining room. The wall coverings are watered silk, the dining table a sleek pedestal of beveled glass. The chandelier shimmers with a thousand crystal pendants and the silver handcuffs of the man who's suspended from it. He's gray-haired, rather distinguished looking, or as distinguished as one can be wearing a blindfold and a sequined pink ballerina's tutu. His feet are bare, save for the magenta nail polish decorating each little piggy, and his wrists, in the steel cuffs, are raw and bleeding from where the ratchets have dug in.

Ronnie doesn't bat an eye.

With great aplomb, he says, "Lost the cuff keys, huh?"

The silent man nods. Only the musical tinkling of the chandelier indicates the bondage ballerina's acknowledgment. We release the man and head back into the storm.

"Don't think we'll be seeing that guy in *Swan Lake*," Ronnie mutters as we head back to the car. "Looks like he better keep his day job."

We take a missing persons report from an elderly lady who's been waiting hours for her husband to come home. It's getting late now, and outside, the storm pummels the windows with icy fists. I sit in the doily-covered, lemon-waxed, immaculate little parlor, watching this woman's gnarled hands wring a damp handkerchief as she struggles not to cry.

He always comes home on time, she says. And the weather is so awful, maybe he had an accident. Maybe he was robbed. He's been gone so long.

I ask the usual questions. Could he have stopped at a friend's house, a relative's? For a beer on the way home?

The lady's quivering lips firms. No, she says. Her husband always comes straight home. In forty-eight years of marriage, she could always count on him. He was very dependable, her husband. Very solid. He went to the store this afternoon for bread and a bag of onions. She was going to make a pot roast.

I ask more questions, jotting the answers in appropriate boxes. Height? Weight? Hair color? Any physical impairments?

My partner's been silent, standing near the window watching the storm. Now he nods to the woman.

Would she mind if we looked around? Maybe he left a note, or a hint of where he was going.

The woman shakes her head. We can look all we want, she tells us. But there's no note, none that she could find. He just put on his jacket, the heavy one with the red and black checks like the lumberjacks wear, and said he'd be right back.

We find the lady's husband in the garage, still dressed in his red and black jacket.

The only thing he's taken off is the top of his head, with a .38 Colt revolver.

His brains splattered clear back to the workbench, where blood and brain matter sprayed over the tool racks and onto the router. One errant eyeball plopped on the note he left behind, which, if you read between the terse, carefully scripted lines, basically says, "The hell with being old, and sick, and struggling through each day. Time to bail out." Which he proceeded to do via a .38 caliber slug.

Ronnie and I look at each other. And begin negotiations on who will tell the lady that we found her husband, this good, solid, dependable man who always comes straight home.

It's getting late in the shift, and we still haven't had lunch. After that last job, neither of us is hungry, but some downtime over coffee sounds good. We slip into a booth at the nearest greasy spoon, away from people, voices, or anything else that reminds us of what's out there. Just coffee for now, and peace, and maybe some innocuous conversation of our own. The floral-design class Ronnie's wife is taking. His daughter's recent engagement. The puppy I'm thinking of getting for my kids.

"Say, Office, you got a minute? I got a problem."

Never fails. The man standing over us lists faintly to starboard, blasting us with beer breath. He's holding some crumpled papers which he shoves under Ronnie's nose.

"It's about my car. See, they said I got these parking tickets—I didn't get 'em but they said I did—and they want me to pay 'em. Six hundred forty dollars' worth, they said."

"That's a matter you have to take up with City Hall—the Bureau of Parking Violations. We don't have anything to do with that." His body odor is making my eyes water.

"Yeah, yeah, I know, but see, you guys are cops, I figure you could—"

"Can't do nothing, man." Ronnie's hand covers his cup, shielding it from random spittle. "You got to go down there yourself and straighten it out."

"Can't go nowhere!" the man whines, grabbing the table for support. "They booted my car, the dirty bastards. Uh, pardon my French, ma'am, but those rotten sons-of-bitches, they—"

"Man, I'm sorry I can't help you, but we gotta go. Got a job." We make our getaway while the man moves to the next table, complaining about the rotten, no-count, lazy-ass police who won't even help a decent citizen.

"1225?"

"'25."

"'25, this'll be the last one before you go in. Take a disturbance, 23— on Taylor, name's Fontana."

Ronnie and I groan in unison.

"Squad, we've been getting that call all night. That's the crazy old lady and her plumbing."

"Not this time. Says here it's a disturbance with a

man. Who knows? Maybe he likes her plumbing? Anyway, check it out before you head in, ten-four?"

"Yeah, okay."

It's still snowing, but Mrs. Fontana is waiting for us outside, bundled in a coat and an old-fashioned shawl.

"I knew it!" She cackles triumphantly. "Don't tell me about roots and plumbers. Thought I was senile, didja? Wait'll you see this!" She leads us down the walk to the street, where she's managed to pry the cover off the sewer. All along the street, neighbors are peeking out of their doors, shaking their heads. Apparently, Mrs. Fontana has a well-earned reputation as the neighborhood crackpot. Now she points to the open sewer and smiles.

"Take a look at that! Then tell me I'm crazy. I knew all along something wasn't right. Couldn't even flush my toilet."

We train our flashlight beams down the dark hole. There are bird carcasses, a pile of them, in various stages of decomposition. Roosters, ducks, some bigger shapes that are hard to identify. The mound of them nearly reaches street level.

"And I know where they come from!" Mrs. Fontana tells us, and points a gloved finger. "See that house over there? Cesar Rivera, he's the one. Lock him up!"

I'm still staring at the rooster pile.

"Mrs. Fontana, you can't accuse somebody unless you know for sure. Unless you *saw* him. . . ."

"I didn't see him, but I know for sure he did it."

"And how's that?"

"Damn fool had a yard full of these things. Used 'em for cockfights. Had half the other fools in the neighborhood betting on them. But the birds used to get loose, come in my yard, eat up all my marigolds.

Rooster shit all over the place. I couldn't take it any more. Told him I was going to report him to Immigration. Have the *Federales* pick him up. Then I went in his yard one night, killed every one of those miserable birds with my late husband's hunting rifle. Nothing like a little buckshot to restore the peace."

"Yeah, so how'd the birds get in the sewer?"

Mrs. Fontana smirks. "He hid them in there, what else? From Immigration. Ever since I told him that, he's been hiding in that house. Thinks they're coming any minute. But you can go on and lock him up right now. Why wait?"

She's still smiling when we radio for a Streets and Sanitation supervisor, who can decide what to do with the mounds of bird carcasses. For good measure, Ronnie asks for Animal Control to be notified, just in case this is beyond the domain of the sewer workers.

"Animal Control is for live animals," the dispatcher informs us.

"You want Mrs. Fontana to keep calling every five minutes?" Ronnie asks tersely.

"Calling Animal Control right now."

"Ten-four. Thought you'd see it my way."

Finally, our tour of duty ends. We pull into the station, even as the radio blares out more assignments. A gang disturbance on the South End. Battery in progress at the liquor store. Shots fired in the tavern.

Ronnie looks at me and winks.

"Nobody says you *have* to quit working now. It's busy out there; they can always use another pair of hands. A young girl like you, another eight hours would be a piece of cake."

"Nah. Don't know if I could handle the boredom."

9

Suffer the Children

Dispatcher:	1225, ride over to County Hospital, take the guard detail for a suicidal prisoner. Name is Eddings, arrested for homicide.
Unidentified Unit:	Is that the one who killed her baby?
Dispatcher:	That's the one. As soon as she knew she was goin' down, she pulled the suicide routine.
Unidentified Unit:	Too bad she didn't try that before she did the baby.

Ask any cop, anywhere, what the most dreaded part of this job is, and the answer will be unanimous. It's crimes against children. It doesn't matter if you're a female cop, or a parent—the effects are the same on anyone who bears witness. After the first tiny body you hold, the fear you see in the eyes of battered children that becomes, with time and repetition, a defeated glaze of acceptance and pain. That's when the nightmares begin. At least, that's when mine did.

It's devastating to handle a child-abuse case, worse to realize that in spite of our best efforts as police, it continues. And nearly impossible to comprehend that, in some quarters, children are as disposable as trash, to be used and abused at the whim of their caretaker, which could be anyone—parent or relative, mother's pimp or neighborhood babysitter. When I handle my first child-abuse case, I find out just how easily I cross the line from "objective professional" to the same blood-lust vindictive fury that demands immediate "eye-for-an-eye" reciprocity. Discover how easy it is to hate the abuser, in spite of the years I spent studying the psychology of human behavior. Realize that my heart has cracked in pieces, with more damage sure to come every time I see another helpless victim. And understand that no amount of game face or callousness will ever protect me from that kind of pain.

So the nightmares begin. I see them in my sleep— tiny falling bodies that tumble through the air, so quickly that they slip through my reaching arms. So many I can't catch them all, can't catch *any*, and the only sound is my screams. Other times, it's a single child who visits me in dreams, with sightless eyes and the vivid wounds of untold torture. A grisly presence that's a silent reproach for what I allowed to happen, what happens more times than anyone knows. I don't scream in that nightmare, only weep because I don't know who the child is, and won't now, or ever. And I wake up with the terror that always accompanies this dream, wondering if that might be my child someday. Wondering about "Stranger Danger," who lurks in every shadow, stalking innocent prey. Wondering if I can ever do enough to prevent it.

It's enough to make me guard my sleeping children, listen to the smooth, slow pattern of their slumber— and feel the terror. I stroke their rounded cheeks and remember what those other children felt like, how no one was there to watch over them. Frustration and fear come in equal measure. Who can save the children? We're cops—the ones assigned to protect. But it isn't enough. It's never enough, not even close. There are no easy answers, no ready solutions. Only the parade of tiny faces that pass before me that I couldn't help, wasn't near enough to keep vigil.

And the nightmares continue. It's a by-product of the job they failed to mention back at the Training Academy. One that cops don't talk about, try not to think about, but it's always there. Because we know, we've *seen* that there are monsters among us. Loathsome, violent creatures who appear to be normal, who possess the ability to walk among us undetected. But the evil they do, the danger they present, is inestimable.

They're baby killers, child molesters, vicious animals who attack kids because they can. And when you arrest the offender, revulsion twists your guts, and every instinct tells you to blow away this conscienceless subhuman who did it, you can't. It's not for you to decide. So you struggle with your game face and wonder how God can permit such atrocities.

One night, we get a call that's fairly common, and often innocuous: "information for the police." Which could be anything from a lady complaining about the neighbor's cat in her begonias to the man who's certain the laundromat's been converted to a crack house.

This time, the call comes from the emergency room of Mercy Hospital. The attending doctor tells us a five-year-old girl was brought in, feverish and crying, complaining of burning "down there." Upon examination, the little girl is found to have syphilis, and enough fibrous scarring to indicate that she'd been brutally penetrated—everywhere—for most of her young life. There are other scars on her body indicating old lacerations, the distinct crescent-shaped scars that mean beatings with electrical cords, and multiple cigarette burns, both old and new.

Because this crime is an "aggravated criminal

sexual assault" of a child, the Violent Crimes detectives are called in and the Department of Children and Family Services notified. After treatment, the child is removed from Mama's care and placed in temporary custody of the state.

The little girl was raped by Mama's boyfriend who, in his everyday life, is a model businessman, his business being drugs and guns. But he's a generous guy, keeps Mama in heroin and coke, even babysits her daughter while she's out turning tricks. When questioned by the detectives, Mama denies everything. She's a working mom. Darrell helps her out, sometimes, when she can't afford a regular babysitter. He'd *never* touch her baby that way. Maybe she got it poking a pencil up there or something. You know how kids are.

Darrell is arrested, Mama's released. At the first court hearing, she shows up in a semiclean, long-sleeved dress that hides most of her tracks, and is accompanied by her church pastor who, for the fifty dollars she's slipped him, testifies that the boyfriend is the demon seed. Mama, on the other hand, is a fine Christian woman, a paragon of motherhood, and the court, in its clemency, should reunite her with her beloved child. A little girl belongs with her mama.

The tired judge has heard it all before, but the court docket is overflowing with abuse and neglect cases. There's so many kids and not enough placement service available. Anyway, this is the first offense reported against Mama, and her pastor seems sincere. The court returns the child to her mother.

One month later, the little girl is dead, beaten to death with a frying pan by her model, crackhead mom.

* * *

One evening, I'm assigned to guard a prisoner who's been placed on suicide watch at Cook County Hospital. It's a common assignment. When a prisoner requires medical treatment or hospitalization, a twenty-four-hour police guard is assigned until the person is released to jail.

When I arrive at County, the wagon guys are waiting for me. It was their job originally—removal of a body.

"Wanna see what they wanted us to remove?" It's Matthews, a salty vet with over twenty years as a wagon man. He swings open the squadrol door and takes out a tiny package tinged with blood. It looks like a butcher's package, just the size of a leg of lamb. He unwraps part of the sheet and thrusts it toward me.

It's a baby, not more than nine months old. He's been decapitated, or very nearly—only the spinal cord keeps his head from rolling free.

"Nice, huh? Whattaya think of that?" He's watching me closely for a reaction. Maybe to see if a woman can handle something like this. Or because he knows I'll be guarding the life of the monster who did it.

"Who did it?" I ask, when I can finally breathe.

"Who else? The loving mother."

"Any particular reason?"

"Yeah. *Because.*"

The cop I'm supposed to relieve is standing in the doorway of the prisoner's room.

"Fucking animal!" he whispers to me. "If there weren't so many nurses around, I'd take the bitch out myself. Let her see what it's like to die. Like her kid did."

His words are savage, but his eyes reflect the same
fear and frustration we all feel: another victim, another instance when we were too late. He tells me
the neighbors called the police originally, and that's
when Mom decided to grandstand a little with a
phony suicide attempt. Grabbed some manicure scis-
sors and locked herself in the bathroom. Just so she
can say she's crazy and beat the rap.

I look past him at the young woman in the hospital bed. Her wrists are bound in gauze and tied in
loose restraints to the bed rail. She's snapping her
bubble gum, raptly focused on the TV—a *Three's
Company* rerun. Not exactly the picture of remorse.

"So did she really hurt herself or what?"

"Are you kiddin'? This bitch ain't crazy. Just a few
hesitation marks is all, not even close to a vein. I've
had worse paper cuts."

When he leaves, I choose not to sit outside the
room, as he did. I want to look at this woman, stare
into her eyes. See if there's anything there besides
evil. *Stare down the demon.*

She looks surprised when I approach the bed, but
unconcerned. A cop can't hurt her. She's crazy, it says
so right on her chart. I flip through the paperwork.
Twenty-six, unmarried. Four other kids. I wonder
where they are right now. Or maybe she's already
filleted them and nobody's found them.

There's a large tattoo on her shoulder: Betty Boop
bending over, baring her Kewpie-doll ass. Red lip
prints on one cheek.

Arrogantly, the woman returns my stare.

"What are you lookin' at, bitch? You some kind
of bulldagger dyke or somethin'?"

I wonder if she ever nuzzled her baby, rubbed her
cheek against that velvety baby skin and blew kisses

on its belly while the child gurgled and laughed. Her eyes are cold and hooded, empty of emotion, indifferent as I watch her. No maternal love, no remorse. It's enough to feed my anger, pull me back over the line toward vindictive "judge and jury." She did it, she's not sorry about it, and now she should pay.

"Nice job you did on the baby."

She doesn't even flinch. "Yeah, whatever."

"You didn't want him, why not let somebody adopt him? There's a lot of—"

"Oh, fuck you! Like I need to deal with another little bastard! Who's got time for all that shit? I got my own life, y'know? So just shut the fuck up. I got mental stress. I been *traumatized* enough." She rolls out the word, savoring it like a fine wine. Her trump card. The shrink says she's traumatized, so she can get away with murder.

Ignoring me now, she returns her attention to her program. I look at her hands again, and the impeccably manicured nails. Long, curving acrylic talons in sherbet colors splay across the bedsheets, sparkling with tiny set-in crystals. Somehow, it's those nails that tip me over. I imagine her checking them for breaks after she cut off her baby's head. Annoyed because her child's blood dimmed the luster of her polish. Washing that blood away, smoothing lotion methodically around each cuticle. The pampered hands of a stressed-out, *traumatized* woman. I picture that baby's tiny hands, fisted in death. The faces of my own kids. The nurse who showed me my baby, right after birth. *"It's a boy!"*

Across the room on the table is a tray with an assortment of medical supplies. A suture kit, rolls of tape and gauze, small disposable scalpels. For a single crazed moment, I imagine carrying that tray back to her bed. And then placing an unsheathed scalpel near each of her hands. Just close enough so she could finish the job on herself. Footsteps behind me interrupt my reverie. It's one of the student nurses, young enough to still believe she's on a mission to save mankind. She collects the scalpel tray and carries it out, gesturing me to follow her.

"Imagine leaving this in there!" she whispers in a horrified voice. "Must have been one of the day crew. Can you believe it? That woman is *suicidal*! Imagine what might have happened if she got her hands on this?" I stare at her dully, and consider the scalpel tray one last time.

"Yes," I say. *"Imagine!"*

Sometimes, child abuse can be nearly undetectable. The perpetrators are clever, masking their work so nobody knows. No obvious indication that would cause a ripple of suspicion. Many times the abuse can go on for years before it's discovered, often inadvertently. The school nurse, the family doctor, an unsuspecting neighbor—anyone who happens to notice unusual behavior or subtle physical signs that indicate a history of abuse and pain. And that's who will call the police.

In Jocelyn Echols's case, there is no one who can call for her. Practically no one even knows she exists. Just three years old, she lives with her mother, Shelby Hodges, in the garage apartment behind a ramshackle three-flat. A part-time shampoo girl and full-time whore, Shelby doesn't worry too much about her daughter. Things like food and clothing cost money. If she doesn't have it, which is much of the time, Jocelyn doesn't get it. There's no shortage of liquor, however—beer and cheap wine left behind from the constant parade of men. So if Jocelyn cries, Shelby pours some down her throat. It shuts the kid up, knocks her out for hours at a time.

Shelby sees herself as a party girl. Most nights she pours herself into a flashy, tight dress, trowels on some makeup, and hits the clubs. It pays to doll herself up. That way she can pass herself off as an "escort," and the men pay more. Before she leaves, she always makes sure Jocelyn won't be a problem. All she needs is a screaming, whiny kid to attract attention, maybe get them evicted. She's already three months behind on the rent and Hector, her landlord, has told her the blowjobs aren't enough, she's going to have to come up with some money. So she doesn't need any more problems, especially with the brat.

There's a dog cage in the unused garage, back from the days when Hector had his rottweiler. So each night she locks Jocelyn into it. She's safe there, Shelby figures. Can't play with matches, can't run away.

One of Shelby's tricks, a fortyish man who works in Sanitation, feels sorry for the kid. Starts bringing her toys and dolls he finds in the Dumpsters, sometimes chips and beef jerky, if he remembers, when he's picking up the beer. The discarded toys he brings are the only ones Jocelyn's ever seen.

One night, after many beers and even more tricks, Shelby counts out her earnings. Pitiful—not even enough to shut Hector up for a while. Somehow, it's Jocelyn's fault. So she stands her daughter on a chair and wraps her neck in the rope she's rigged from a curtain rod. And holds up Jocelyn's favorite toy, the ragged *Sesame Street* doll that she loves most.

"Wave bye-bye, Jocelyn. Wave bye-bye to Cookie Monster."

Jocelyn is surprised and delighted. Her mother never shows her such attention.

"Bye-bye!" she says, waving her tiny hand. "Bye-bye, Cookie!" And is still smiling when the chair is kicked out from under her.

On the midnight tour, we get the call to meet a citizen in the alley. He's there waiting near the Dumpster, a handkerchief held over this mouth. Even in the dim light, I see that his eyes are swollen and damp.

"I was walkin' my dog," he tells us. "We got around here, he started to bark. I thought maybe it was a cat—you know how they dig through the garbage. But it was no cat." Not trusting his wavering voice, he points.

It's a chicken box, the fast-food, cardboard kind that holds an individual meal. A couple pieces of chicken, mashed potatoes, a roll, and, in this case, a dead newborn baby, crushed into the box with someone's discarded dinner.

Even my partner, a hardened vet, can't handle this one. He averts his eyes quickly, goes back to the squad on the premise of getting his gloves. *Fighting back the tears and nausea, getting a tighter grip on his game face.*

Later, he admits that tiny body conjured up images of his own three kids—his daughter the aspiring gymnast, his Little League-star son, his older boy who's already weighing college choices.

"I see something like this, some dead little baby who never had a chance, a whole life thrown out with the garbage. And then I go home and listen to my kid talk about what he wants to be, how he's gonna conquer the world." In the privacy of our car, the veteran eyes are misting. "And I'm supposed to say, 'Go ahead, son. Get out there and make a difference.' Like there *is* a difference. There's people out here doing this to babies, and I'm supposed to tell my son, 'The world is your fucking oyster!'"

If he had it to do over again, Eddie Flowers would never have opened the door. Mama had warned him about it, said there was never anyone on the other side but the police, bill collectors, and them damn pests from Social Services. No reason for him to open the door, unless she or one of the kids was out of the house. Or if Cornelius, her current boyfriend, was on the way over.

On this particular day, Mama was sleeping. The other kids were outside, and the knocking at the door was loud, insistent. He couldn't ask who it was—then they'd know for sure he was there. The sharp knocking continued. Maybe it *was* Cornelius.

He eased the door open a crack and peered out.

"Well! I was beginning to think no one lived here anymore. Good afternoon, young man." A woman's voice, loud and determinedly cheerful. A white woman.

"This is the Flowers residence, right? May I come in?"

Eddie held his ground. Social workers were never this cheerful, but maybe she was new. What else would a white woman be doing in his building?

"Mama ain't home."

The lady shook her head and smiled. She *must* be new.

"Actually, I don't need to see your mother. I just want to drop something off."

Maybe she was a cop, coming to take someone to

jail. That happened at the Robinsons' downstairs. One day they showed up at the door waving papers; next thing you knew, Dante Robinson was doing five to ten in Stateville.

Eddie squinted into the gloomy hallway. This woman didn't look like a cop. And what was she doing with that basket?

"I'm from the Urban Food Coalition," the woman chirped. "We're delivering food baskets to needy families in this area."

"We ain't needy," Eddie mumbled. Maybe it was a trick. Admit you're hungry, and the social worker comes and hauls away all the kids.

Juggling her basket, the lady kept her bright smile firmly in place.

"Of course you're not, sweetheart. But why don't you take it anyway? You'd be doing me a favor." She winked at him like they shared a secret. "So I don't have to carry it back down all those stairs, I mean. How about if I set it down right here, and then you can bring it inside?"

"Don't want it!" Eddie called, but the woman was gone, doing double-time down the stairs, leaving behind the basket and the faint scent of flowery cologne.

Cautious, Eddie waited, listening for the retreating footsteps, the slam of the door three floors below. Only then did he swing the door open to examine the basket.

He ignored the tag that was wired to the handle— some stupid picture of people holding hands over a loaf of bread, and a printed message he didn't bother to read. It was the food that commanded his attention: cans of vegetables, boxes of rice and cereal, a bag of apples. Snagging one, he chomped down.

"What the hell is you eatin', boy?" Mama stood glowering in the kitchen doorway. She was rumpled and sour-smelling, in clothes that hadn't been washed in quite some time. And she looked ready to cuss out the devil himself. There was no telling about Mama's moods. They changed so fast Eddie couldn't keep up—from tearful to nervous to hell-raising mad, depending on if she'd been drinking, or dipping into the little plastic bag Cornelius brought. This time, her overbright eyes and dripping nose meant she'd gotten an early start.

Shoving her son aside, she upended the basket.

"What the hell is this shit?" she slurred. "Beans? Crackers? Where all this come from, boy?"

Eddie told her. Even though he'd opened the door— a cardinal sin, as far as Mama was concerned—he thought she'd be pleased with the groceries. They'd never had this much food in the house, not as long as he could remember. That should be enough to make her happy.

A harsh punch to his head told him he was wrong.

"Why you open that door?"—*slap!*—"I tol' you, boy!"—*punch!*—"What I gotta do to make yo' simple ass mind yo' Mama?"

Before she could deliver another blow, something among the scattered groceries caught her eye. A canned ham, five pounds of cooked meat sealed in a metal jacket.

"Look here, Eddie!" Mama picked up the can, cooing at its colorful picture. "I loves me some ham! Back when I was comin' up in Mississippi, Big Mama made us ham ever' Christmas. Easter, too. Collards, cornbread, beans and rice. . . ." Her glassy eyes softened at the memory. "Don't you love you some ham, boy?"

Eddie couldn't remember ever having ham. Most of the grocery money went up Mama's nose. But he was willing to go along with her. Anything so she wouldn't hit him again.

"I like ham, Mama. Now we got some, you can make it just like back home, like Big Mama did."

Abruptly her glassy eyes narrowed, cooing lips stretched into a snarl.

"What you say, boy? You don't like my cookin'? Think my mama do it better 'n' me?"

Before the startled boy could respond, her hands swung up, still holding the weighty can. Grunting from the exertion, she brought it down on Eddie, again and again, striking out at whatever demons capered before her drug-glazed eyes.

In the hospital intensive care unit, Eddie stares unseeing through one swollen eye. A tube breathes for him, bleeping machines track his heart rhythms. His prognosis is bleak. Too hard to tell with multiple skull fractures, the doctors tell us. Surgery reduced some of the intracranial pressure, but still . . .

When the detectives approach her, Mama is reluctant to leave Eddie's side.

"He's my boy," she says vaguely, to no one in particular, staring at his bandaged head. "I can't leave him alone."

"Should've left him alone before *this* happened," an angry nurse mutters, adjusting a monitor.

"Ain't my fault," she returns dully. "I tol' him not to open that damn door."

10

Animal Attraction

Dispatcher: 1071? Squadrol 1071?

1071: At your service.

Dispatcher: '71, transport a patient to Cook County Hospital. Name is Richmond. He's at 15— South Keeler.

1071: What about the paramedics? We don't usually transport patients in the meat wagon.

Dispatcher: The fire department's refusing on this one, and the patient can't afford a private ambulance.

1071: Okay, we're on the way.

Dispatcher: Uh, '71, be advised that this might be an AIDS patient.

1071: *Might* be? He doesn't know?

Dispatcher: The guy's wife says he hasn't been diagnosed, but she's sure it's AIDS.

1071: Right. Or maybe it's just a summer cold.

Animal-rights activists take note: Your work is cut out for you. That is, if the increasing incidents of crimes involving animals is any indication. In Chicago, animal-related crimes are on the rise. We're not talking about Fido knocking off the local butcher shop, but people intent on hurting animals. Animals become victims, hostages, and the objects of torture so heinous the average person can't begin to fathom it. It happens every day. Sadly, the perpetrators of such sickening acts are so skilled, they're usually able to victimize the animal before it ever gets a chance to take a bite out of crime.

During one particular month, police crime-reporting statistics indicate a significant increase in the loss or theft of pets in the Albany Park area. Reports are made by citizens who claim their dog's been taken out of their yard, their cat never returned from a midnight prowl. Analysis of the reports indicates there's no clear pattern for the pet crimes. No specific preference with regard to breed or pedigree. Mutts of undetermined origin are being snatched as often as the purebreds.

This pattern continues for another month. The only criteria for the crimes seems to be that the animals are house pets, four-legged, and fairly accessible. So far, a home break-in to acquire the animal has not occurred.

Finally, a call comes through 911: "Information for the police." An anonymous citizen instructs us to check out the storage freezer at the Lotus Hut, a popular Chinese takeout restaurant frequented by the neighborhood residents, the beat cops, and students from Northeastern University.

Mr. Woo, the restaurant's owner, is puzzled when he sees tactical cops trooping in, search warrant in hand. And is even more confused when he learns the nature of the visit. Lapsing into his native Cantonese, he can only babble while questions are asked and the walk-in freezer's inspected.

Mr. Woo, it turns out, is a pet lover from way back. Loves them in chow mein, loves them in just about any dish his cooks can whip up. Judging by the stacks of frozen dog and cat corpses that fill his freezer, the patrons of the Lotus Hut have become inadvertent pet lovers too.

Witnessing all the frozen little bodies, the tact team members are doing some quick mental calculations, trying to recall the last time they've had Lotus Hut takeout. Some poodle chop suey, maybe, or sweet-and-sour kitty, the schnauzer and peapod special.

Mr. Woo is perplexed. In Asian cultures, dog and cat meat are considered delicacies, and it was his intention to serve only the finest to his customers. It's not his fault if the American palate can't recognize a gourmet treat!

The Board of Health shuts down the Lotus Hut. But, just one month later, while Mr. Woo's attorneys prepare his defense for his theft and criminal-damage charges, the restaurant reopens.

"I don't get it," one of the tact team says. "The guy's serving up people's pets and they give him a play? He'll probably start doing the same thing all over again. Wonder how heavy his clout is, to reopen so fast?"

"Yeah," agrees another member. "Must've paid somebody off big time!"

No one glances at the calendar, a complimentary one provided to all Lotus Hut customers at the beginning of the year. It hangs on the tact office wall and offers a colorful if jarring note of irony regarding this case, by proclaiming this the "Year of the Dog."

The North Side's Lincoln Park, along the breathtaking Chicago lakefront, prides itself on the famous Lincoln Park Zoo. Working the zoo beat is a gravy

detail for cops in the Eighteenth District. While enjoying the wafting lake breezes, visitors and cops alike
can stroll through the scenic grounds, viewing elab-
orate displays of animals both exotic and familiar. A
popular attraction is the Farm in the Zoo. There's a
working dairy barn there, cows, bulls, pens of pigs,
and sheep—a charming rural counterpoint to the
nearby skyscrapers. Kids love to pet the cows, watch
the milking process, giggle over the snorting piglets.

For Lloyd Akins, the Farm-in-the-Zoo is his favorite attraction. He's a good ol' boy from Georgia, and
when the stress of city life reaches critical mass, he
relaxes at the zoo. It takes his mind off things, he says.
Reminds him of home. He visits there three, sometimes four times a week. Nothing like a bit of the
country to relax a man. Except that he visits only after closing time, when there's no one to witness just
how seriously he takes his country comforts. Which,
usually, is in the form of a relatively placid dairy cow
who, except for the occasional moo, doesn't seem to
mind when Lloyd has his close encounters of the
bovine kind.

We're called one night to meet security officers at
the zoo. A disturbance in the barn. We find Lloyd
and his lady of choice engaged in a most intimate
act. Despite whatever else can be said about him,
Lloyd is focused. Even when we walk in—two cops
and two security guards with weapons drawn—he
doesn't miss a stroke. And appears to be unconcerned about the criminal charges his act will earn
him. Burglary, for starters, since he broke into the
zoo after hours, which might carry a felony conviction from an unamused judge.

Afterward, he's relieved and unembarrassed. What's
the big deal, he wants to know. Folks back home

wouldn't even blink. And anyway, he wasn't hurtin' anything, least of all the cow.

The security guard signs complaints. Lloyd is arrested and placed in a squadrol. He offers no apology or justification to the zoo officials or the police. And, in case you're wondering about the charge for an intimate encounter with a farm animal, it's "criminal damage to property."

In this city, miles of shimmering beach stretch along Lake Michigan from the Indiana border all the way to the exclusive North Shore. Winter and summer, residents enjoy the lake, strolling, biking, jogging, and swimming as the weather permits. There are times, though, when early-bird joggers get the shock of their lives. Like when they're loping along, enjoying the beach and the blooming sunrise. The breeze is gentle, the early rays warming, they're at target heart rate, and everything's fine. Until they nearly run over the animal's head staked out on a pole, like some ghastly pagan emblem. There's blood on the sand, a little dried gore, and drag marks to indicate the animal wasn't a willing victim. There's also some unusual marks painted within a large circle.

A pentagram, it turns out, drawn by a band of Satanists who've used the beach for their evil ritual. The sacrificed animal is a goat, usually, but if they can't procure one, a dog or a lamb will do. The important thing is that it's alive, that they get to slaughter it, feeling some sick empowerment when the dying eyes bulge, roll back into a blank stare. And then anoint themselves, and each other, with the thickening blood.

These incidents usually occur in the early spring

and summer, presumably to observe the spring equinox and summer solstice. But the same grisly tableaus have been found at other times throughout the summer and autumn months. Maybe the devil worshipers, like everyone else, just want to get out and enjoy the weather. And although there's a twenty-four-hour police beach patrol, these groups have been difficult to apprehend. The locations and crime pattern are random enough to make tracking difficult. The only thing that's known for sure is that in the deepest part of night, while most of the city sleeps and the lake laps at the sprawling sands, there are those who gather in the absolute dark, killing and fornicating, drinking the blood of helpless animals.

In the Twelfth District, there's a cluster of high-rise projects positioned in a loose circle over a three-block area. Fifteen-story monoliths circle quadrants of parking lots and some dismal patches of dirt originally intended for gardens and lawns. Instead of roses and pansies, broken liquor bottles cover the ground, some trash, used syringes, and random bullet casings from the latest shooting.

To the north of these buildings are more "jets"— grids of two-story row houses just as oppressive, equally crime-ridden. To the south is an embankment leading up to the railroad tracks, and a reliable "shopping" source for any enterprising person daring enough to risk it. The tracks are guarded by the railroad police, a squad of cops specially hired by the train companies to make sure the boxcars get to their destinations intact. A tough job, considering that the cars move along long stretches of poorly lit tracks and often stop, sporadically, and for just long enough to provide ample opportunity for pilferage. Anything can happen and usually does. So theft from the trains continue.

The embankment around the jets is wooded with enough trees and growth to block out most light sources. And any good boxcar thief knows how to work in the dark, efficiently, with a very small window of opportunity. So when the trains slow down for their ten-minute stop near Morgan Street, the thieves are ready. Bolt cutters make quick work of the boxcar door locks, the seal is broken and—voilà!—one-stop shopping. The thieves grab as much cargo as they can and hightail it back to the safety of the jets.

Since the contents of the boxcars varies, the thieves never know in advance what they're stealing. Doesn't matter. One thing's as good as another to fence on the street, after you've taken out your share and sell some to the neighbors. On a Monday night, the train might be robbed. By Tuesday night, every little girl in a six-building radius might be sporting new gym shoes—the cargo du jour. Bicycles, clothing, hardware, food supplies—everything goes. Everything's got a price.

One night a group of young thieves get a brilliant idea. They're tired of playing shopping roulette with the trains. Last time, they hit a car full of frozen butter, and that took *forever* to fence, hauling it around to various restaurants. They want something different, something big. Something none of their homeys have done.

They decide to knock off a cattle car full of steers bound for slaughter. The perfect crime, they think. They'll lure a steer down the embankment, lead it back to the jets, and shoot it in the head with a 9-millimeter Glock. After that, it's barbecue city. Enough to eat, and store, maybe sell some to the neighboring buildings. And if that bad boy's got a nice-looking hide, maybe a jacket and boots might come out of it as well.

It never occurs to them that they've overlooked a few critical points. Like the size of the steer, and its potential *attitude*. Maybe it won't want to follow them placidly. And maybe there's a few more steps involved between steericide and prime rib for everyone.

When the ambitious thieves break into the cattle car, their plan goes awry. Not just one, but *all* of the cargo are ready to make a break. And proceed to stampede over and around the foolish thieves, down the embankment, and toward the jets. The size of them, their sheer force is a complete surprise. Somehow, they look much bigger in person. And when they overturn a few cars that get in their way, it draws the neighbors' attention. Heads appear in windows. Shrieks are heard.

A few people are certain they're hallucinating. Stampeding cows down 14th Street, like it's some kind of goddamn roundup? Yeah, right. Good weed and a bottle of cheap wine will do that to you.

Many people see it as a photo op for some good eating. And grab knives, baseball bats, a Saturday-night special or two—anything that'll get 'em their share of the steaks.

Our dispatcher can't stop laughing.

"1235?"

"'35."

"Cattle roundup, 14th and Loomis."

"Sure. Right after we retrieve the space shuttle from the Maxwell Street hot-dog joint."

"I'm not kidding, '35. Says here there's a bunch of cattle stampeding around the jets. We're getting a lot of calls on it. We'll get some other units to ride with you. Ten-four?"

"Damn, and on the night I forgot my spurs!"

"Oh, and '35 . . . ?"

"Yeah?"

"Make mine medium rare, mushrooms on the side. A modest porterhouse will be fine."

"No problem."

Without question, it's a stampede. People are pouring out of the buildings with clotheslines, extension cords, jump ropes—whatever they think will truss up an animal for the impending barbecue. Just grab an unsuspecting steer, tie it to a light pole, and start the fire. Swab on some barbecue sauce, wait an hour or two, and let the feasting begin.

Other folks, who take their hunting more seriously, have opened fire, from ground level, from fifth-floor windows, from the branches they balance on after being treed by an irate steer. Bullets are flying, people are screaming; the frightened steers are demolishing anything in their path. Another typical day of serving and protecting.

Our sergeant, a new guy, arrives on the scene to make an executive decision. It's his first night in the district, having been transferred unwillingly from a cushy desk job at Headquarters. He'd heard it was a jungle out here, but this is more like the Wild West! Nothing in Sergeants' School prepared him for anything like this. And after a steer gouges his squad car, he's completely clueless. Better wait for the field lieutenant, who can make *his* command decision.

"Circle the squads!" the lieutenant orders. "Contain the area. Then you can capture the animals."

Which has us all looking at each other. When did a lasso become a standard feature on our gun belts?

"Circle *this*!" my partner growls. "Does this fucker think it's *Wagon Train,* or what? I say we shoot 'em."

"It's not the steers' fault."

"The lieutenant, not the steers. Let the railroad cops head up the roundup. We're out here playin' cowboys, where the fuck are they?"

Good question. The lieutenant is now bellowing new orders to the assembled troops. Under no circumstances are we to fire at the animals. They're considered the property of the railroad. Only a railroad official can give the order to shoot.

One of our squadrols is charged and tipped over by rampaging cattle. The wagon guys, up in the safety of a tree, are laughing hysterically. By now, most of the livestock have charged off beyond the confines of the area, into the main streets, under viaducts. And will probably be sashaying down State Street before a railroad official finally shows up.

The local citizens are disgusted. Not one of them managed to snag a steer. They pack up their barbecue sauce and head back to the jets, complaining about the useless, no-count muthafuckas who call themselves the *po*-lice. The same shiftless muthafuckas whose salaries these good people pay.

Gorski and Malone thought they'd seen it all. With a combined thirty-five years as wagon men, they were certain that nothing could surprise them. One early morning in August, they were proved wrong.

The dispatcher assigns them to transport a patient to the hospital—not a normal assignment, since the squadrol has none of the amenities required to comfort the sick or injured. The back of the wagon has two steel benches bolted to the side walls, and a lingering stench from the corpses, drunks, and other transports who have gone before. Not exactly the optimum in creature comforts.

The patient has AIDS, the dispatcher tells them. Undiagnosed, but the wife is sure of it. Gorski and Malone know what *that* means. When a patient can't afford a private ambulance, and the fire department dispatchers, for some arbitrary reason, won't send the paramedics, they call the cops. And usually feel the need to embroider the truth, make it sound like a *real* emergency. After all, the police department can't refuse anyone. Aren't they supposed to protect and serve?

Mrs. Richmond is waiting at the curb when the sqaudrol pulls up.

"He got AIDS!" she barks without preamble, hands on hips in a defiant stance. "And you better not tell me you won't take him. We're citizens, we got rights. I'll get your badge numbers, report both of you and—"

"Hold on, lady," retorts Malone, but Gorski, senior partner and designated diplomat, steps forward. His voice drops into his patented croon, guaranteed to soothe the hysterical and befriend stray animals.

"I know you're upset, ma'am, but just relax. Nobody said we ain't taking him." He meets the woman's combative glare with an easy smile. "Now, why don't you tell us what we got here."

"AIDS," she says again. "Are you deaf? My husband's got AIDS, and I got to get him to the hospital."

"Did his doctor tell you it's AIDS?"

"Ain't seen a doctor yet, but I know. Know where he got it from, too."

Malone shoots his partner a look. *Careful how you handle this. You're treading on delicate ground.*

"Got it from his job," Mrs. Richmond announces. "They had a blood drive there last week and, like a fool, Nate went and donated some. Now he got AIDS."

Gorski considers the angry woman. Both he and Malone, and *all* police personnel in the city had attended the department's in-service AIDS education classes. The information presented (by a team of medical specialists who'd spent years studying diseases and immunology) was enough to provide a basic knowledge of how the virus could be contracted.

"You're saying he gave blood last week, and now he's got AIDS?"

"That's right, and believe me, those bastards are gonna pay. I'm gonna get me a fancy LaSalle Street lawyer and—"

"Mrs. Richmond, what are his symptoms? See, it takes a lot longer than a week for noticeable symptoms to appear."

"Oh, he got symptoms, alright. Got real bad cramps—doubled over in pain for the past three days. And there's a god-awful smell comin' out of his butthole, 'long with all kinds of pus and goo. If you don't believe me, I can show ya."

The men are willing to take her word. And load Mrs. Richmond and her feverish, moaning husband into the truck for the trip to Cook County Hospital.

In the emergency room, Mr. Richmond is given a preliminary exam and found to have a fever of 104 degrees. The stethoscope pressed against his belly by the tired resident reveals "abnormal bowel sounds." The cubicle curtains are drawn for a more thorough exam.

Lounging near the nurses' station, Gorski and Malone hear a scream. It's Mrs. Richmond, who shrieks out a string of expletives so ripe, she could pass muster as a Marine drill sergeant. A scurry of rushing feet, and then a squad of struggling orderlies assist her down the hall.

Mr. Richmond, it turns out, does not have AIDS. What he *does* have is a dead gerbil trapped in his lower bowel. How long it's been there is anybody's guess, but the severity of infection means that surgery is a distinct possibility. The ER staff agrees that this takes top honors as the weirdest admission on their shift.

"A rat up his ass?" Malone wonders. "Haven't these people heard of exterminators?"

"He *stuffed* it up his ass," the tired resident corrects. "A fetish thing. They shove one up there, then yank it out while it's clawing and fighting. Part of the thrill, I guess. Only this guy forgot to pull it out. Or couldn't. Either way, this is one he won't forget."

The two cops are astonished. They've run into some strange things on the street, but this is a new one. Who'd have thought?

"Gerbils are *rodents*, right?" Gorski asks his partner. "Like hamsters and rats?"

"Yeah. And they're not small, either." Both men lapse into silence, shaking their heads at the images this suggests. Months from now, Gorski will admit that it's a very long time before he can pass his son's hamster cage without shuddering.

11

Wholly Holy

Dispatcher: 1434? Beat 1434?
1434:   '34.
Dispatcher: '34, they're holding a couple shoplifters for you in the security office, Caswell's Department Store, 16— North Milwaukee.
1434:   Okay.
Dispatcher: Security guard says he wasn't sure whether to call the cops or a priest.
1434:   Why? Are they dead?
Dispatcher: Nope. They're nuns.

During one particular February, it's announced at roll call that all beat officers should be aware of a particular crime pattern that's developed on the North End of the Twelfth District. The North End is comprised of meatpacking houses along Fulton Market, multi-floored businesses and new lofts in a seminal "artists' community," and the infamous Madison Street. For those who never visited the Windy City, Madison Street is the geographic center of the city, dividing North and South sides. When you follow it west, away from the downtown "Loop" area, it becomes something much different.

West Madison Street is a famous whores' stroll where you can get whatever you need, when you need it, from any one of a number of women, men, or gender undetermined parading down the gritty streets.

On one memorable night, I'm cruising the side streets off Madison. A particular MO in crime has been seen here in the past two weeks. Female impersonators (known as "he-she's" in cop jargon) have been robbing their tricks. They'll get in the car with an unsuspecting john and, after the price of a blow-job's been negotiated, instruct him to drive to a remote area. That's where they unzip the witless customer, whip out a straight razor, and threaten to slice off his equipment if he doesn't hand it over—cash, credit cards, the whole deal. Most victims don't quibble. Many of them are too embarrassed to make a police report. So a special detail has been assigned to catch the bad guy-girls.

I'm working alone, nosing my squad behind factories, around the warehouse docks—all the known spots where tricks are taken. In the darkened alley behind a printing company, I notice a parked car with the brake lights flashing sporadically. A common occurrence with a trick-in-progress: The john will remember to put his car in park, but, while business is transacted, at least one foot keeps hitting the brake pedal. A knee-jerk reaction when you're being serviced by someone who could suck the chrome off a Harley.

The car in the alley is nondescript, a beige four-door sedan. I run the plates, standard procedure in these circumstances. The car comes back registered to an anonymous post-office box, which usually means the vehicle belongs to a larger corporation which provide company cars for their employees.

When I tap on the window, the man goes rigid. Which may or may not be from the efforts of his companion, who raises her head, wipes off her mouth, and smiles at me. It's Desiree, one of the regulars on the Madison stroll. One of the girls who's just out here to make a living.

I instruct the horrified man to step out of the car, keeping his hands up and in plain view. More standard procedure. The guy can't zip up his pants, but he also can't grab a weapon. And once it's been established that the man is not armed, and that Desiree isn't wielding a straight razor, we move on to the question of identification. The man is deeply embarrassed, but still takes a shot at a plausible excuse. He's lost, he tells me, just asking this kind person for directions. Desiree was glad to assist.

"It's not really necessary to produce a license, is it, Officer?" The man's voice is pleading.

"Afraid so, sir. You're operating a motor vehicle. If you don't have a license, I'll have to take you in to the station."

The man looks at me, at Desiree, at his crumpled clothing on the ground. And, finally, with a submissive gesture to indicate his intent, bends slowly to retrieve his wallet from his pants pocket.

His driver's license identifies him as Stephen Grelet, residing at a North Side address I immediately recognize.

"The cathedral?" I ask him. "You live *there*?"

"Yes."

"Groundskeeper? Maintenance staff?"

The man's muffled response can barely be heard.

"I'm sorry, sir, I didn't catch that. What did you say?"

"Priest," he manages in a faint voice. "I'm assigned to the cathedral."

Desiree slaps her leg.

"Lawd, Jesus, y'all mean to tell me I been doin' a priest!" She cackles delightedly until another thought clouds her face. "Wait a minute. Don't that make it some *special* kind of sin?"

While she ponders this, I stare at Father Grelet. And a whole childhood of Catholic-school memories come flooding back, and the lessons we learned about sanctity and chastity, and the holy men and women who spread the holy word. Who pass out communion and anoint the sick. And one of whom, at this moment, is standing in front of me shivering in the breeze. Unlike Desiree, I don't want to ponder the breach of Divine Rules that's occurred here. Instead, I return his license and rattle off the standard safety warning so fast, it sounds like gibberish even to my ears. The only thing I'm thinking as I drive away is, *A priest, for God's sake!* It'll take me a little while longer, at least until the shock has worn off, to realize that, this time, God's sake had nothing to do with it.

Midnights again, and this time, the dispatcher instructs us to meet the pastor of a local church. Possible information about a burglary, we're told. The pastor will be waiting in the driveway of the church.

He's wringing his hands when we get there. And points to a battered Nissan that's parked in the driveway.

"I thought it was a burglary," he tells us. "The church basement door is unlocked, and this car . . . well, I was sure it was burglars!"

"Okay, Father, we'll take a look."

"Wait! While I was waiting for you, I called the convent. There was an Altar and Rosary Guild meeting earlier this evening. I thought maybe one of the sisters had forgotten to lock up."

"And?"

"They locked up, alright, but one of the sisters says this car belongs to the heating repairman. He was here earlier today, fixing some ductwork. I didn't see him, though. Mother Superior's the one who talked to him."

"She the one who identified his car?"

"No. She's asleep now. One of the other sisters told me."

By now another squad's arrived on the scene. Our backup, in case it's a bona fide burglary. We enter the darkened basement, moving cautiously. At the far end is a closed door, with a sliver of light along its base. Our flashlight beams dance as we move along the walls. Finally, a light switch is located, the basement illuminated.

There are rows of folding tables stacked with piles of clothing—donations for the poor. There is a rickety card table holding old church bulletins, an out-of-order soda machine. No burglars, and nothing worth burglarizing. But the light still shines under the far doorway. Maybe the inept burglars have taken cover.

There's a wall switch just outside the burglars' door. We draw our weapons, take position, and flip the switch. The inner light goes off, and we hear some muffled sounds.

"Who's there?" Is that a woman's voice?

"Police!" My partner shouts. "Open the door, nice and slow, and come out with your hands on your head."

More muffled noises.

"Open the door, you slimeball, or we'll kick it in!"

"Don't shoot!" Definitely a woman's voice, high-pitched, strained, very shaky. "Don't shoot, Officer. Everything's under control here. I'm alright."

"Who's in there?"

We hear more voices, a male voice muttering urgently. Then it's the woman again. "It's just me, Mother Evangelina. I'm fine. You can be on your way now. I'm just . . . taking care of some paperwork."

"You keep some strange office hours. It's 2:30 in the morning. Who's in there with you?"

"Uh, no one. You can leave now. Really, I'm—"

"We're not leaving until you come out, Mother. Gotta make sure you're okay. Open the door so we can see you—then we'll leave." Is that shock in my partner's eye? Another casualty of Catholic education.

When Mother Evangelina finally emerges, some five minutes later, with the heating man cowering behind, her face is scarlet and her habit and wimple are more than a little disheveled. She's mortified; the priest looks close to fainting. And the heating guy, who managed to get only one of his shirt buttons fastened, has completely overlooked his gaping fly.

More Catholic-school flashbacks. This time, I can hear all the lectures delivered by nuns anxious to rein in our class of eighth-grade girls. *Never slow-dance with a boy. Never sit on a boy's lap. No sweaters; they're immoral. No makeup. No anything.* The whole patent-leather-shoes stigma that had us all fearing an eternity in the fires of hell.

Even my partner, the senior officer with nineteen years' experience, is momentarily speechless.

"Well, Father . . . I guess everything's under control here."

"Thank you, Officers. I think you can go now." The priest is struggling with his composure. A losing battle.

We wait until we're back in the squad before another word is uttered.

"A nun!" my partner says. "Wow! Should've seen
the look on your face!"

"Yours, too!" I shoot back. "And the priest. *Everybody!*"

"Yeah. And what d'ya say at a time like that?
What *can* you say?" He guns the squad's engine as
we head back into the night. "One thing, though,
about a situation like that. Wonder if the same old
punishments apply?"

"What? You mean, like having to go to confes-
sion?"

"No . . . like getting cracked on your knuckles
with the yardstick."

As my experiences on the street continue, I learn that
one of the most difficult things to deal with is all the
death that cops encounter—not just the termination
of life, but the death of hopes and dreams. Dreams
are a fragile lot to begin with; but mix them with
reality, whim, or a chance encounter with true evil, and
they go the way of the dinosaurs. I see the defeat, the
painful acceptance in the eyes of parents, spouses,
old people, anyone who's witnessed the transition
from hopeful optimist to cynical realist. But it's always the worst when you see it in a kid. For them,
it's not just the inevitable crash and burn of a secret
wish they've nurtured, but the forfeiture of a piece
of their innocence as well.

Like Miguel Valadez, who wanted to be an altar
boy. It was a promise he'd made to his father a long
time ago, when Papa would tell him stories about
the old days. How Papa had served the mass, back

in Mexico, at the Church of the Holy Virgin in To-luca. It was an honor, Papa said, to serve the Lord and help the priest bring His body and blood to the faithful. Jesus had blessed Papa for his service by giving him a fine wife and children. And a strong first-born son, *Miguelito*, who would continue the blessed tradition. Basking in the light of his father's love, Miguel had promised.

Now Papa was dead, gone too soon to his reward. It couldn't be helped, the doctors said. The tumor grew too big, too fast. Now Miguel must honor his father's memory and the promise he made.

The first meeting for new altar servers is held in the church after school on Tuesday. Miguel is the first one there. Sitting in a polished pew, sniffing the in-censed air, he's eager, but careful not to fidget under Sister Margaret's eagle eye.

This is serious business, she sternly informs the gathered children. No fooling around here. This is the Lord's work.

The children are ushered into the sacristy, where Sister Margaret points out the sacred vessels, the pristine vestments hung and ready for the next mass. Miguel imagines himself bowing and kneel-ing, ringing the sacring bells as the priest elevates the Host. Papa would be proud.

Miguel attends every meeting. He's diligent at practice, careful under Sister Margaret's scrutiny. And delighted when he's informed that he can serve his first mass in one week's time.

On the way out of the church he meets Father Marty, the new young priest in the parish. The one who plays touch football with the kids during recess, who jokes with the nuns. Who held Miguel's baby sister at the funeral while Mama said her rosary.

"Yo, Father Marty! Guess what I'm doin'?"

They walk together, the priest and the boy, past the church grounds and through the empty lot. Miguel is excited to share his good news, thrilled to be walking with Father Marty. It's because I'm an altar boy, he thinks. I'll be helping him serve God. When they reach the corner, Father Marty leads him toward the viaduct. On the other side is an old truck lot, mostly empty and overgrown with weeds.

"I live the other way, Father," Miguel says, but he follows him anyway, through the gloomy tunnel, into the cinder lot where rusted shells of old trailers hunker in the weeds. Father Marty seems to know where he's going. He points to a pile of old tires in a remote corner.

"Race you!" he challenges. Miguel is off and running, beating the priest by a good ten-foot lead. And barely has time to flash a victor's smile before Father Marty is on him, forcing him over the tire mound, dragging off his clothes. Crying, whimpering, Miguel writhes, struggling against the pain, the grunted commands in his ear.

"I won't hurt you. I'll be your special friend. But you can't tell." More cries, a desperate shriek. "Nobody would believe you if you did. I'm a priest. And you'd go to hell."

On routine patrol, our squad circles the truck lot. We hear a scream, can barely make out the figures back around the bushes. We exit the car quietly and make our way across the lot. Creeping around the trailers, we're unobserved by the terrified boy and the rutting man. My partner hauls him off, throws him face down on the gravel, where he's handcuffed before we even notice the cleric's collar. I gather up the trembling, bleeding child and bundle him into the squad. Away from his attacker, away from the horror, and his broken dreams of serving the Lord.

The twinkling lights make it official. The tent is pitched, the folding chairs arranged in curving rows, and on the makeshift stage, the crucifix is erected— eight feet of Jesus writhing on the cross with acrylic blood clots so real-looking you'd swear he was dripping! It's Saturday night, and the first annual All-Faiths Prayer Congregation Revival of the Holy Spirit is officially under way.

People are crowding into the tent, drawn by curiosity, the thumping music, and the carnival atmosphere. There's a gospel quartet on the stage, a minister shaking and testifying that he's seized with the spirit, and a crew of ushers who work the crowd, praising Jesus, shouting hallelujah, and passing the collection baskets so the crowd can give thanks to the Lord.

Ruth Gibbons is among these sweaty faithful, listening to the words of salvation. She's a widow who usually spends her weekends alone. Not too much for a lonely Christian lady to do come Saturday, not in her neighborhood. Not many places to socialize or maybe, God willing, meet a decent companion to pass away some afternoons.

She comes to the revival on a whim. A good way to pass the time, rub elbows with other Christian people. At some point, her eyes fix on the man standing off to the side of the stage. His white shirt is spotless, molded to broad shoulders, a barrel chest. A *real* man. She looks down, away, but there's something about him that piques her interest. His bow tie is perfect, his finger-waved black hair as lustrous as a raven's wing. Down South, they'd call him a fancy man. Ruth just calls him gorgeous.

At the intermission, he moves down the aisles, speaking with the congregation. When he comes to Ruth, he takes her hand, bending low in a courtly bow. He introduces himself. Wesley Simon. The *Reverend* Wesley Simon. He thanks Ruth for coming out, and praises Jesus for the chance to meet her. The touch of his hand is enough to weaken her knees. She watches him, discreetly, through the rest of the service. While the other ministers preach and pray onstage, Reverend Simon moves around the audience, singing and clapping.

After the revival, Reverend Simon seeks her out.

"There's an afternoon revival tomorrow, Sister Gibbons. I'd sure like to see you again. Any way you think you can make it?" She can, and she does. And the next evening, when the revival's over, the reverend invites her to dinner. Just a little bite to eat, he tells her. Share a meal and some pleasant conversation. Nothing fancy, and no way he could afford to be, anyway, not on a minister's salary.

Over short-rib specials at the local diner, they swap life stories. The reverend ("Call me Wesley") is courtly, attentive, drawing Ruth out. She tells him about her ten long years of widowhood, her quiet life, her home just blocks away. When Wesley looks wistful, speaks of his lonely life as a traveling minister with no family, no home of his own, it seems uncharitable not to invite him to hers.

She offers brandy in the tidy parlor. Sipping from the delicate glass, he can't compliment her enough. The house is lovely, her garden a glory. So much to keep up for a woman alone! And so costly, on a widow's pension! It must be hard, a woman like her, making ends meet.

Warmed by his attention and a second glass of brandy, Ruth smiles. It seems so natural talking to Wesley. Like she's known him all her life. Like she can tell him anything. So she does.

She's been lucky, Ruth says. Her late husband, rest his soul, knew how to save a penny. Between the investments and his railroad pension, she doesn't have to worry, thank the Lord.

He must have been a fine man, says Wesley, praising Jesus. Ruth agrees. He was a good man, always looked out for her. Worried about every little thing.

She laughs, pointing to the antique sideboard in the dining room. Why, he even built her a little safe, right there behind that sideboard door. Slid open, right into the wall, so she could store her valuables and such. Money, too, for emergencies. He said you couldn't be too careful. Who else would have thought of such a thing?

"Not many." Wesley smiles. "The Lord bless his soul."

When he strokes Ruth's hand, it seems natural. Not much later, he's kissing her, feeling her, whispering words and wishes she hasn't heard in too many years. It's been so long, and feels so good, that soon they're in bed together, rolling and thrashing, calling out God's name for an entirely different reason.

Afterward, he stems her embarrassment by telling her it's the Lord's will. Such a wonderful thing was meant to be. Why, he'd been lonely so long, Jesus had sent him a fine woman with a name straight out of the Bible. It was a sign. And he reaches for her again. Once more, and then she drifts off, wrapped in the reverend's arms.

It's morning before she wakes, stiff, groggy, and just a little disoriented. Then she remembers, and reaches for Wesley.

The Reverend Simon is gone, along with her wallet, the sixty-five dollars in it, and all of her credit cards. She runs through the house, calling his name, but there's no sign of him. Only the empty glasses in the parlor and the open door of the sideboard safe. He cleaned her out—the money, her jewelry, even her late husband's gold pocket watch.

When we take the report, Ruth is numb with grief. She sits stiffly in her tidy parlor, holding a lace-edged handkerchief in her clenched hands. Her eyes are teary as she glances around the spotless room, where she and Wesley shared dreams and brandy—and so much more. A *reverend,* she keeps repeating. *A man of God.*

During the follow-up investigation, detectives learn there is no Reverend Simon affiliated with the All-Faiths Prayer Congregation of the Holy Spirit. Church personnel who are subsequently interviewed state they've never even heard of a Reverend Simon. No Wesley Simon, either—not now, not ever. Only the holy are employed there. The good and the righteous, dedicated to spreading the word of the Lord.

When the investigation is finally concluded, Ruth is informed that Wesley was never a minister, a man of the church, or associated with the prayer revival in any way. He was nothing more than an enterprising hustler, in fact, who attended church functions in hopes of fleecing naïve believers. A common practice of con men skilled at robbing unsuspecting souls of a few dollars, and sometimes, as in Ruth's case, a lot of dreams.

* * *

Caswell's Department Store is one of a dying breed: an old-fashioned, family-oriented establishment with creaking wooden floors and wares spread out across rows of long tables. Some of the salesclerks are nearly as old as the ornate brass fixtures, but the customers don't seem to mind. Caswell's has it all, from clothing to drug sundries to toys—maybe not the latest thing, but good enough for the local crowd. It's a neighborhood place where friendly service is valued over high-tech convenience.

On one particular Saturday, the store is crowded with shoppers. It's just after Thanksgiving, so the Christmas bargain-hunters are out in numbers. The narrow aisles are filled with parents and their children, browsing senior citizens, the random cluster of teens. Among the shoppers are two nuns, dressed in traditional habits, moving slowly through the store. Without breaking rank, they nod to the courteous salesclerk and head down the main aisle toward the door. The man entering through the revolving door never sees them. Propelled by the impetus of the pushing crowd, he stumbles forward, smashing into one of the good sisters, who goes down with a thud.

The anxious manager hurries forward. "Sister! I'm so sorry!" he breathes, extending a hand. "Let me help you." Once he helps her to her feet, the nun is sorry, too. On the floor are a pile of items that were knocked loose in the fall: stolen items that were secreted in the folds of her voluminous habit. A silver pen set, dusting powder, a woolen scarf. Two bras, a pack of note cards, hemorrhoid cream, and a box of laxatives. The green shards of a broken glass candy dish.

Assuming that these thieves are impostor nuns, store security escorts them to the ladies' room, where a female officer searches them both. She confiscates three pairs of women's cotton underpants, a tape measure, a bag of malted-milk balls, lip balm, a pack of batteries. And, finally, identification that states the cowering crooks are Sister Joan Marie and Sister Annunciata, respectively, from the order of nuns residing in the nearby parish convent.

Security officers call the police, but by the time we arrive, the astonished store manager has decided not to prosecute. More an embarrassment than anything, he tells us. The items they stole didn't exactly amount to a felony theft. Better to just let them go with a warning. After all, he's a Catholic. A man who's learned the value of forgiveness.

Watching the shamed nuns scuttle out of the store, one of the security officers shakes his head.

"Guess they forgot the Ten Commandments, huh? The one about 'Thou shalt not steal'?"

"Or one more important than that," the manager observes wryly. "'Thou shalt not get caught.'"

12

Babes in Gangland

Dispatcher: Here we go, sports fans. All units in Twelve, all units on citywide, we have a gang fight, a gang fight in progress in the north alley of 21 and Winchester. Citizens are reporting shots fired at that location. Units to ride?

1222: '22. It's our beat, guess it's our party.

1227: 1227. We'll drop by for the festivities.

1263C: '63 Charlie. We're riding.

Dispatcher: Okay, '63 Charlie, ten-four. Units, be advised that civilian-dress officers are also responding. Repeat, civilian-dress officers will be on the scene.

1224: 1224's going too, Squad. What's springtime without a gang war?

1227: Right. Like the swallows at Capistrano.

The names are exotic, enticing. They sound like the titles of boys' adventure stories: the Spanish Cobras, the Counts, Insane Unknown, Latin Dragons, la Raza, the Vice Lords, Trumbull Boys. These are some of the street gangs of Chicago, more than 140 known gangs, but the numbers grow daily. Asians, Hispanics, blacks, Caucasians—*all* ethnic groups can now boast representation in the city's gang society. Like an ungainly pie, the city is divided into turfs fought for and presided over by resident gangs. In the most simplistic terms, Chicago gangs pledge their allegiance to one of two main groups. There are many subgroups, minor factions, and spin-offs of larger groups, but all of them are part of either "People" or "Folks." In Los Angeles, it's the Crips and the Bloods. Whatever the city, the outcome is the same: Invade the turf of a rival gang, and you're teasing the Grim Reaper. Gang members are fiercely loyal, quick to defend, quicker to kill. It's not just a question of survival, it's about respect. And, increasingly, it's about big business. The name of the game is drugs, a never-fail supply-and-demand empire that can launch a gang's economy into the stratosphere. Drugs need dealers, suppliers, and runners. A gang supplies all of that.

Initially, most kids join gangs for support. They feel they're not getting it at home in their single-parent or absent-parent families. Or they're getting hassled on the street. In communities where the strength lies in numbers, the gang offers them everything that's missing: loyalty, support, protection. *Fuck with me, fuck with my brothers.*

Some kids start young. At the age of eight or nine, when they're just "shorties," they're recruited by older gang members. Young kids make good "mules"—the ones who transport money and drugs. They're too young to be locked up if they get caught, too young to do any real time in the Audy Home, Chicago's juvenile detention center. So they run the money—sometimes four, five thousand dollars at a time—between the dealers and the dope houses, learning the hustle. By age ten or eleven, they're junior gang members, as adept at gun usage as the older guys.

By now they've had a taste of the wares: the drugs, the girls, more highs than they ever imagined. They're part of the gang now. They run with the pack. For many, the story ends in death. Others are lucky enough to get out, reclaim their lives.

For Rigo DeLeon, it was the fast life, a golden, glamorous ride that shot him light-years beyond the boredom of home. His daddy, Guillermo, was a mechanic who worked hard every day, came home each night to his wife, Alicia. His home where, amid the chaos of five lively children, he was happy to forget the long workday with some family chatter and a couple of cold *cervezas*. Devout Catholics with a strong sense of family, Guillermo and Alicia tried to instill the same values in their kids. Not the usual family profile for what Rigo would become.

He was the oldest child, a smart boy, quick in school, quicker on the street. He saw how much money the gangbangers and dope dealers were raking in, saw how hard his own father slaved to put food on the table. What was the point of killing yourself? Why be poor when you could be rolling? For Rigo, it was a no-brainer. He wanted to be his own man and enjoy the finer things of life: a flashy car, a flashier woman, and a big wad of cash in his pocket. So when gang members approached him, just after his eighth birthday, and asked if he wanted to be a mule, he said sure.

Smart kids learn fast. At nine, he's running guns. At ten, he's a junior gang member. And is careful to hide from his family the gang's official pitchfork tattoo that's his pride and joy—proof that he runs with *real* men.

These real men wean him on marijuana, and then hash, and reward him with lines of coke when he's very good. Like good enough to knock off the mom-and-pop grocery store, or pistol-whip a decrepit old lady for the seven dollars she had buried in her purse.

By the time he's twelve, Rigo is ready to move on. Show us you got some *huevos,* his fellow members tell him. Time to ride the horse, man. Get some hair on your balls. Be a man.

Rigo is pretty sure he's a man already. Just a week before, they'd fed him some Benzedrine—an amphetamine that made him feel like he was flying, like he could do anything. So he did. They put a revolver in his hand and told him to kill somebody—anybody—just to prove himself. He shot an old man walking his dog in the alley, and then, because it felt so good, he shot the dog, too.

Now he has to prove himself all over again. It's time to ride the horse, court the Lady Heroin. And so the seduction begins. At first, he just snorts up. Somehow, that isn't as scary as needles and anyway, the high's the same, isn't it? Skin-popping comes next and, finally, the needle that slides into his vein bringing white heat and red lust. At twelve years, Rigo falls in love.

Now Rigo becomes a lover possessed. More needles, more hits, more orgasmic blasts of ecstasy. So besotted is he, so eager to prove himself as a lover, he vows to devote himself to his new mistress. Every waking moment is spent thinking about her, every dream of sliding into her sultry embrace. But it costs. The money he makes with his gang doesn't cover it, nor do the proceeds from the purse snatching and petty thefts. His lover is a demanding one. If he wants to be with her, he has to find a way. He decides that way is his father's car. He can steal it, sell it for a lot more money than he'd find in any old lady's purse.

A few nights later, we're sent to a "domestic disturbance with the family." When we pull up in front of Rigo's house, a crowd of neighbors congregates, murmuring in Spanish and English. Once inside, we shoulder past the screaming Alicia, the wailing children, to the bathroom where Guillermo is.

He'd been taking a bath, relaxing in the warm water while listening to his favorite music on the Spanish station, WOJO. And Rigo had gone in, on the pretense of relieving himself, but really to take the car keys from his father's pants pocket. When Guillermo shouted at him, Rigo grabbed the radio—still plugged into the bathroom outlet—and threw it into the tub.

When we put the cuffs on him, Rigo rotates his hand defiantly, so we can see the pitchfork, his beloved emblem of manhood. And when we lead him outside, he swaggers, sneering at the gathered crowd. And waits until he's inside the squad car, behind the thick steel cage before he asks, "So now what? Where you takin' me, huh?" The twelve-year-old murderer's voice quivers. "You can't do nothin' to me. I'm just a kid."

The street is the best teacher for any cop. Lessons learned are quick, harsh, and, if you're smart, never forgotten. You learn to read the streets, notice the rhythms of crime patterns, the players who figure most prominently in the commission of those crimes. And when, as a cop, you're assigned to a district with a heavy gang population, or to the Gang Crimes Unit, you learn that gangs, like crimes, are equal opportunity. And that, like the cycle of nature, gang activity heats up with the weather. For gangs, spring marks the time to come out in numbers, jockey for position in the hierarchy of gang power. Membership recruitment is stepped up, drive-by shootings begin as a way of displaying dominance. Gang fights break out, and another bloody cycle of rivalry and vengeance begins.

On one mild spring afternoon, a beat-up old car is parked strategically, on a corner near an empty lot that provides a clear view of the intersection. Important for the car's occupants—four girls who watch the passing traffic. The oldest girl, the driver, is sixteen. The youngest is thirteen. She sits in the backseat with a gun in her hand and her baby daughter asleep beside her.

These girls are Lady Pythons, the female satellites of the Latin Pythons, a South Side gang. They're on the corner, smoking, drinking, watching. Each car that passes through the intersection is tracked by four pairs of brown eyes probing, identifying the occupants as friend or foe, potential invaders of their turf. The girls are petite, dressed in the same baggy jeans, the same oversized T-shirts. The same tattoos decorate their arms and hands, identifying them as Pythons.

Most days, they sit on the corner, defending their turf. "Presenting" to the low-riders who cruise by, challenging. Flashing gang signs, popping off a few rounds sometimes, so folks know they're not punkin' out.

On this particular day, the girls are watching for a specific reason. Li'l Queen, the fifteen-year-old in the front seat, has a score to settle. There's a new girl in the 'hood, some bitch named Marisol whom she wants to burn. Marisol is new to the city, new to the country. She came here with her family from Mexico, and doesn't yet understand the ways of the 'hood. So when Li'l Queen and her homegirls tried to recruit her, she said no. She has family, brothers and sisters to take care of while her parents work. She's not allowed to run the streets.

Some girls say no to gangs. Girls like the "party crews," who like to hang out, but don't affiliate. They stay neutral, but remain friendly. This bitch, Marisol, she just turned her back, fronted Li'l Queen off like she was some kind of garbage. To make things worse, some of the male Pythons have been checking the new girl out. Even Li'l Queen's boyfriend, Tico, said Marisol is one fine bitch who he'd bone in a hot second. So enough is enough. Time to do something about Marisol.

Li'l Queen spread it around that Marisol secretly runs with the Ambrose, a rival gang. And that she's trying to get close to *their* boys—the Pythons—so she can set them up. Which, in gang society, is tantamount to signing her death warrant. More than anything, Li'l Queen wants to burn the bitch herself. So she sits in the car with her homegirls, Flygirl and Nas/T and G., and waits. Sometimes Marisol walks this way. Today might be the day.

While they wait, they drink, swigging from "40s"—huge, forty-ounce bottles of beer. And discuss other ways to take Marisol out.

They know she's preparing for her *quinceañera*, the traditional cotillion held for fifteen-year-old Mexican girls. It'd be a shame if she didn't live to see it, Nas/T snickers. Which gives Li'l Queen an idea.

Later that afternoon, a car pulls up in front of Marisol's building. The driver gets out, holding a spray of flowers wrapped in florists' paper. Before opening the door, Marisol peers cautiously through the peephole. *Cuidado,* her mother had told her. *Be careful.* She sees the floral paper, the tiny envelope stapled to the corner. A delivery, she thinks, for her cotillion. A surprise from her father.

She opens the door, smiling. These are the first

flowers she's ever received—and the last. The flowers are thrust against her and a gun aimed at her head. Marisol drops to the floor, felled by a single bullet through her brain. The card stapled to the flowers, which now lies soaking up the seeping blood, is scrawled with a quick slash of graffiti: the street symbols for the Lady Pythons.

It's encounters like this that amplify the ways this job is changing me. Working the street makes time seem to accelerate, make a month seem like a year. I can barely remember the person who joined the department because it was a good salary and benefits . . . but just a temporary gig until something better came along. I can't believe I once sat in an office, working as a therapist, and thought I understood about people's pain. Anything I experienced in the confines of that office pales in comparison to what exists out here. Could a therapist—or *anybody*—soothe the pain of parents whose beautiful vibrant daughter has been gunned down on the threshold of their own home? Can anyone use theories and research to explain to families who tried their best, worked hard—why gangs exist, claim the lives of countless innocent victims?

The district I work in is tough, gang-infested, on the lowest end of any socioeconomic scale. It's an area populated by people who've never had any breaks, or been given much chance to make their own. More people on welfare here than on employment rolls. People who are familiar with the feeling of falling through the cracks in the system that's supposed to provide opportunities, pave the way toward the same advancement that other people in other neighborhoods know and enjoy.

Here, the only equal opportunity that kids understand is crime. The credo of the streets is a tough "live hard, die young" proposition that only a precious few manage to escape. Here, it's hard to entertain dreams of college and careers when you're concentrating on getting to school alive. Dodging the gang recruiters who follow you home, who might shoot you if you don't join.

Kids on these streets live and breathe fear. And learn to combat that with violence, through gang membership, through crime, through anything that will help them through the labyrinth of hopelessness the streets afford them. Education is tough in an environment focused on day-to-day survival. Employment? Where can you get a job with no experience, no skills? Even the fast-food restaurants have thirty applicants for every job here, and that's with *previous* experience. Kids trying to claw their way to a better life meet with rejection and despair at every corner. Eventually, some of them find it easier to stop fighting, simply surrender to what's all around them. Why fight the system? Gangs have power, money, respect, all the things missing from a desperate kid's life. Unfortunately, gang members also have the life expectancy of a radio battery. Life is cheap on the streets. *Live hard, die young.*

Cops know all this, see it every day, feel the same helplessness because we can't stop it. We see our own kids in the faces of crippled fourteen-year-olds who were in the wrong place at the wrong time. Bring parents to the morgue to identify their children and wonder what we could have done— what *anyone* could have done to prevent it? And know there are no answers, not today at least. Or any of the other days you strap on your gun-belt and go back out there, try and do damage control on a problem larger than all of us.

I feel the frustration, and witness the fallout. Some

cops hang in there, do the best they can in spite of incredible odds. Those are the ones who understand the street life, how it can beat you down. Those who want to see these kids beat the odds, make it out to a better life. Other cops become emotional casualties of these same mean streets. Their experiences have left them angry, and bitter, and finally apathetic. For them, the job has diminished to nothing more than eight hours in exchange for pay.

My first encounter with a cop like this comes on a steamy Saturday night in July, when the district is up for grabs. Street fights, shootings, disturbances in every sector, and there's not enough of us to go around. Manpower's at a dangerous low, with injured cops on the medical roll, people on furlough or calling in sick. Job assignments have been switched, adjusted to accommodate.

I'm paired with a traffic cop who usually works alone on the accident car. Which means he spends a good part of his tour at Dunkin' Donuts, supposedly to finish writing his accident reports, but really to swill coffee and bullshit with the waitress. His preferred way to pass a tour of duty.

Now, he's not exactly thrilled to be pulled off his regular car and lets me know it. He hasn't worked the trenches in years, he tells me. What good is having seniority if you still have to deal with the scum? He doesn't even have a safety vest, for Chrissake. What if the shit hits the fan?

Too late to worry about it, I tell him. It's *already* hitting the fan, all over the district.

Our first job is an in-progress call: damage to property at the 18th Street 'El' station. Teenagers up on the tracks, spray-painting graffiti. There's five of them up on the platform, so engrossed in their work they don't even see us. And are too scared to scatter when my partner fires off a round.

"God, Vince! What are you doing? These are just kids. Put the gun away!"

He circles them, a cowering bunch with spray cans, and laughs nastily when the smallest pees his pants.

"Yeah, you little bastards, you *should* be scared. I should blow you all away right now."

I can see the headlines now: "'Crazed Cop Slaughters Innocent Children.'"

"Vince, listen—"

"Whattaya think we should do with these scumbags?" he growls at me. "I say we throw 'em on the tracks. Watch 'em fry on the third rail."

Is this Psycho-Cop I'm working with? If so, I understand why they usually assign him to the relative isolation of a traffic car. Obviously, he's forgotten what it's like on the streets. And if this is his version of "good-cop, bad-cop," he's been watching too many movies. Maybe he hasn't been reading the papers, but cops are getting indicted for less.

"Vince, I think we should—"

"I think you're right. Let's take 'em down to that piece of shit they call a car. See what else they got."

It's a '79 Chevy, a low-rider belonging to the oldest boy, identified as Jaime Ayala, seventeen years old. The car is obviously his pride and joy. The rust spots have been sanded, carefully patched with Bondo, and sanded again. The layers of primer that cover it now are temporary, awaiting the final coats of flaked enamel that will transform it into a badass machine. In the trunk of this badass machine is a carton containing a dozen more cans of spray paint.

"So, you all think you're fuckin' Michelangelos,

want to do some paintin', huh?" Vince swaggers around the boys, Captain Bligh surveying his mutinous crew. "Little gangbanger motherfuckers, got nothin' better to do than destroy public property?"

He circles again, considering, and then stops in front of Jaime.

"Well, you wanna paint, I think you should paint."

"W-what?" Jaime stares at the ground, unwilling to look up.

"I said, I think you should paint. Don't let me stand in the way of your creative urges. I'll give you two choices. We haul your sorry asses to jail, or you paint. Which is it?"

"Uh . . . what do you mean, Officer?"

"I mean, you paint or we lock you up. What's it gonna be?"

Dumbfounded, the boys exchange furtive glances.

"Uh, paint, I guess."

"Good." Vince swings up the trunk, points to the carton. "Get your shit there and get started. Only you're not gonna ruin any more property. You wanna paint, you're gonna paint this car. Looks like it could use a nice paint job."

An anguished cry from Jaime.

"I said, paint!" Vince barks. "Only, you're gonna paint exactly what I tell you. Otherwise, I'll haul you all to the shithouse."

At this point, I'm certain Vince has lost his mind. But he's the senior officer, and our manpower shortage means that I can't go in to the station and request another partner. I'm stuck with him now for another six hours.

While the boys work, Vince shouts directions, heckling, threatening. And flashes his blue-steel Smith & Wesson when progress is slow.

When they're done, the car is completely covered. From bumper to bumper, over every inch are slogans in foot-high letters. All of them dictated by Vince, all offending the rival gangs the boys will pass on their way home. "Vice Lords Eat They Mamas!" proclaims one fender. "Latin Kings are Dick Smokers." "Gangsta Disciples are Pussies." "Imperial Gangsters Suck Dog Dick."

The boys are nearly in tears. Jaime's prized possession is ruined. There's no way he can drive it now and expect to go more than a block without attack. There's also no conceivable way they can make it safely on foot. They're on rival turf here. Enemies on every corner.

"That was amusing," Vince says as we drive off. "Did you see the looks on their faces? I guess *that* fucked up their night, huh?"

"*If* they have a night. If they don't get killed on the way home. Why not just bring 'em into the station, call their parents?"

Vince looks at me like I've lost my mind.

"You realize how long that'd take, paperwork for those five little pricks? And then calling a Youth Officer, and waiting for the sorry-ass parents to show up? *If* they show up? Who needs that shit?" He settles back, satisfied, and gestures to the radio.

"Tell 'em we're clear from this job, and we're gonna do a premises check at 18th and Western."

"That's the coffee shop."

"Yeah, I know. All this work's makin' me thirsty."

The Blood Brothers are a white gang that originated on the Southwest Side and was started for one basic reason. The niggers and the spics, they said, were getting all the glory. The founding members were a bunch of blue-collar skinheads who liked to think of themselves as white supremacists. Only there was nothing very supreme about cruising the manicured neighborhoods of the Southwest Side in their pick-ups, maybe spray-painting a garage now and then, and talking about how bad they were. Not when the black and Hispanic gangs made the papers and the news every other night for shootings, drive-bys, all the glamour stuff. Goddamn shitheads were stealing their thunder. It was embarrassing.

They decided to get a plan, bring the attention back to the white boys, where it belonged. So they stepped up their recruitment, made sure they left their graffiti calling card at the scene of every crime so when it made the neighborhood papers, the community would know how mighty the Blood Brothers were. But a few burglaries, a shooting here and there wasn't enough. They wanted something more, something flashy that would distinguish them from the rest. And decided that infiltrating the police department was the best way to do it.

What followed next was very clever, and potentially deadly. People affiliated with the Blood Brothers were employed by the city and placed in sensitive positions, like the Department of Personnel, where they could access classified information. The names and addresses of all sworn police officers, their assigned districts and watches, all were made known to the Blood Brothers, who then instituted a new initiation requirement for gang recruits.

They had to break into a cop's house, steal his guns, and bring them to the gang leaders, *after* they'd been used in the commission of a crime. There was a special kind of kick using a cop's gun to do their gang business. Cops' addresses were supplied, as well as their work schedules. The only thing left was to do the deed.

A string of burglaries followed, all with police as victims. The hunters became the hunted. Nobody was sure what would happen next. But the plan was logical: Don't hassle the police, *become* the police.

Within a short time, other gangs followed suit. It was the perfect strategic move: Work from the inside. Soon there were reports of cops working with dope dealers, fronting rings of car thieves. Cops stealing guns, cops taking down cops. The media had a field day. How could the city expect protection from a department that can't police itself?

On one occasion, a gang-member cop (who previously had been covert about his affiliation) was called before a disciplinary panel to answer charges of alleged racketeering. He strolled in, wearing his gang colors, and flipped gang signs at the flabbergasted review board. *Police THIS!*

Officially, the police department acknowledges that there is "a disturbing number of current department members affiliated with or an associate of gangs" and that "a thorough investigation is being made to identify these persons and take necessary action."

Yeah, right. And the check is in the mail.

The reality is that there are enemies in our ranks. All on a very covert level, of course, so nobody is really sure who's who. Bad guys and good guys, all working together, all looking over their shoulders so nobody gets the jump on them. They're all wearing the uniform, and they all carry guns. Not much different, when you think about it, than the way it's always been.

13

Wagon Ho

1271:	1271
Dispatcher:	Yes, '71?
1271:	Squad, hold us down transporting some prisoners from Vice down to Women's Central Detention.
Dispatcher:	A prostitute transport again, huh? Are they picking on those poor girls again? They're just trying to make a living!
Unidentified Unit:	That's what they all say.

We all have to do it sometime. Every Chicago cop, at some time in his or her career, has to work the wagon aka squadrol aka meat truck. The idea is to make us well-rounded cops, give everyone the experience of what the *other* guys do, like hauling stiffs and transporting prisoners. For some, the experience is one they don't care to repeat. Others claim it's the best job in the department. All will agree that working the wagon is an acquired taste.

The prerequisites for a wagon man (or woman) are a strong back, a stronger stomach, and a sense of humor. It also helps if your nasal passages are permanently blocked for those times when you're assigned to remove a "stinker": a body that's been dead and decaying a week or more before anyone discovers it.

Seasoned wagon vets will tell you there's nothing like the wagon assignment. It's safer, since wagon personnel are usually not in the line of fire, and very seldom in shoot-outs. Health risks are lower, outside of a few ruptured discs or the heart attack that might strike when you're struggling to haul a three-hundred-pounder. Wagon guys are not required to participate in high-speed car chases. Few have been known to scale a ten-story fire escape in pursuit of a bad guy. And it's rare for them to throw a punch, since the people they deal with are usually dead or handcuffed.

Even the prisoners they transport generally present few problems since, by the time the wagon arrives, they've pretty much resigned themselves to the fact that they're going to jail. As for the corpses, it's even easier. They don't talk back, don't beef to OPS (Office of Professional Standards) and *never* ask, "What took you so long?" And, as most wagon personnel tell me, once you get past the smell, you've got it beat.

Driving a squadrol for the first time is a unique experience. Just recently the department decided to phase out the original squadrols and gradually replace them with sleeker, more functional vans. But nothing will ever match the old meat wagons. They're big, clunky things, a box on wheels that trundles along like a pregnant snail. The prisoners are transported in the rear compartment, which is outfitted with a back door and a steel bench bolted to each wall. The wagon cops ride up front in a small cab with a tiny window to monitor the passengers. Not the height of comfort, but heavy on basic practicality. Speed is not part of the equation in one of these babies—turn a corner too fast, and the whole thing tips over.

My first time as a wagon woman ("wagon ho" in copspeak) has me partnered with Mack, a twenty-five-year vet with twenty-two of those spent on the wagon. He's chomping a massive cigar, the standard prop of many wagon drivers ("Cuts the smell," he informs me), and he seems most interested in testing my mettle.

"Hope you're not the squeamish type," he informs me. "Sometimes it can get pretty brutal out here. Ever see how bad it can get after a four-car pileup? Or see what's left after a shoot-out?" *Ever think about keeping your mouth shut, Mack?*

We roll along streets where the early-hour quiet is marred only by Mack's incessant gabbing. War stories, gore stories, every disgusting call he's ever gotten are passed along to me with obvious relish and billowing clouds of cigar smoke. My stomach is starting to turn, more from the stink than the stories, and it's almost a relief when we get the call for a removal.

"Hope you haven't had breakfast yet," the dispatcher tells us. "Landlord's calling this one in. Says there's something dripping through his dining-room ceiling. And coincidentally mentions he hasn't seen his tenant in a few weeks."

It's worse than I imagined. The stench hits us from half a block away. It's July, the middle of a record heat wave, just the thing to nudge the dear departed toward maximum levels of putrefaction. The landlord is waiting on the porch. His tenant is an old man, he tells us, seventy-five if he's a day, with no family that he's aware of.

He points to a stack of mail on the stairs leading to the second-floor apartment, mail that the old man hasn't picked up in more than three weeks.

"That didn't strike you as unusual?" I ask. "You

didn't think to go upstairs, check to see if he was okay?"

The landlord shrugs.

"I stay outta his business," he says. "He's quiet, he pays the rent on time, I don't ask questions. I got my own problems."

"Didn't you notice the smell?"

"So maybe the ol' man got some hygiene problems. What do I know? But when somethin' started drippin' through my ceiling, I figured, hey, this ain't right. Better call the police." *No shit, Sherlock!*

The apartment upstairs is tiny, airless, filled with the stench of decay. For whatever reasons, all the windows are not only closed, but painted shut, so it's impossible to ventilate the rooms. Using his nightstick, my partner breaks out a window.

"Otherwise we'll keel over too," he mutters through the handkerchief he holds over his nose. He moves into the kitchen, rummages along the counter until he finds a can of coffee. Setting a frying pan on the stove, he pours in dry coffee and turns up the gas. Burning coffee grounds, an old wagon trick, meant to temper the overpowering stench.

The old man is found, facedown on the floor of the bedroom. He's been dead long enough for his body's natural gases to erupt in jagged bursts of rotted flesh, for the body fluids to drain out onto the floor, *through* the floor, and the first-floor ceiling as well.

"You'd think the landlord would've called before now," Mack says disgustedly, and turns back to the kitchen. He points to the open cabinet doors, the kitchen drawers, the opened lids of assembled canisters.

"You looking for more coffee, Mack? There's still some in the can."

"Not coffee. But it looks like somebody's been looking for *bread*." Moving toward the bedroom now, he gestures toward the open bureau drawers. "Looks like our friend downstairs was having a field day."

Pictures previously hung on the wall are scattered on the floor with their backings torn open. Stepping around them, Mack shakes his head.

"Sometimes these old guys hide their money in crazy places. And when they die, it's open season for any bloodsucker who's close enough to hunt for hidden treasure." He points to the closet, where clothes hang askew after what must have been a recent, hasty pat-down. "Lot of these old people have no family, no one who'll know if they get ripped off after death. Sometimes it's the landlord who does it, sometimes the neighbors, I sometimes even the wagon cops if they're the first on the scene."

"They rip off a *dead* person?" I realize how naïve I sound, but I'm appalled by what my partner is saying. Grave robbers of a guy who's not even buried yet.

"Damn straight. These old coots, sometimes they don't believe in banks, keep a bankroll hidden in the icebox, a coffee can, who knows where. Y'never know where you'll find it. And this guy cashed his pension check just before he croaked. I saw the check stub on the kitchen table. Landlord—or whoever was in here before us—must have seen it, too. And decided to liberate the cash while they could." Moving through the living room, Mack points to the sofa cushions tossed on the floor. "Think I'm kidding? Whoever did this wasn't gonna stop until they found something."

"That's really sick!"

"Sick? You want to hear sick? Check the old guy. See if he's got any jewelry on. Rings, watches, a chain . . . anything. Bet you don't find any of that. You think that's a coincidence? It isn't. You know what I—oh, *you dirty bastard*!" His deep voice rumbles from the other room. "Come in here, kid! I wanna show you something!"

It's not hidden treasure my partner's found. His expression is sour as he points to the empty television stand, the rectangle of clean on a dusty table.

"Fucking thieves! Look at this. . . . Here's where the guy's radio probably was. And look there—see that empty video box? Where the guy's TV and VCR used to be. Goddamn weasel—whoever did this!"

For Mack, the preliminary investigation is over. The *only* investigation, even though this is clearly a theft, but a crime that's not reportable. There's no victim to sign complaints, no family members to insist that justice be done. Just an dead old man who departed the world just a heartbeat before his earthly possessions.

Now there's nothing to do but remove the remains of the remains. As we strip the shower curtain down—a makeshift tarp to cover the oozing body, Mack is philosophical. And more than willing to impart a few pearls of wisdom to his partner, the new kid.

"Be surprised the things you come across when you work the wagon as long as I have. At first, I couldn't believe it myself. 'Specially the partner I had when I first started out. This guy was like a human metal detector—except it was money, not metal he was after. Any job we went to, if there was money in the place, he'd find it."

Stepping back from the body, Mack blows out a labored breath.

"One time he found ten thousand dollars in an

old lady's cookie jar. And a pair of diamond earrings that he gave his wife for Christmas."

"You never said anything? You let him do it?" Another naïve question, but I really want to know.

"Let him? What could I do? He was the senior man on the wagon. I was just a green kid. Nothing I could've said or done." He nods sagely before delivering what he clearly considers the best advice of all.

"On this job, first thing you learn is to keep your mouth shut. You don't say *nuthin'*! If you do, you get a reputation as a crybaby and a snitch, and nobody will work with you. Or if they do, your chances have just increased by about 200 percent that you might just have a little accident. Know what I mean? You're working with guys who have big guns and bigger attitudes. That's nothing to mess with. So you keep your eyes open and your mouth shut, and hope for the best." *Echoes of Sergeant Woods's speech back at the Academy.*

The images Mack described are so grim there's nothing I can do but keep my mouth shut while I consider them. An extended silence that my partner takes for license to continue his wagon war stories.

"Another time, we had this guy, ninety-four when he died, and a real wacko. He collected silver dollars, see, but he didn't keep 'em like anyone else would. He glued 'em to the pages of magazines, then painted each page blue. Maybe he thought nobody'd notice them that way—who knows? Anyway, when we got there, here's piles and piles of magazines all stuck together with blue paint."

"Don't tell me he—"

"Hell, yes, he did." Smiling sheepishly, Mack ducks his head. "*We* did, my partner and I. Nearly broke our backs carrying those magazines out to the wagon, but it was worth it. We split it, of course, even-Steven. Got around eight thousand dollars apiece." He pauses, eyeing me, before his next question.

"You know how long it took to get that blue paint off so much money?"

"No idea."

"It wasn't easy. I looked like a damn Smurf for a week."

It would be unfair to assume that everyone who works the wagon is an opportunist. Some wagon people just like the fact that the people they serve don't fight back. For them, the glamour of playing supercop simply doesn't stack up to the prospect of working the wagon assignment which usually guarantees regular hours with no overtime, and (most of the time) getting to go home with the same body parts you started with. Which is not always the case for the victims we transport.

One afternoon, I'm working with Yolanda, who's worked the wagon for ten years and is, by her own description, happy to stay away from the bullshit on the streets. She's perfectly content to "bag 'em, tag 'em, and drag 'em," and tolerate the catcalls and whistles of surprised prisoners who discover they're being chauffeured to Central Detention by a female cop, an attractive female cop who prefers French perfume to smelly cigars and who doesn't bat an eye when they call her a wagon ho?

The dispatcher directs us to the intersection of 39th and Racine. We're to pick up a "package" from the traffic car.

The package turns out to be someone's head,

rudely removed from its body in a six-car pileup. The paramedics removed all the victims, the traffic cop tells us, except for this head. Nobody could find it, and it didn't make sense to tie up traffic looking for the damn thing. He figured it'd turn up sooner or later.

He figured right. A lady called it in, screaming and wailing over the 911 line. Her cocker spaniel sniffed it out in the alley, was slurping away at it before the poor woman realized what it was. And is now convinced that an ax murderer is stalking the streets of her neighborhood.

I carry the head, now wrapped in newspaper, back to the truck. No sense in putting it in the back, Yolanda points out. It would just roll around like a bowling ball.

Holding someone's head (without benefit of the body attached) is a truly unique experience. Ghastly when you think there's a part of a person in your lap, the part that was thinking and talking and laughing not very long ago. A spiral of queasiness begins to unwind in my gut. It's sickening to think about, but there's also an awful curiosity that shocks me. I'm not ghoul enough to unwrap the paper, but the reality of holding someone's head is horrible and preposterous at the same time.

Yolanda is watching me.

"I know that look," she says. "You're not going to throw up, are you?"

"I'm okay."

"Sure?"

"So far."

She's still staring at me. "Let me guess. This is your first time for something like this?"

"You mean stuff like this happens *often*?"

"Depends on what's happening out here." Shrugging, Yolanda throws the truck into gear, and we head out. "You never know. Accidents are always bad, or explosions. Had one once at a chemical plant that was a bona fide mess! Even guys who worked the wagon twenty years had a hard time handling that one." *Please, God, let her spare me the details.*

We drive in silence. I know that she's watching me, little sneak peeks to ensure that her rookie partner doesn't lose her lunch out the wagon window. And decides, like Mack and all the other wagon vets, to offer the wisdom she's picked up along the way.

"You gotta have a sense of humor, girl. Otherwise you ain't gonna make it on this job." She nods toward the grisly parcel. "I know there ain't nothing funny about that, but whoever this person was can't feel it now. And you gotta get through your day, so you better lighten up. Else you're gonna go crazy or quit . . . whichever happens first."

Pulling up to a traffic light, Yolanda chuckles.

"This happened to me once, about two or three weeks after I first started working the wagon. Same situation—a pickup from a traffic accident, only nobody had the courtesy to wrap it for me. And my partner at that time—Harris was his name—decides it's immoral to transport a head that isn't covered. So we end up going through the drive-through of the chicken takeout joint, asking them for a spare bucket. And Harris lifts up the head to show them what size bucket we need, and the poor little girl at the takeout window fainted—just passed out cold!"

"So what did you do?"

"Do? What could we do?" Yolanda smiles wryly. "He went inside—without the head—and got the bucket. And we drove on to the morgue. And finished

our job. That's the bottom line, honey—that's all
we're supposed to do. Just make sure we finish our
job."

It's a bitter winter night, too cold for the snow that's
beginning to fall. We're sent on an "injured person"
call, with possible transport to the hospital.

"Aren't the paramedics ridin' on this one?" my
partner asks the dispatcher. I'm working with Tony,
a wagon vet seasoned enough to weed out the un-
necessary jobs.

"Not this time. The information we're getting is
there's a possible weapons charge on this one. Let us
know what you got when you get there, ten-four?"

"What we *got* is a friggin' heart attack!" Tony
pants as we climb the four narrow staircases of the
victim's building. "How come this shit never happens on the first floor?"

The injured man is lying across his sofa, moaning.
He's enormous, a quivering mound of flesh, and he's
buck-naked. Tiers of flab cascade in quivering,
sweaty rolls down to his massive thighs, which are
so meaty he can't close them. His hands are buried
there, under one of the subbellies. Protection, or a
display of modesty?

"My balls!" He roars. "I done got shot in my
balls! I swear 'fore God I'm goin' to die!"

With game face intact, Tony steps forward.

"We're not gonna let you die, man. Let's see what
happened. . . ."

The man's scrotum is the size of a grapefruit, swollen and purple, smeared with blood. On the coffee
table is a .22 revolver with one spent casing, one
round chambered. He's been shot "through and

through": a small entry wound, a jagged exit hole. A silent woman stands calmly in the corner of the room, oddly detached from the scene. Progressing to a howl, the man reaches and claws, shredding a cushion in his agony.

"Relax, man, c'mon. Tell us what happened. Whose gun is this?"

"My brother's—oh, *Jeezus!* This hurts like a motherfucker! . . . he's a . . . a security guard."

"With a .22? Yeah, sure. Is it registered?"

"Don't know. Ain't my—uuuugghhh!—ain't my gun."

"So what happened?"

"I—uh . . . ah . . . oh, man, y'all better get me to the hospital 'fore I die!"

The woman steps forward. "He was cleanin' the gun," she says. "And it went off, just like that. Shot hisself. Nearly shot his dick off, too." And shifts her face away, but not before we catch the satisfied smirk.

"Went off just like that, huh? Amazing!" Tony looks at the moaning man. "That the way it happened, Chief?"

"Uhnnnn . . . uh, yeah. What she said."

"Is *that* right? Well, tell me this. How often do you clean a gun in the nude? A gun that ain't even yours?"

The man is swelling at an alarming rate. By now his scrotum is approaching the size of a cabbage.

"Look Office . . . get me to a doctor. . . . *Ahhhhh!*"

"And an entry wound like that, you must've have been holdin' that gun with your toes." Tony glances back at the woman, who can barely suppress a smile.

"You his wife?"

"Naw. But he my man. Least, that's what he call hisself. But—"

"Yeah, yeah. A love thing. I know." And to the man, "I guess you don't wanna sign complaints, right?"

"Just get me to the hospital, Office. I'm 'bout to fall out from the pain."

Nodding, Tony steps back.

"Okay, man. Get yourself a robe or something, and let's go."

"*Go?* What you mean? Ain't you got to bring the stretcher or some-thin'?" Tony barely spares me a glance. He knows that there's no way the two of us will be able to negotiate all those stairs carrying the weight of this man. And his experience prevents him from trying. Other cops in similar situations have tried, and failed with disastrous results. And there is no way you can justify dropping an injured person down several flights of stairs.

Tony musters up his best game face.

"Man, you never had a gunshot wound before? You get shot someplace like the nuts, that bullet can lodge in there, cause so much swelling your dick'll fall out. You want to keep moving, keep the circulation going in your pecker. Know what I'm saying?"

"For real? I could lose my dick?" Aghast, the man cradles his swollen sac.

"I seen it happen. Be a shame, too, a man like you in your prime—"

"*Fuck that!*" the man bellows. Straining forward, he heaves himself up. "Tasha! Go on and get me a blanket to wrap up in! I got to get outta here!"

Swathed in a comforter that almost covers his tremendous girth, the man limps down the stairs before Tony can say another word. After he's settled in the truck, we head for the ER.

"Interesting," I remark. "'Swelling up and falling off.' Seen that much in your years of practice, Doc?"

"Did you feel up to carting him down all those stairs?"

Whatever works.

There are things no one should ever have to witness. Things so truly awful it makes you question the existence of a merciful God. Like the mother who opens up a closet door to find her fifteen-year-old son, naked and hanging strangled from the clothes pole. A homicide, we assume, and notify the Violent Crimes detectives.

When the crime lab people arrive, they shake their heads. Not a homicide, they tell us. Not even a suicide, or at least, an intentional one. What we're looking at is another victim of autoerotic asphyxiation. A fetishist's peculiar sexual practice in which the person chokes himself while masturbating. The strangling sensation is supposed to add to the excitement. Ideally, orgasm is reached just before passing out. In some tragic cases, the victim gets carried away, literally.

The victim's mother is hysterical, fighting us, her husband, anyone who tries to drag her away from the purplish, dangling body. Who tries to protect her from the final horror of strangers in uniform measuring, marking, snapping photographs of her dead child, trussed up with his father's toolshed extension cord.

The call is to "assist the inhalator" for a removal. That means someone's dead, but the fire department ambulance has been summoned instead of the squadrol. But the police still have to be on the scene to make sure that nobody gives the ambulance people a hard time.

The address is on the East Side, an area overrun with drug dealers, junkies, crackheads, an assortment of the chemical undead who hang out on the corners, in the alleys. Waiting for death, or the next high.

The stench of urine and rancid grease hits us as soon as we walk in the building's vestibule, a place obviously used for more than checking the mailboxes. Used syringes, pools of vomit, broken muscatel bottles—the winos' beverage of choice—litter the filthy floor. Skittering roaches join hollow-eyed junkies in the shadowed corners where vermin of every description leave their fetid droppings.

The smell of death is everywhere. It's a smell that defies description, like rotted meat, festering wounds, the most noxious combination of hell's worst gases all mixed together. We start up the crumbling stairs, stepping carefully around the piles of excrement.

The apartment is empty, except for a stained, bare mattress stinking in the corner. A motionless woman sits hunched against the cinder-block wall. Parchment-dry lips stretch in a final grimace over gray gums. Her eyes are open, glazed with the dull sheen of death. It's hard to tell how old she is. Nineteen? Thirty? Her body is wasted, shriveled in the filthy clothes that hang in tatters like the last flag of a defeated nation. Track marks snake along her skinny arms, thick and twisted as sin. A length of rope ties off her forearm, from which a used spike still protrudes.

" 'Bout time y'all got here." The belligerent voice comes from the doorway. An obese woman in straining orange sweatpants struggles to plant pudgy hands where, in another lifetime, her waist used to be.

"I'm the one called. The baby in here." She waddles past us and into the bathroom. My partner reaches for his pack of Winstons, extracts four cigarettes, and passes me two. We break off the filters, put one in each of our nostrils, a field version of a gas mask. Anything that will dilute the smell of death.

It's a baby—or what used to be—in the tub. The tiny body is rotted, half-eaten by the resident rats, so it's impossible to determine its gender. Where the face was is now a crusted hole. I clamp my jaws, thinking of my babies at home, wanting to scream. Thinking of this baby, and what kind of life it had. What kind of death.

My partner uses his nightstick to bang on the tub, which sends the rats scampering. By the time the inhalator arrives, we've already pulled on our disposable rubber gloves (standard equipment for street cops, carried inside your hat, right along with your prayer to St. Jude) and begin the gruesome task of putting the tiny corpse in a plastic biohazard bag.

"How long's the baby been here?"

The fat woman shrugs.

"I don' know. Never saw the mama too much. She usually be getting high, and it ain't like we socialize. Know what I'm sayin'?"

"When's the last time you saw the woman alive?"

The woman rolls her eyes.

"I tol' you, I don' know. Ain't nobody seen either one of 'em too often. A while ago, the welfare woman come around, lookin' for the mama. I ain't seen neither one of 'em for so long. Then Eugene come cryin' in the hallway. Say his mama sleepin' and she won't wake up. Then this horrible stank be comin' from the door—"

"Who's Eugene?"

"He her other baby." The woman points to the doorway, where a tiny boy watches us silently. His body is emaciated, his huge eyes solemn. Eyes that watched his family die.

"I been watchin' after him 'til y'all got here. I don' know if he got any kin. He only four. Don' know who his daddy is. But then, neither did his mama." She glances over at the woman's body.

"Sky-Dog, he the one be sellin' rocks and such on the corner, he used to come up in here sometimes." The woman nods vigorously, pleased with her role as informant. "You know how it be. She buy a rock sometimes, but if she don't have the money, he give her a little taste if she give up some pussy. She liked that heroin, too. Look like that's what finally kilt her."

"When's the last time you saw Sky-Dog?"

"Don' know. Maybe a week, two weeks ago. He say he wasn't comin' up in here no more cuz she was a stank ho. Said she smell too nasty to be dealin' with no mo'."

The fat woman gives the paramedics wide berth when they remove the mother's body. And watches skeptically when we approach the tiny boy. In his thin, filthy clothes, he's shivering in the drafty hallway. His breathing is labored, hampered by congestion and crusted mucus around his nose. In the yellow hallway light, we see lesions on his skinny arms, more on the back of his neck. I wrap him in a blanket from the paramedics and lift him, whimpering, into my arms.

"How come y'all never come before?" the woman

demands loudly. "Or don't y'all care about our babies dyin'?"

Doors open in the hallway. Heads poke out to stare at the police.

"They finally come," the woman yells to her neighbors. "Now it's too late, they come. Y'all muthafuckas get paid for nothin' and we up in here dyin'!"

She plants herself at the top of the stairs, shouting down at us. Other voices join in, softly at first, then louder.

"Why y'all ain't come sooner? Lock up the dealers, them muthafuckas that be poisonin' us! Do y'all jobs for a change!"

Voices boom off the walls as people gather in the hall.

"I'm talkin' to y'all, goddammit! Why ain't you come sooner? That baby might be 'live now, if you did. You the *po*-lice. You s'posed to be doin' somethin'!" The shouting voices follow us through the hallway, down the narrow stairs, down to the portal of hell.

Sometimes the wagon assignment offers some interesting diversions. Besides the brawling prisoners and sick or deceased transports, there's sometimes a lighter note in the evening's work. Like when we're instructed to transport prisoners from the prostitution unit down to Women's Central Detention located downtown.

Most times, these working girls are resigned to the fact that they have to take an unscheduled work break until their pimps bond them out. Usually that means an overnight stay in "the Penthouse," the women's jail facility on the thirteenth floor of the Police Headquarters building.

Getting arrested can be almost a relief to someone who's been out all night, especially in winter, shivering in the brutal cold, mincing along in cheap stilettos between tricks. The regulars know all the cops in the women's lockup, know they'll have a chance to kick back, munch on a bologna sandwich du jour, rest their aching feet, and visit with the other girls until Mack Daddy goes their bail.

Many of these ladies have been arrested so often they know the wagon people by name. Like a flock of chirping, exotic birds, they're led out of the holding cell in Vice and into the squadrol, laughing and joking with the female cops, flirting with the men.

"Careful of my dress, sugar. I paid thirty bucks for this on Maxwell Street. I can't afford to get me no grease stains!"

"Ooooh, baby! Y'all done grown a mustache since I seen you last! You lookin' fine!"

"Wish you woulda picked me up a little earlier. I had me a crazy man, dick was so big that now I'm a drive-through! Child, I like to died!"

Giggles, banter, the lighthearted mood of a teen slumber party more than jail-bound prisoners. And in that spirit, we sometimes take a detour from the normal routine. These girls are in no hurry to get downtown, and neither are we. A Central Detention run means we get to leave our district, away from the routine drudge work for a while. Why not stretch it out?

Simply meandering along, taking the scenic route won't do it, not for our passengers, at least, since there's no windows in the wagon. Instead, we head to the famous Maxwell Street hot-dog stand, a land-mark, as seen in countless Chicago-based movies. The stand is open every day of the year, round the clock, and the menu never changes. Hot dogs, Polish sausage, burgers, and pork chops (bone in) all lov-ingly fried in the same sputtering grease, all slapped on white-bread rolls and buried in a mound of drip-ping fried onions. A cardiologist's nightmare, but it's hot, it's filling, and for some of our passengers, it's their only meal of the night.

We pick up a huge sack of food and drive over to the lakefront. A little ambience while we clog our arteries and gab with the girls. To these ladies, pork-chop sandwiches are ambrosia. It's been a while since most of them have eaten, and if they did, it was just a "listen sandwich" (a pig's ear on a slice of bread) grabbed at some dingy food shack along Lake Street. Now they can relax, enjoy the gorgeous view, savor their food, and swap shoptalk with their uni-formed chauffeurs. Where else would we hear the most intimate details of the red-light life?

It's not a practice condoned by the department. This would *definitely* fall under the category of "con-duct unbecoming" and, if we got caught, we'd be looking at some suspension time. But a little down-time is imperative for anyone who works the streets, whichever way you work it. In that way, hookers and cops are similar: Sometimes, after giving everyone else what they want, you have to take what you need.

14

Live from Dead-End Street

Dispatcher: 1212? Double 12?
1212: Double.
Dispatcher: You got some working girls on the corner, Madison and Bishop.
1212: Yeah, so?
Dispatcher: Citizen's complaining. Wants you to shag them off. It's the same guy who always calls.
1212: Probably mad cuz he can't find his change purse.

Like the finest sweets, they come in all flavors. All shapes, all colors, something for every budget. When the mood strikes for something unusual, something different, of simply *something,* they're there, ready and willing to satisfy—for a price. They're prostitutes, members of the world's oldest profession, delivering a product that's always in demand: relief, satisfaction, or maybe just a warm body. Called hookers or whores, call girls or hos, they're out there, plying their trade.

They parade along the notorious whores' strolls like West Madison Street, South Stony Island, North Clark Street, East 63rd. On other corners, other streets, anywhere a potential customer might pass, they're out there, ready, waiting, inviting.

Prostitutes can be invaluable information sources for the police. They're always out there; they read the streets. They know who's doing what, and with whom, when and where. For a nominal exchange of favors, like a bag of doughnuts in the early-morning hours when they haven't had a fix and their sugar jones is kicking in, they're usually happy to share what they know.

In my first months on the street, I learn that they also like to talk about themselves, a subject most people don't ask about. On a slow night, they're happy to shoot the breeze with a congenial cop. Trading jokes, stories, insights on the Life. Whether girls or women, men or gender indeterminate, these are people who've seen it all.

Talking to the prostitutes—male and female— helps me personalize the nameless faces that skulk along the avenues, waiting for a fast trick. Teaches me not to generalize or accept the stereotypes associated with streetwalkers. For each person out here, there's a separate story.

Before becoming a cop, I believed, like most people, that prostitutes are basically the same: strung-out junkies selling themselves for dope money, or broken-down whores with no source of income other than their bodies. Just a few months on the street is enough to prove me wrong. There are those types, of course, and more—a variety of men and women from different backgrounds, different worlds. Any cop who's ever worked Vice will attest to the fact that there is no standard profile for a prostitute. Secretaries, medical students, housewives or husbands are some of the streetwalker's "occupations" we run across out on the street. And when we arrest them, some will say they're simply "moonlighting." Others are hooked by the prospect of excitement, and some quick cash. Many will say they never intended to do it on a regular basis—it just turned out that way. Their stories vary, but the reason is always the same: money. Which is a strong enough motivator, both for the prostitutes or the pimps who manage them, to return them to the streets, and the risks, in spite of countless vice arrests, savage beatings by unknown customers, or the diseases that kill as efficiently as bullets.

The hard-core whores—those who've been on the street so long they can't remember any other life— usually have a drug habit. It's the only thing that insulates them from the reality of what they face, and the dangers involved. In the brutal street hierarchy, prostitutes are easy targets for robbery, or rape, even homicide. But while they're out there, nobody thinks about death. Only the next trick, the next high, the next hot meal if finances allow. And the next vicious beating from a pimp who's never satisfied, no matter how good business is.

I learn some of this from Tiffany, who's been in the Life since she was fourteen. She's nineteen now, with three children, a heroin habit, and a razor blade she carries in her shoe. For the customers who get a little crazy, she says. You can't be too careful on the street.

It was the money that first attracted her. Quick money, and a boyfriend with a taste for the finer things, like designer drugs and cars he couldn't afford. Tiffany was young, she was fine—a definite asset. And a commodity on the street, something that an enterprising young man like DeShon recognized immediately.

It wasn't bad at first, she says. She gave DeShon

her money; he bought her food, drugs, and looked out for her. Something her parents never did, wherever they were. She got tired after a while, wanted to quit after the first baby. The customers were nasty, rough sometimes, and she'd been beat up more than once. DeShon told her to keep working. And gave her more drugs, harder drugs, to keep her quiet and numb.

"It's real boring out here," Tiffany says. "Just a parade of dicks, limp, hard, big, small, don't matter. They all the same. Just lookin' for a place to squirt they stuff. And then act all pleased with themselves after, like they gave you the big prize. And all the time I be thinkin' how hungry I am, when can I get a sandwich, how bad the cramp in my leg is from these cheap-ass heels. But the tricks never know what I'm thinkin', cuz all the time I'm moanin' and sayin', 'Oh, baby, yeah! This is good, baby, gimme some more!' Actin' like I never had anything better. That's good business.

"That's all it is, a business. You got to know how to act, how to dress. Keep 'em comin' back. First time I came out, I had on some blue jeans, a sorry little blouse, and gym shoes. Now I know what to wear. Somethin' that goes up and down real quick, no time to be messin' with buttons and zippers. And no underwear. Takes too long to get it on and off. A little makeup, not too much. Not a lot of it, like those hard-ass old hos who smell bad as they look. Mens like that I look young. Sometimes they ask if they the first, and I always say yeah. Good business."

Tiffany is a regular on the Cicero Avenue stroll, a mostly industrial area with factories to the east and west, and Hawthorne racetrack just a mile away. A good spot, she says. She gets the men from the track ready to spend their winnings, the factory workers just getting off.

She's waiting on a corner at 42nd and Cicero when we respond to a call of "a man slumped over the steering wheel." She waves toward a glossy red Camaro parked halfway down the block, and follows us there, as fast as her wobbly stilettos will carry her.

The car's engine is still running, the driver's door open. The man inside is indeed slumped over the wheel, since most of his brains are sprayed over the dash. A close-range gunshot wound has ended the short career of DeShon: small-time pimp, part-time drug dealer, *last-time* drug thief.

"He tried to rip off a big dealer," Tiffany tells us. "Thought they wasn't gonna catch up with him, with his thievin' ass. But they did." Her nineteen-year-old eyes display no regret, no grief. Only the matter-of-fact acknowledgment of basic street justice.

"You see it happen, Tiffany?"

"Naw, but I heard it. The gun, I mean." She nods toward a group of men outside the nearby factory. "They seen it, tho. They can tell you."

She's off and running, back to the corner. A whistle shrieking in the distance means it's lunchtime, when all the factory workers will be hitting the streets. Where Tiffany will be ready and waiting to handle the customers. Good business, she says.

In some ways, the jobs of a prostitute and a cop are surprisingly similar. They both give their bodies for a fee. They're never quite sure, going into a job, if they'll come out intact. The services required of them depend on the needs or whims of their customers.

Most people look at them in a derogatory manner, and their outward appearance often hides the sensitivity and heartbreak within.

We get a call one frigid winter night to disperse the prostitutes gathering on the corner. It's not unusual to shoo the random hooker off the street, especially if citizens are calling to complain, but we almost never see a bunch of prostitutes clustered together. It's not good business, unless they're offering a group rate.

There's a tight knot of working girls and he-she's huddled on the corner when we pull up. Some of them are kneeling. All of them are straining to see whatever's in the middle of their circle. Someone's been shot, or stabbed, we think, and push through the group.

There, sitting on the icy sidewalk is Jovette, a 6'4" Donna Summer look-alike, complete with disco wig and sparkly eye shadow. In his lap are a bunch of squirming puppies only hours old, judging by their appearance. He's cradling them against his chest, letting them suck the tips of his fingers. Tarika, one of the other regulars, crouches beside him, holding a paper cup of milk.

"Hey, Office!" Jovette says, offering a dazzling, if toothless smile. "Ain't they precious? We heard 'em cryin' underneath that car over there. They mama dead. Look like the poor thing froze herself tryin' to take care of her babies."

It's obvious that business has been concluded—or at least suspended—while these streetwalkers tend to their newly adopted brood. In spite of the whipping wind, the relentless cold, they're not going anywhere until the safety of these new lives is ensured. My partner and I exchange a look. This is one of those decisions that doesn't require a single word of discussion. We call for a squadrol to transport Jovette, Tarika, and all the proud aunts and uncles to the animal shelter, where the newborns are given their birthday exam.

The outcome of the puppies? After worming, shots, and a lot of nurturing by many willing volunteers, they're all adopted by loving families. I can personally report that one of the males, Madison (named after the street where he was born), has a passion for cheeseburgers and prefers sleeping at the foot of my older son's bed. And we've noticed that his sister, Tricks, seems to have absorbed some of the characteristics of her aunt/uncle Jovette. In the presence of anyone male, she becomes an outrageous flirt, batting her eyes and twitching her little canine rump.

On another night, we spot a sleek new Mercedes sedan, parked in an alley behind a factory. The driver's door is open and the engine is running. We kill our headlights and cruise up behind it. It can't be a working girl, we figure, since most johns would be careful to close the car door. Who wants the interior lights on, advertising just how they spend their money?

When we run the license plate, it comes back registered to a Celeste Mitchard, with an exclusive Gold Coast penthouse address. And it's Celeste we find in the car, providing some very innovative personal service for her postal-employee trick. With surprising composure, given the circumstances, the woman steps out of the vehicle and gestures toward her purse.

Without a hint of embarrassment, Celeste offers

us an embossed card from a distinguished firm in the financial district. She's an executive in investments, she tells us airily. A good job, with decent benefits. It pays the rent. It pays more than that, if the car and jewelry are any indication.

The glittering stones at her ears and throat are real, as is the elegant platinum bracelet that could pay my salary for a year. Tossed across the front seat's buttery leather upholstery is a sumptuous fur coat that would launch animal-rights activists into cardiac arrest. Celeste doesn't seem the least bit concerned that the postal worker left a special delivery now oozing down the coat's left sleeve.

Life on the Gold Coast isn't all it's cracked up to be, Celeste informs us. A boring life, a boring, predictable job. Even high-stakes finance don't provide the excitement she needs. Which is why she seeks a cash flow elsewhere, on her own time, for a different kind of thrill. Sometimes it's more fun to walk on the wild side.

My partner, a twenty-something single woman, looks dubiously at the rumpled man, the garbage-strewn alley. And then back to the immaculate Mercedes.

"Don't knock it 'til you've tried it," Celeste says defensively. "I've met some very exciting people this way. Some *real* men!"

"If you say so."

Which is just enough to put Miss Gold Coast's nose out of joint.

"Look, Officer, there's no need for harassment. If you're going to arrest me, get on with it. I'm perfectly capable of paying my own bail." And while my partner handcuffs Celeste, she glares at me, at both of us, and huffs, "Figured the two of you would understand, being women and all. But I guess you can't be very womanly working *this* job. Or maybe you like acting like men. Should have known!"

We place her in the back of the squad, for her ride downtown to Women's Central Detention, where Celeste will be booked on misdemeanor prostitution charges. As we drive off, she continues her tirade of sneering remarks.

"Is this how you get your kicks? Harassing a *real* woman? Or maybe you two don't know how to take care of a man." And finally, "So what's the bail going to be? And do you take American Express Platinum?"

One night we go in to the station with a simple disorderly conduct arrest. The area around the front desk is crowded with cops from the previous watch, people who would normally be halfway home by now, or a least two beers along at their favorite gin-mill. Everyone's muttering, but it's not the usual jokes and insults you exchange after putting in your eight on the street. There's a tension that's almost palpable, a static charge that travels from desk crew to the waiting crowd.

When the watch commander's door swings open, I see why. There are suits, lots of them, and everyone's got the same grim expression that means one thing: These are the big boys from downtown, and some unfortunate soul has stepped in some serious shit.

I'm told that it's not just Internal Affairs in our presence, but people from the Office of Professional Standards as well. And when they walk out into the hall, ushering two handcuffed cops between them, I know it's not the standard "conduct unbecoming . . ." beef.

Once the big boys have adjourned to an interrogation room in the back of the building, we get the whole story from our desk sergeant. The two cops now in custody had been partnered together on the afternoon watch. While on routine patrol, they passed some hookers out on the whores' stroll and decided, Why not? Only the concept of "paying customer" never entered the picture. There are some girls (and guys) who, in the interest of future favors, are glad to provide the police with freebies, but the girl they selected wasn't one of them.

They grabbed her, tried to force her into the back of the squad car, and, when she resisted, slapped her enough to take the fight out of her and then told her she was under arrest. After that, she was driven to a secluded location where she was forced on her knees, confronted with two unzipped pairs of regulation police department trousers, and ordered to service the two cops. With the barrel of a service revolver glinting near her head, she didn't have much choice.

She did the first one, and by the time the second stepped up, she had a plan. She was going to give him the best blowjob of his life—and the worst fucking of his career. While his pants were around his ankles, she scribbled in his underwear with her lipstick. Gasping, grunting, moaning for more, he never knew. Afterward, satiated, he yanked up his slacks, slapped her around some more and told her to take off. Promised to lock her up if they ever saw her again.

The woman went immediately to the police station, demanding to see the watch commander. She showed him her swollen eye, her bleeding mouth, and extended a handkerchief holding department-issue ejaculate. She supplied her attackers' names, their beat number, even the license plate of the squad. And then she told him about the lipstick.

When the two men were called in, they denied everything.

"She's a common whore," they said. "Just some junkie bitch trying to start trouble. You know how is it, Captain."

The captain *did* know.

"So you never saw this woman before?"

"Never. We were out there on our beat writing parking tickets. You can check our ticket books if you want." It sounded plausible, written proof that they'd been actually working. A good way to cover their asses.

"You want me to check your ticket books?"

"Sure, Cap. Here's mine and—"

"I'd rather check your drawers instead. Both of you drop your pants." The lipstick was there, in full dime-store Ravishing Red glory, in the shorts and now smeared on the guilty party's shriveled weapon as well. Proof that they'd just taken part in a felony, an "aggravated criminal sexual assault" at gunpoint.

The two men were flabbergasted. Couldn't believe that some simple street ho had tricked them, and were shocked speechless. Which was okay, because, as two sets of handcuffs were snapped on, the boys from Internal Affairs were saying, "You have the right to remain silent. . . ."

What was once apprehension has become acceptance. Running up ten flights of project stairs *alone* doesn't faze me anymore, or stepping between two combatants in a raging domestic. It's just part of the job, just something I do. What all cops do. These streets I work are strictly inner-city ghetto, tough streets where tough and angry and sometimes hopeless people reside. None of them expect a break, or much of anything beyond the struggle of day-to-day existence. Police are not welcomed in these quarters. Here, cops aren't viewed as friends or heroes or "Officer Friendly." We're met with attitudes that range from low-grade hostility to raging contempt, and understand that a fight or two in the course of our workday is as expected as the sun rising each day. Just something that happens. Part of the job.

I can't remember when the changes started. When the knots of fear that came each time I walked into the projects relaxed, or when I became so casual about the frequent rides to the closest hospital ER for yet another quick patch-up after yet another injury on duty. What's a little blood, a few stitches when you're a cop? Nobody else whines about it. It's just something that happens. Just like it happens that one day, you notice the difference in the way you walk, the way you talk to people. The confident swagger that cops have, the authoritative word. And you realize, with just a little bewilderment, that you're one of *them* now, these cops who command respect, symbolize authority, instill fear.

These months and years have taught me the rhythm of the streets, and how to "walk the walk." Instead of questioning *why* things happen, I'm more concerned with *how*. Out here, observations serve better than analysis. Cops are spin doctors of the first

15

Changes

1233:	Squad, hold me down at 13— Halsted. Got an on-view disturbance on the street. I'll let you know what I got in a minute, ten-four?!
Dispatcher:	'33, you're a one-man unit. Let me get you a backup unit over there.
1233:	Negative, Squad. It's just a couple citizens duking it out. I can handle it.

The weeks and months on the street, as a street *cop*, have flown by so fast I can barely keep track of the time. A year gone by already, and then two. I know I'm changing—it's impossible *not* to change out here, and most of the time, I don't even think about it. Sometimes though, I can step outside reality and glimpse what I've become, and where I'm heading.

Streets and neighborhoods that once filled me with apprehension in my civilian life are my regular beat now. I don't see things the same way. Driving past squalid row houses marked by graffiti and urban blight, I see only what cops see: a suspicious man loitering, a group of teens too young to be driving the brand-new Cadillac with the punched-out trunk lock. Or maybe the young boy casually sizing up the passing traffic at an intersection for his next smash-and-grab robbery.

order. Crime prevention is as important as criminal apprehension, which takes sharp eyes and sharper instincts. It takes a long time to realize that I have both, that I'm doing a job I never thought I could, or would, and doing it well. And *enjoying* it besides. And even though the streets I work are sordid and crime-ridden, with none of the glamour or affluence of other areas of the city, this is my home now. My beat, my turf—a dark world with an energy as strong as my pulse. And every night I'm out there, feeling that energy, I can mesh with it, read it . . . and make a difference.

My transition to the "us versus them" mentality is gradual—in increments so small I barely notice them. I share a war story with a civilian friend, a domestic disturbance that ended with three people arrested after a fearsome fight, and me in the ER, getting stitched up again. The friend is aghast. How can you do that, I'm asked. Go to work every night and face that kind of garbage? All you see is misery, and it's not safe. What kind of rewarding work is that?

How can I explain? How can anyone know what it feels like to pull up to a fight scene—and see the relief flood a victim's face? Know that this person is relying on you to save them, to *rescue* them. To be the cavalry in a world of raging savages. Or how it feels to deliver a baby in the back of your squad car because you couldn't make it to the hospital. Feel that new life in your hands and see joy replace the terror in the young mother's eyes as she reaches for her child.

Or cradle the head of a gunshot victim as you try in vain to stanch the blood flow, knowing you're the last person he'll see and feel, that you're the only one who will witness his passage from this life. Or how your job brings you to families in crisis, lives in chaos, and your presence brings the only order they've known. Their only hope that, maybe, things can be made right again.

It sounds too idealistic to explain, too sappy to say out loud. So I say nothing. Just retreat into my "cop identity"—the one that's beginning to separate me from anyone who isn't. There's no way to feel what I do, not unless you've been there. And I think of my father, his silences and stoic behavior, and I begin to understand.

This job brings other changes, to people who never strapped on a gun belt or pinned on a badge. I notice them first in my children. Although they're still very young, they understand why their mom wears a .357 Magnum on her hip and a snub-nosed revolver in an ankle holster. And why they shouldn't cry when they see me come home bruised and bloody from another injury. The important thing, I tell them, is that I made it home. Harsh lessons for small children, but it's the rules of a cop's life, for cop's kids. Both boys seem to accept it, develop their own stoicism to handle it all.

They learn earlier than other kids about Stranger Danger, about the evils that lurk beyond the safety of their home. In our house, lessons in street smarts and basic survival skills are ongoing. I know what's out there; I want my kids to be aware, and ready. And protected, when I can't be there, by their own instincts and ability. Which means there's a tradeoff—childhood innocence for wary vigilance. Naïveté for cold reality. It's a tough choice, but one I can't avoid, one I *won't* avoid, not when I see another beaten or murdered kid on the street, and visualize my own sons' faces. I want my children alert. I want them alive. I want to save them, like all those other kids that no one could save.

So the lessons continue, and my sons become cops' kids. And pick up, along the way, other things I never meant to pass along. By observing my behavior, they add it to their own. How you don't make a big deal out of a little blood or injury. How you accept the good with the bad—it's the way of the world, so you'd *better* get used to it. How you never show fear, even though it's natural to feel it. Fear can paralyze, get in the way of action. So you hide it, along with any other emotion that hints at vulnerability. It's all about protecting your physical safety, your emotions. Better to have a game face. The stoic one that no one can see behind, that no hurt can penetrate.

I don't realize the impact of these tacit lessons until the first parent-teacher conference at my older son's school. The drawings of his first-grade classmates decorate the walls of his room, along with neat examples of homework and art projects. The teacher inquires whether I've seen my son's drawing, and points it out with grave concern. The kids had been instructed to draw a picture of their house and family. My son's drawing depicted our house, with both boys inside, standing at the window. I was drawn outside the house, dressed in bright blue and vivid red.

"I asked him to explain the picture," the teacher told me quietly. "He said that was his mom. I asked him why she wasn't with him and his brother inside the house. He said because she was bleeding, and this was the day she wouldn't make it home."

What words can describe what I felt then? Pain, first, that I brought this fear and turmoil to my kids.

Guilt that I invaded their children's hearts with the grim realities of my harsh world. Confusion because somehow, in trying to protect them, I've become my father; while my son becomes the child I was, watching and waiting for the next time, the next horror. The tears that come are hot and bitter, more so because I know I can't change, not as long as I'm a cop. It's part of the job, it's what comes with the turf. Another of the sacrifices that alter our lives.

There are other sacrifices along the way. I spend my first year on the job assuring my civilian friends I won't change—that it's just a job that I leave behind when my tour of duty is finished. By the second year, I realize I see them less frequently, and tell myself it's my demanding schedule. There's shift rotations, court appearances, depositions, and grand-jury testimonies that cut into my personal time. Rotating days off that mean I'm working when everyone else is free, or catching up on sleep when I finally get time off. Holidays? Sorry, I'm working. Party invitations are returned with regrets—manpower shortages mean no day-off requests are granted. That's how the job is. Cops understand it. Why don't civilians?

That's when I understand how surely I am changing. My friends are now "civilians," now part of the uninitiated, the group labeled *THEM* who resides on the other side of the thin blue line reserved for *US*. I find myself editing my conversations with them, deleting all but the most innocuous part of my job experience because they won't understand. Or can't accept. Or are horrified at the things I see, or what I'm becoming. Which is probably why, eventually, I start to avoid them, withdraw from their circle. They've seen what I'm becoming. Maybe I don't want to. Maybe, at this point, I still can't.

The social fallout spills over into other parts of my life. I discover just how difficult it is to maintain a relationship with a man who isn't a cop. Or, more precisely, for him to have one with a woman who is. In a culture that equates uniforms with power, it's a little unnerving to be with a woman who carries a weapon, and has the power of arrest—who *has* arrested leagues of felons violent enough to scare the pants off the average person. To a middle-management executive working a desk job all day, this is more than a little intimidating. At one point, the man in my life observes that it's ironic to watch me cry at a mushy movie, knowing that, at work the next night, I might be stepping around bloody corpses without batting an eye.

And that it's interesting that I depend on him to open stubborn jars, but think nothing of wrestling a burglar to the ground. And that while other women are slipping into filmy camisoles, I'm strapping on a Kevlar safety vest. He's right of course. There's nothing I can say to refute any of it, no words that will salve his wounded pride. He's supposed to be the man, the protector. How do you protect a woman with a 9mm tucked into the waistband of her jeans? I have no answers, and neither does he. I'm hurt that he believes my femininity's been compromised; he's upset and intimidated. Both of us separately nurse the same thought; "If you loved me, you'd *understand.*" Eventually, the only thing either of us understands is that this won't work. I'm a cop, he isn't. That's the reality, and the end of the relationship.

Other relations will follow, all of which will be revelations. I'm a woman until he discovers I'm a cop. After that, I can't be anything else. To some, it's a novelty at first—("My girlfriend carries a gun! She can lock you up!") . . . but eventually that gets old. Over time, I learn to recognize the pattern. Acceptance at first, or what he claims is acceptance. Dismay ("You did *what* at work last night?") followed by equal measures of judgment ("You cops are all alike!") and censure ("Why can't you just do a *woman's* job? Like a nurse, maybe—or a secretary?") And the final parting, justified by the observation that he's a man, but I'm a cop. It isn't a job for a woman. You can be a woman or a cop—but not both.

I don't remember them teaching us that back at the Academy. I believe I'd recall if they did. What I *do* know is the number of times I've seen "the Look" in a man's eyes when he discovers I'm one of *them*. Or maybe it's just the reflection from my own look when I realize, sadly, that he's not one of *us*. And then count another casualty of this job; another sacrifice I never anticipated.

Part Two

Being

16

Partners

1220:   Squad, get us a wagon and an ambulance over here, 17— West Cullerton. We got an injured officer, and one prisoner for transport.

Dispatcher: Ten-four, Sarge. You're over on '25's job?

1220:   Yeah, and you can give a slowdown to all the other units coming in. These girls had this wrapped up before the rest of us got here.

A police partnership is like a marriage. In the best of them, you're teamed with someone you like, someone you can tolerate for a few hours at a time, who'll be your friend, your confidant, who understands your weaknesses and is willing to pick up the slack. You work well together, you respect each other, and you can count on that person to be a friendly voice in a cold world. Worst-case scenario is someone who makes your skin crawl simply by breathing, who makes eight hours together seem like a year. A person you can't depend on, don't trust, and toward whom you nurse a low-grade resentment that, at any time, might escalate into full-scale warfare.

In a bad marriage, you might end up in divorce court. In a bad partnership, you could very well end up dead. With cops, it usually takes a while before you find the right partner. Sometimes, you never find the "perfect" one; there are too many variables to ensure that everyone gets their dream match. The most you can hope for is someone who'll watch your back and not be too obnoxious the rest of the time.

At the beginning of a cop's career, rookies are routinely assigned to a variety of partners for a reason. Different cops have different styles, and all of them can contribute invaluable experience that's part of the rookie's ongoing education. From some partners, you learn the fine art of diplomacy, or patience, or skill in conducting victim and arrestee interviews. Some cops are masters of street stops, others can spot a drug deal going down from a mile away. Aggressive cops don't wait for trouble to come—they go out looking for it. Others would prefer to pass their tour of duty in or near a tavern.

As a rookie learns, he develops his own style, discovers his strengths and areas of interest. After a year, he may be ready to find a partner whose work style matches his own. For a female cop, finding the right partner can be more difficult. Some guys mistakenly assume that having a female partner means they won't have to work as hard. Women aren't into the "kick ass and take names" routine, they figure. They're too worried about breaking a nail. So it's always a shock when they witness some bad guy's takedown by a cute little thing who barely looks strong enough to tote around a nightstick.

For some guys, having a female partner means a built-in secretary/maid. She's the one who writes the reports, gets the coffee, and sits in the squad monitoring the radio for job assignments while he stops at his girlfriend's house for a quick jump.

There are some female cops who'd rather not work with women, for any number of reasons. Some of them prefer the "protection" of a male partner, even though it's been proven ad nauseam that, on the street, women are as capable as men. Some feel other women are competition. And some women just like feeling like one of the guys, hanging out with them, acting like them, outdoing them.

When it came to partners, I'd worked with enough different people to figure out what would suit me best. My needs were simple. Someone who wasn't allergic to work, whom I could count on and, preferably, no cigar smokers—the *worst* in the close quarters of a squad car. Everything else was negotiable. Gender was not important.

We became partners by accident. Diane was new to the district, coming in on a last-minute transfer order after everyone on the watch had been partnered for the night. I'd been scheduled to work a one-man unit that night. Diane was added to make it a deuce.

Nobody was quite prepared for her when she breezed into the squad room for roll call. Tall and thin, with precisely sculpted features and the natural flaxen hair of her Swedish ancestors, she looked more like a folk singer than a law enforcer. Dresden blue eyes completed the look. Immediately, every guy on the watch fell in lust. The women hated her on sight. Great, I thought. Joni Mitchell does John Wayne. But once in the squad car, we hit it off immediately.

I found out she'd put in six years in the toughest district on the South Side. She knew how to handle herself, how to defuse an incendiary situation. She'd seen enough upper-echelon bullshit to have a realistic view of department politics, and she wasn't particularly thrilled with the police department as a whole. But that didn't stop her from doing her job, and doing it well. She had heart, guts, and a highly developed sense of the absurd, which meant she didn't take much seriously, least of all, herself. The belly laughs that issued from those sculpted lips kept us rolling on that first night, and for years thereafter.

On that first night, we got a call for a domestic disturbance. Pulling up to the given address, we heard a scream, followed by shots fired. Instinct and teamwork kicked in as though we'd been together for years. She crept down the gangway to cover the back of the house. I went through the front.

In the rear of the house was a door leading to a yard, and a ramshackle garage. Diane eyed the door, knew that's where the shooter would make his exit. But except for the garage, the yard had no cover, nothing that would shield her if he came out shooting.

The shooter *did* run out the back door, but instead of making his escape, he turned around, gun cocked and ready to shoot me as I followed him. Crouched on the garage roof, Diane made her move. Screaming like a banshee, she leaped off the roof, airborne for a few impressive seconds before she landed on the gunman. Or, *most* of her landed on him. Some of her—specifically, her left knee—landed with a sickening crunch on the concrete walk that bordered the yard.

Later, at the hospital, she was exuberant. She couldn't stop laughing, either from the painkillers or adrenaline, or the heady combination.

"Wasn't that cool?" she asked. "Just like Batwoman! Guy never knew what hit him! Did I tell you I'm afraid of heights?"

"You're afraid of—so what the hell possessed you to climb up the garage?"

"I knew he was going to shoot one of us. Over my dead body! So I figured, why not the garage? Do a little kamikaze number. And it worked. Wasn't that cool?"

"Diane, you split your kneecap."

"Yeah, but we're not dead. I would've loved to see that guy's face when I landed on him! Whoomp! So cool! Didn't you think that was cool?"

One week later, after the shooter is released on bail and has consulted an attorney, he files a lawsuit against the department for police brutality, personal injury, and "excessive emotional trauma." Diane and I are brought up on disciplinary charges of "official misconduct" and ordered to appear before the Complaint Review Board.

"Don't worry," she tells me. "We're cool."

She's right. As long as we're partners, everything is cool.

Later, when all charges are dismissed as "unfounded"—department-speak for "more petty crap that's a waste of time"—I realize just how cool we are. We like each other, we watch out for each other, and we get the job done. Qualities some cops never experience in the whole of their careers.

Working together, we learn each other's strong points. Experience teaches us who will step forward, who provides the balance. Almost intuitively, we know how the other will respond, what's necessary to make what we do together work.

One night we pull over a late-model cream-colored Cadillac that's cruising down a side street near the jets. It's got all the signs of a hot car: broken passenger window, four young occupants, and a neighborhood that doesn't match the vehicle.

With weapons drawn, we get the occupants out, line them up for a pat-down. They're teenagers, not much past sixteen. None of them have weapons, and, except for a small amount of marijuana, the search is fruitless. But the boys are nonchalant, joking and taunting, cockier than they should be considering that a gun is trained on them.

When Diane approaches the car to search it, they exchange a leering grin. This is more than game faces, I think. There's something else. . . .

"Diane! Get down!" I scream, just a heartbeat before the fifth passenger appears in the car window, the one who was crouched down in the backseat, cradling his gun. It's a machine *pistol,* a handy little technological advancement more portable than a machine gun, and just as deadly. Its rapid-repeater blast, which takes out the back window, is a burst of blue flame and spraying glass.

Facedown on the street, Diane is showered with shards of window, but otherwise unhurt. The four boys are not so lucky. Their hidden triggerman, it seems, has the heart of a lion but the aim of Mr. Magoo. And can't seem to differentiate his homeboys from these five-O bitches. Before I can get off the shot that quells his shooting frenzy, his misdirected gunfire kills the first boy, injures two more. The fourth boy decides that *no* ride—not even a Cadillac—is worth taking a bullet for, and makes his escape, streaking for the safety of the jets.

Later, while the bodies are loaded into ambulances, Diane is back to being Diane.

"Wish you'd told me *before* I ate gravel," she says. "I just got these pants out of the cleaners."

"Maybe the guy whose car was stolen will make it up to you. Dinner and a ride on his fine Corinthian leather."

"Wrong car, goof."

"Whatever. Maybe he'll offer a small token of his

appreciation. Nothing gaudy. A simple ten carats should do it."

"Right. And maybe I'll win the lottery, too."

Our sergeant, recently arrived to inspect the crime scene, points to a staring corpse.

"Looks like you had plenty of luck for one night. You're not the one that'll be wearing the toe tag."

Another time, we answer a burglary call in the jets. The victim, an elderly woman in a wheelchair, watched helplessly as three young boys kicked in her door, trashed her apartment, and stole everything they could fence: her television, her radio, and her wedding ring. They also took all the money she had: thirteen dollars left over from her Social Security check. And, on the way out the door, one of the boys took the carton of eggs from her tiny refrigerator and smashed them all over the kitchen.

"I couldn't stop them," the weeping woman tells us. "They just come up in here and do what they feel like. I was too scared to scream. Ain't nobody gonna come if I did."

Diane soothes the weeping woman while I check the rooms. Young boys, the woman had said. Fourteen, fifteen at the most. They ran out, just before we got here.

I find a scrap of red fabric stuck in the pried-off burglar grate at her door, probably left behind by the boys as they rushed out. Footprints in the slimy egg muck, indicating the clear imprint of athletic shoes, lead out of the apartment and toward the stairwell. A no-brainer this time. They left everything but a calling card.

Downstairs, just outside the entranceway, are a

group of young boys, one holding a portable radio. The tallest wears a Bulls jacket with a substantial rip in one red sleeve. They're laughing and high-fiving, don't even notice us until we're next to them.

"Yo, baby, easy now!" One of them says as Diane pushes him against the wall. "You ain't got to grab it. I'll give you some for free, fine-looking woman like you." He rolls his eyes suggestively, smirking at his homeys while we search them.

"Y'all is some *fine* bitches!" another says. "I like to get me some of what you got, sweet thangs."

We find the woman's wedding ring in one boy's pocket, the thirteen dollars in another's. Standing behind the tallest boy, Diane jerks his arm back, presses up against him.

"I got a pair of handcuffs for you, my man. How's that for starters?"

"Awww, baby! Why you got to be like that? I ain't did nothin'!" After his friends are cuffed, he looks hopefully at me.

"I ain't did nothin', miss. Tell your friend here to let us go." He grins, trying for some zero-hour bravado. "I could be sweet to you, baby. We could work somethin' out. You and me together. Don't that sound good?"

"Sure. We'll start with breakfast in Juvie Hall." I point to his high-top sneakers, still smeared with gooey egg yolk. "I like mine over easy."

One of the advantages of working with another female is the built-in sensitivity factor. There are some situations that benefit from a woman's touch, especially when we're dealing with kids. One night we pull up in front of an abandoned building bordering the expressway. Plywood sheets are haphazardly nailed over what once were windows. Random shutters hang crazily askew, banging in the gusting wind. Our job is to check on children left alone.

"Check the address," I tell my partner. "Nobody lives in that dump. It's got to be a mistake." But there's no mistake. We walk up stairs sagging from termites and rot, through the doorless threshold and into total darkness.

"She just be gone for a little while. She comin' right back." The tiny, shivering girl, clearly terrified of the uniforms who've trooped into her home, fans her arms backward, trying to gather and protect the smaller kids. There are five of them, five tiny bodies huddling together in the dark on a drenched mattress. It's only by using our flashlights, and following the stench of ammonia—and worse—that we find these kids.

It's past midnight, but there are no lights on in this place, no light-bulbs, no lamps. And even though it's January, there's no heat either, as cold inside as the arctic temperatures outdoors. Garbage, broken bottles and used hypodermic syringes litter the floor. Between the piles of feces and old beer cans, insects skitter across the floor. When we lift the smallest baby from the mattress, we find a hole underneath where a mother rat and her babies have nested, taking advantage of the human body heat.

The oldest girl—Sharonda, she tells us—is seven. Her emaciated body is barely as big as a normal three-year-old's. She doesn't remember when they've eaten last. She doesn't remember when her mother left. A broken bottle of molasses lies on the floor, its blackish ooze spread and drying and covered with bugs. When the kids get hungry, Sharonda says, they crawl over and lick some molasses. There is no other food. But Mama's going to bring some when she comes back, which should be any time now.

Blankets are brought from the car and the children are wrapped up snugly, preparing them for their trip to the station. Sharonda is terrified. Where are we taking them? What if Mama comes back? How will she find them? The trembling girl tearfully explains that she'll get whipped for leaving with the kids. That's why Mama takes their shoes, so they don't go nowhere. Well, she don't take *all* their shoes. Sharonda is the only one who had a pair, and those don't fit anymore. And none of the kids have coats.

On the way to the station, we radio the dispatcher to have a DCFS caseworker meet us there. I sit in the back with the kids playing "Itsy Bitsy Spider" while Diane makes a few necessary pit stops: the convenience store for milk and disposable diapers, Maxwell Street for a bag of hamburgers. It's pedestrian fare, but enough to dazzle our tiny passengers. They never ate burgers before; they're astonished that they can each have a whole one. When we tell them they can eat as many as they want, there's shocked silence, and then, nothing but the sounds of little mouths munching.

At the station, warm and fed and squinting in the bright light, Sharonda is reluctant to talk to us at first, and insists on holding the smallest child in her arms. But when we produce crayons and paper for the other kids, she softens. And actually giggles when Diane shows her how to make shadow bunnies on the wall. When she sees her brother nestled in my lap, scribbling happily with a yellow crayon, she relents.

Mama just went out for a little while, she tells us. Sometimes she do that, stay gone for a time, but she always comes back. Maybe she just went to get her hair did. Her mama is pretty, Sharonda says wistfully. She likes to get her hair did with all them braids.

She doesn't know where her daddy is. Not sure she *has* a daddy. Mookie, he's five, his daddy dead. And Darnell's daddy—he got other children, he stay on the South Side—he don't come around. Darnell is four.

She points to the toddler with horrific burn marks on her face.

"That's Olivia. She two. Don't know where her daddy is. That burn? She got that when she fell against the radiator one time. Mama was sick then. Couldn't get out of the bed to come pull her off. That's why come we don't have heat no more. Mama say she ain't payin' the bill if we gonna act like fools when it's on."

The baby in Sharonda's arms begins to fuss. She coos at him, stroking and soothing with practiced gestures.

"This here Jerome," she says proudly. "He almost one. His daddy be the pastor, down at the Baptist church."

"The pastor?"

"Uh-huh. He used to come around, sometime, be with Mama. Bring us clothes once in a while, for Mama and the babies, even me. Things from what the church people give away. He ain't come around in a while. Say Mama be too sick all the time, he can't hang no more." She kisses the baby, smoothing the tiny tufts of matted hair.

"Y'all got some pretty hair," Sharonda tells us admiringly. "My mama had her some nice hair, 'fore she started getting sick so much." The old-lady eyes in her waif's face dart around, checking on the other kids. And then shift back to the uniforms, wondering if she's said too much.

It's not our job to tell Sharonda her mama's not coming back. That she, like hundreds of other parents, have abandoned her children, and will never be found, despite the best efforts of the police. Or that there's a strong probability that Sharonda's brothers and sisters will be sent to separate foster homes. All we can do now is comfort her, try to divert her from the reality of her sad life.

"Mama comin' back," she tells us. "Y'all better take us on back now. She be real worried if we ain't there." She clutches the baby tighter, watching us. The tiny voice grows louder, panicked.

"Y'all don't want my mama to worry herself. She ain't been sick in a long time. 'Fact, she just fine, so y'all need to take us back."

Olivia, the burned child, clutches her sister's leg and starts to whimper. Sharonda shifts her load of baby and pulls her sister close.

"You hush up now, girl, hear? Cuz we goin' home in a minute. And Mama gon' be waitin' on us, and she gon' be all pretty, and have some food there. Grape pop, and beans, and some fatback, and she gonna give you the biggest chunk. And you can eat it all up, cuz you my baby." Sharonda rocks the smaller children, crooning to them as the tears roll down her cheeks.

"And Sharonda gon' take care of you, and it's gon' be alright, cuz you and Jerome, and Mookie and Darnell, you gon' be right wit' me, and I ain't goin' nowhere. Y'all are my babies."

17

What's a Nice Girl Like You . . . ?

Dispatcher:	1225, are you up and rolling yet?
1225:	Just coming out of the parking lot now, Squad.
Dispatcher:	Okay, '25, gonna start you off with "information for the police," 111— South Oakley. Citizen says they'll be waiting on the porch.
1225:	Ten-four.
Dispatcher:	Oh, and . . .'25? Be advised they asked for you specifically.
1225:	They asked for the beat car?
Dispatcher:	Negative. They said, "Make sure you send the redhead and the blonde."

Now that Diane and I are regular partners, I find my professional identity undergoing more changes. I'm part of a unit now, half of a whole. A regular beat patrolled by a regular team. And because my partner happens to be a woman, I'm no longer the "token" female, the one male cops expect to automatically assume the responsibilities of nurturer and sympathetic ear. As cops, as women, we're equal partners, each doing an equal share of the same work. And the fact that we're two females puts a whole new spin on our approach to policing. It's an adaptation most female cops discover out of necessity. In lieu of raw muscle power, or the ability to intimidate in the face of conflict, we have to find an alternative approach. With Diane, I discover a whole new repertoire of approaches that range from ingenious to hysterical. Tactics all founded on that golden rule learned back at the Academy: "Whatever works."

In the beginning, Diane and I work in uniform, assigned to a regular beat car. Our supervisors, dispatchers, and most of the men on our watch refer to us as "the Babe Car," a title that's not, in any way, meant to be derogatory. Because I've been partnered, at various times, with most of the men on the watch for the past two years, they know my work habits, know I'm not a "bimbo with a badge." As a result there's a mutual respect and support among us, which makes facing what's out there a lot easier.

When we answer routine calls, Diane and I get a lot of double takes, even more clichéd analogies to *Charlie's Angels*. When we show up at a burglary victim's home to take the necessary report, it's not unusual for the victim to blink and hesitate, and then blurt out, "Jeeeeeez, I never saw any cops that look like you two! Whatever made you wanna be the police?" A variation of the same question we hear endless times in the course of our careers: "What's a nice girl like you . . . ?" A question which, to us, poses another, unspoken question. Can't *nice girls* be cops? Or is it that, because of the job, people assume we become less than nice?

In the process of doing our job, it's ironic how the attitudes of the public we serve sometimes shift. One of the bloody combatants in a bar fight will say, "Sorry you girls had to see this. I ain't the creep you must think I am. Most of the time, I'm a real gentlemen." A citizen reporting a garage theft will offer us tea and cookies, and then play surrogate parent when we leave. "Be careful out there, girls. The streets aren't safe these days for women. Make sure you take care of yourselves."

Sometimes the sight of two female cops can bring out a sense of gallantry that most feminists would swear has long been dead. Men open doors for us, offer us flowers, attempt to buy us coffee, or lunch. Try to press business cards or hastily scribbled phone numbers in our hand in exchange for the traffic ticket we've just written. Will instruct other, less gallant men to shut up if they happen to utter a profanity in our presence ("Watch your mouth when there's ladies present, you jerk!") In the course of routine patrol, we experience some surprises that show there are still some people who notice the woman behind the badge.

One day we observe a sleek Jaguar rumble to a stop at a traffic signal. The driver notices us noticing him and, grinning, he roars through the red light. When we pull him over and approach his car to write the inevitable ticket, he's still smiling. And tells us he couldn't help himself; he just wanted the experience of meeting two babe cops. Which is enough to have us all smiling—but he still gets his ticket. And a month later, he shows up in traffic court, completely willing to pay the fine, and bearing a bottle of champagne and a dinner invitation for the officer in question. An interesting experience, and one that I find, over time, is not at all unusual.

People—and men, in particular—are curious about female cops. And there are some who find a woman in uniform particularly sexy, something that those of us who have to wear them find a little absurd. Just a short time on the street familiarizes me with most of the standard lines men use for female cops. I'm certain that, at the time, the guy thinks he's being clever, original, and charmingly innovative. I speak for all the ladies in uniform when I say these lines have been done to death.

It's *not* original for any man, any time, to ask leeringly, "Wanna frisk me, baby?" Or to inquire if we do it with handcuffs, or if calling 911 will indeed make us come. No female cop that I know will take up a man's offer to "check out a *real* gun" or to hold his personal "nightstick."

Less common but equally stupid lines I've heard all refer to what the guy obviously believes is a woman doing a man's work. In response, I can report that, no, my bra isn't bulletproof—but my safety vest is, same as it is for all of us! And, despite expectations to the contrary, making comments about my breasts, butt, or the length of my legs will *not* prevent you from getting a ticket, and is *not* a guarantee against arrest. No, I'm not a leather fetishist—the gun belt I wear, and all the equipment that attaches to it, is regulation. And being a cop does not make me a dominatrix, a control freak, or possess a questionable gender orientation. It's just a job, just like yours. My job description just happens to include keeping a lid on criminal behavior and upholding the peace. Not something that's easily accomplished by passive or submissive behavior.

Working with Diane, I hear all the lines, all the suggestive remarks—and all the ripe curses from people who wrongly assume we're just two chicks in uniform. Sometimes, it might be an easy, if false assumption to make. Going into a job, we're generally calm, assessing the situation before we make a move. No need to go in like gangbusters if something can be resolved peaceably. To the observer, it might look like weakness—one woman watching, the other woman acting as negotiator. In many instances, the people we serve are appreciative of this approach. It's refreshing to have someone listen, without the *attitude*. Without any of the authoritarian posturing they'd expect from a male cop.

Criminals are sometimes deceived by it. To them, we're two bimbos with no clue about their real agenda. Which allows them to switch into the "rap mode," the "Yo, baby, you and me, we could get together" routine that's offered when it's time for them to go down. But once the cuffs have been slapped on and they're in the squadrol on the way to jail, their perception changes. Then Diane and I are no longer babes, or bimbos, or even "the redhead and the blonde." We're bitches, and, ultimately "goddamn cops"—just like everyone else who wears the uniform.

There are plenty of others who don't see us as babes, as chicks, or anything relative to the female gender. To them, we're just a pair of uniforms, two cops who deserve—and are given—the same amount of contempt, or hostility—and the same combative behavior. The punches tossed our way, the weapons pointed in our direction are equal opportunity, meant to take out a cop, regardless of gender. In those instances we, like everyone else who wears the badge, are authority figures, targets, potential victims.

In this job, which for decades has been the domain of men, it would be wonderful to report that times have changed for female cops, that our supervisors and department brass consider us to be officers before women, equal in every way to our male counterparts. It would also be a huge lie. Going into the millennium, women are still considered inferior and, despite continued job performances that indicate otherwise, still regarded as backup more than first-string.

Diane and I learn this first hand when we decide to apply for our district's tactical unit, a plainclothes operation that, so far, has been limited to men. At this point, we've worked together for two years, during which time we've amassed one of the highest records for felony arrests in our district. It's up to our watch commander to approve our application before we can be considered, a bit of department politics that ensures women—or anyone—won't go anywhere we're not welcomed. In this case, the watch commander is a long-standing member of the boys' club mentality which means, in his estimation, we're better suited as watch secretaries than tac officers. He vetoes our application initially, and then three more times in six months.

When Diane and I finally confront him, he's evasive, but tries for a diplomatic note. It's too dangerous out there for women, he tells us. Working plainclothes is a whole new ball game. He's not sure two "girls" like us are ready for it.

Diane points out that no one thinks we're *girls* when we're out there in uniform. And that our duties and responsibilities are the same, regardless of dress requirements. And that people shoot at us just the same, in regulation attire or in jeans. The watch commander is unimpressed. In our district, the tac teams are all men, he says. They wouldn't feel comfortable working with girls.

Then we'll work alone, I tell him. It seems to be working so far, judging by our arrest record. For just a couple of *girls,* we must be doing something right.

The watch commander is still doubtful, and it's only when Diane suggests filing a grievance—that "sexual discrimination in the workplace" charge that's become the bane of union officials everywhere—that he decides to strike a "compromise." And informs us that, before he allows our applications to be considered by the tactical lieutenant, he wants to see "what we're made of." And assigns us to an "incident car"—an unmarked vehicle we're to work during our regular tour of duty. The only difference is that we'll be in plainclothes, we won't be assigned regular jobs from the dispatcher, and we'll be expected to bring in a higher percentage of arrests than our uniformed counterparts. After completing this assignment for a full period (28 days), he'll evaluate our performance.

What the watch commander *doesn't* tell us is that the car we're assigned, while indeed unmarked, is also without a siren, an emergency light, or any other apparatus that will distinguish it as a police vehicle. No loudspeaker, no microphone, no antenna to facilitate radio transmission. Which means there's no way we can pull over an offender's vehicle, no siren that will indicate our pursuit of a felon, no pulsing light to help part traffic on a high-speed chase. What we *have* got is a seriously rusted four-door sedan with balding tires and a lethargic transmission just this side of meltdown. And the only thing we'll catch in this baby is a cold, since the heater doesn't work either. Not an auspicious start for the burgeoning tactical career of the redhead and the blonde.

"Typical department bullshit!" Diane hisses that first night, as our sluggish "incident car" trundles along. "Would've been easier if he just said no. At least that way, we'd have some recourse."

"Exactly what he didn't want!" I point out. "And

anyway, why should this stop us? So what if he gave us a dog car? Just think how pissed he'll be when he finds out we can do the job anyway!"

Between the two of us, we have enough experience both on the street and in dealing with departmental politics to know what the score is. This time, it's about screwing over the "girls," giving us enough rope to hang ourselves so we'll fade into the background of uniformed patrol. Something neither Diane and I are willing to allow, not now or at any time in our career. It's not about winning as much as maintaining our identities as law enforcers. We wear the badges; we carry the weapons; we take the risks. And if we have to accept the sacrifices and all the other "downsides" that come with the job, we should at least be accorded the same opportunities to succeed. Or, in lieu of that, to have the smarts to know how to step up and take what's ours.

In this case, it proves easier than we imagined. The watch commander wants arrests, that's what we'll give him. The only thing we have to figure out, with the decrepit vehicle we have, is how to do it. We're starting off with a handicap; but since the boss considers us "girls," then we'll do what girls do to get the results we want.

On that first night, we leave the dinosaur sedan in the station parking lot and opt for a more "covert vehicle"—Diane's sporty gold Trans-Am. Any bad guy on the street can make a cop's car—with or without markings—on sight; who else drives around in groups in dark-colored Crown Victorias? In the Trans-Am, we're just two more babes cruising the streets.

We roll along slowly, scanning the action. And decide to head down 18th Street, past Blue Island, toward Harrison Park. All gang turf, all guaranteed to have arrest possibilities for anything from narcotics to weapons violations, and anything in between. The first nibble comes when we're stopped at a light. The low-rider Chevy that pulls alongside us has five occupants: all Latino men, all gangbangers, all intensely focused on the two babes in the gold ride.

"Yo, baby, whattup?" the driver asks, flashing a blinding grin. His dark eyes rake over us, first me, then Diane. Encouraged by our inviting smiles, he makes the next move. "You looking to party, or what?"

"Depends," I coo. "What kind of party? Not too much goin' on around here. Looks like this 'hood is dead!" That's all it takes. That, and a little lash fluttering, a little lip-licking, and the gauntlet's been tossed down. These gang members are bound by pride and the code of the street to show these two babes just how fine a 'hood this is, and what a great party they can throw.

We're instructed to pull over—an ironic twist: gangbangers curbing the cops—and the driver comes over to our door, where he stares shamelessly at our cleavage while inquiring just what will constitute the right kind of party. After determining that we have no gang affiliation, that we're an independent "party crew" strictly out for a good time, he describes the delights he can offer us. Whether cocaine or heroin, crack or crystal meth, the choice is ours, as long as we allow our "hosts" the pleasure of our company. We're instructed to follow his car to an address on the border of the district. It's easy, en route, to use our mobile radios to request uniformed backup at that location, and for an available squadrol for prisoner transport. Easier than that to sail into the apartment with our leering hosts, allow them to preen and swagger and lay out enough narcotic "refreshments" to constitute a felony narcotic arrest of major proportions.

And then, after our backup arrives and our hapless hosts have been arrested, cuffed and transported for processing, the easiest part of all—to scoop up all the evidence, both narcotics and weapons, which we'll inventory back at the station in what will be one of our biggest arrests of the year.

On another night, while driving near the projects, we notice a Lexus with black-tinted windows and Indiana plates. It's cruising slowly down the littered streets like a prowling panther amidst the battered and burned-out vehicles that line the curbs. From previous experience, we know that a lot of weapons are brought into this area by gunrunners from Indiana, which would account for such a high-end car in this squalid location.

We pass the Lexus slowly, smiling blandly in no particular direction. In this area, the only reason two white women would be cruising the streets at midnight would be to score some dope, or as "working girls" looking for customers. Either way, we're not made as cops.

In the rearview mirror, Diane notes that the Lexus has turned, is now following us. She pulls over to the curb and watches me pull my already-dipping neckline down a little lower, a lot tighter, before I climb out of the car. And then stand near the rear of the car, bending over as if to inspect the tire, and to afford the Lexus a full profile of my undercover-cop's ass.

The Lexus pulls up alongside us. The window lowers to reveal a passenger in a cream-colored suit and a diamond-encrusted tooth that flashes in the moonlight when he smiles at me. I return the smile and shrug helplessly in my best clueless-female imitation.

"Y'all having a problem there, miss?" he rumbles. I'm assaulted with a variety of odors that pour out of the car: coconut air freshener, musk cologne, marijuana. Still bent over, I raise up just a little—enough to afford him a view of cleavage and skin that's beginning to prickle from the audacity of what I'm doing. Anything could happen now, depending on luck, or fate, or the amount of drugs these guys have ingested. I know that Diane's already radioed for backup, which will arrive momentarily. And I know that now, as she steps out of the car, fluttering and flirtatious and adjusting a tank-top strap that just *happens* to keep slipping down, she'll provide even more distraction that will buy us some critical minutes. But in that moment, intuition tells me it's too much to leave to chance. To these guys, we could be party favors—or their next victims. It's up to me to swing the odds in our favor.

So I pivot slowly, running my tongue over lips that should be desert dry, given the fear I'm feeling, and slink over to the car. And bend lower again, enough to see the other passengers, the glint of the weapons on the front seat. And feel the hair raising on the back of my neck as I purr, "I just *love* a man with a fine ride! We're having a little trouble with ours. Any chance we can get a ride?" The man smiles and leers, watching my lips that are scant inches from his face, so close he never sees the 9mm I raise and press to his temple as Diane drops into a crouch, leveling her weapon at the driver.

By the time our backup arrives, we have all the occupants out of the vehicle and facedown on the ground. And once they're cuffed and en route to the station, we're able to do a thorough car search, which reveals not only a crate of high-tech Brazilian submachine guns, but more than a pound of uncut heroin as well. The uniforms on the scene congratulate us on our great police work. The sergeant who stops by the scene tells us how proud he is of our arrest. No one notices, or mentions, how my hands are shaking, how Diane can't stop shivering. And how the fear that clawed our backbones with icy fingers while we confronted our arrestees has left us in a cold slick sweat. All part of the job, you say? Yes. It's also part of what we have to do, as women, as "girls" to prove our ability.

By the end of the period, the watch commander is presented with arrest statistics that indicate we've more than surpassed the uniformed cars on our watch, and also the entire district. He has no choice but to approve our application for the tac team, which is then submitted to the tactical lieutenant for *his* consideration.

Four months later, we're notified that we've been accepted to the tactical unit, but because everyone else is already partnered off, we'll have to work together. Not something the tac lieutenant approves of, especially since we're women. After all, he tells us with a frown, working plainclothes is a whole different ball game. Something he's not certain *girls* might be able to handle.

18

Adrenaline Junkies

Dispatcher: All units in the Twelfth District and on citywide, be advised we have a vehicle chase going on, eastbound on Washington from Loomis.

1210: 1210.

Dispatcher: 1210 coming in? Go 'head, Sarge.

1210: Squad, what unit's involved in that chase?

Dispatcher: It's 1265 Edward, Boss. They're in pursuit of a green Plymouth eastbound on Washington.

1265E: '65 Edward—make that Southbound on the expressway.

Dispatcher: Ten-four. Okay, Boss, they're on the expressway now, southbound.

1210: Squad, advise them to discontinue the chase. Repeat, they are ordered to discontinue the chase, authority of Beat 1210.

Dispatcher: Ten-four, Boss. Okay, '65 Edward, do you copy? Sergeant's ordering you to discontinue the chase.... Uh, no response from them, Boss.

1210: Those damn girls are probably at the Indiana border by now!

As with most defense mechanisms, it's not something you notice immediately. And when family, or friends, or the people you work with happen to point it out, you deny it ... at first. *Adrenaline junkie? You? Not*

a chance! Sooner or later, though, it occurs to you
that it *must* be true, and that's when you try to rationalize. If it *is* true, it's only another way of dealing with the job, an outlet for the stress that might
otherwise build to dangerous levels.

Like water that seeks its own level, most street
cops find their own way of coping with the changes
this job brings. Not just changes in their lifestyles,
but in what they believe in, and their perceptions of
other people. At some point, cops understand that
they have to find a way to compensate for the disil-
lusionment that comes, in small measures and huge
leaps, for as long as they're on the job. Either from
failed expectations, or unrealistic goals, or just a
sharp dose of reality, the day comes when you know,
in spite of your best efforts, that your life, and your
work, will never equal your dreams.

So you learn to compensate. If a cop is feeling bitter, disillusioned that he's passed over for promotion
once again, in spite of consistent good work, he
might just give up, sink into a laissez-faire approach
that borders on lethargy. He decides it's just a job, just
a paycheck, and not worth getting killed over. Since
he's knocked himself out all these years, without any
kind of recognition, what's the point of continuing?
No chance of his winning this one, since department
politics have a way of defeating the most ardent opponents. Better to let the young kids just coming on
the job take up the slack. He's tired and bitter. So he
performs his police duties, but just barely. No acts
above and beyond the call, and no danger zone from
which he may not emerge. Just go through the motions, collect the paycheck, leave the hot-dogging to
someone else.

Other cops are fully aware of the same setbacks

and disappointments, but they handle it another way. At the point when they realize this job isn't all they would have wished, maybe wondering why they didn't become a plumber or an electrician instead, they're generally at the point where their pension is vested and understand that jumping ship mid-career would be a financially foolhardy. So they swallow the disappointment and muddle through, developing a sharp cynicism, a gallows humor that appears, to others, almost as apathy. But it's mostly a way to protect those raw emotional spots that come from too much reality, and the death of too many dreams.

For others, like Diane, like me, adaptation comes in a different form. We see the tragedies, the atrocities, the street theater performed live, each night we hit the streets. Every possible aspect of the human condition parades before us faster than we can keep track, sometimes. Babies are born, people are killed, homes burned to the ground, all in between the celebrations of the ordinary that occur in every neighborhood of the city. Sometimes, the jobs we handle are on the next evening's news broadcast, or a front-page feature story in the morning paper. The news that other people are viewing or reading is our work history from the previous night while we face something completely different twenty-four hours later.

As the police, our worlds have narrowed to the fast-track pace of cops 'n' robbers, the good versus bad struggle that continues at warp speed. It's a hectic, delirious tempo that makes *ordinary* life, by comparison, look boring. Which also makes the people who exist in that world a little less interesting. How many *other* workdays might include scaling buildings in pursuit of felons, swinging off fire escapes, and high-speed car chases? Throw in a few shots fired, a gang fight or two, and it's not a gig most folks will envy. Our jobs are dangerous, fueled with adrenaline. It's a rush that's exhilarating—and addictive. It's also a phenomenon difficult to understand unless you've tasted the fear and the thrill in equal measures, managed to survive what surely should have been your last call on this earth—and then gone out and done it again. Adrenaline junkies thrive on the chase and the challenge. It's a way to stare down the demons that lurk around every corner, to push the envelope each time so you can validate who you are. It's also a preventive measure against boredom and apathy—occupational hazards in any job, but potentially deadly ones in a cop's life.

Some might call it a death wish. I think it's a way of keeping your focus in a job where lines and distinctions become easily blurred. And when the lines are blurring in every other part of your life, the guaranteed thrills and chills of an adrenaline junkie's job performance are the only thing that remain a constant.

Take one freezing February night, for example. Diane and I leave the district parking lot for another night of the unknown. She slides a cassette into the tape deck as we hit the street—the mellow blues of B. B. King to warm the frigid night. As the music throbs like a heartbeat and B. B. croons about "Paying the Cost to Be the Boss," we come across our first job, an "on view" street disturbance. The man's furious shouts can be heard up and down the block as he gestures from the sidewalk. The woman has taken it to the streets, all three-hundred-plus pounds of her, wearing only a wobbly smile. Oblivious to the cold, she's dancing in a drunken circle, belting out an unintelligible country song at earsplitting decibels.

And responds to our suggestion to cover up and go home by bursting into tears. We're women, she sobs, we must understand what it's like to be in love with a no-good, cheatin' man.

Meanwhile, the man in question has decided he's heard enough of his personal business on the street, and starts blasting away with the .32 Colt pistol he pulls out of his pocket. Which has us diving for cover—except the woman, who simply plops down on what happens to be Diane's foot. Luckily, the man is drunk enough to miss us all, and doesn't put up much of a fight when we lock him up on assault charges. But after facing a barrage of live rounds, our adrenaline meltdown feels like at least a year shaved off our lives. And once the woman is back in the house, and we're transporting our prisoner to the station, B. B. is warbling about watching out for big-legged women.

Our next job is a heartbreaker. We see a late-model Toyota, pleated like an accordion by the truck it crashed into. The car is crushed so efficiently that only the blood seeping through the passenger door tells us the occupants are still inside. We wait for the arrival of the accident car—whose offices will take the report and process the scene. Also on the scene is the fire department emergency team, who work feverishly to extricate the passengers, and who find the evidence that tells the story. The three teenage occupants had used a paper bag and a rag soaked in Trauline, a liquid engine cleaner known to produce a zombielike high by "huffing" the fumes. Kids who will now never see their eighteenth birthdays. It's another instance when I think of my own kids, and my quick silent prayer for their safety doesn't seem like enough. When Diane and I get back in our car, the cassette clicks back on, and B. B. is crooning, "How Blue Can You Get?"

The night grows colder, with relentless winds blasting out of the north. While driving through an alley, we observe a cluster of people near an auto-body shop. The wind has knocked down a powerline which dangles, still sparking, near the ground. Near it lies a man who smells like roasted meat. His face is frozen in an obscene death mask, with teeth bared in a futile snarl. Witnesses tell us the man, a regular at the corner tavern, was seen wandering down the alley when he stopped to relieve himself, and apparently decided to play "fire extinguisher" with the power line. It was an awesome thing to see, one witness says. Like a one-man fireworks show.

We disperse the crowd and wait in the warmth of our car until the squadrol arrives to remove the body. "I Pity the Fool," B. B. is singing, and this time, I agree completely.

Next stop is the Steak 'n' Egger, where we stop for a much-needed coffee break. The place is empty except for a truck driver hunched over a plate of pancakes, gearing up for his morning run. Mimi, the waitress, brings our coffee—hot, black, and strong enough to take the chrome off a Harley, but tonight it tastes like ambrosia. I sip it slowly to savor the heat and dilute the fatigue, smile when Mimi leans a well-padded hip against the counter and asks how our night is going. And slides slices of fresh apple pie toward us as she listens intently. She's heard it all, a thousand times from a thousand cops who sit on these stools and brace themselves before hitting the streets again. She knows how to listen, and when *not* to pry, so tonight she just smiles and cracks a few corny jokes.

And for the umpteenth time, I reflect that this grease-filmed little diner is our sanctuary, and Mimi with her platinum hair and tired eyes is the brief respite that comforts us on these long nights. So we trade wisecracks, tell a few more jokes, and drain our coffee before heading out. And somehow it's enough to get us through whatever comes next.

B. B. King is singing "We're Gonna Make It," and with only three hours left to go, we think that maybe we will. Until we hear the next radio transmission, with the dispatcher announcing a burglary in progress, just three blocks from our location, at a men's clothing store. We're already en route before the transmission is finished. More adrenaline, especially when we arrive on the scene and determine that neither the store's front or back doors have been opened, which means the entry was made through the roof. Without a word, we're scaling the walls, depending on luck, impetus, and, please God, enough traction from our running shoes to make it up two levels of icy bricks.

The burglars, two wiry young men in their twenties, are still inside. One busies himself scooping up counters full of silk shirts into a pillowcase while the other hammers at the cash register. Neither of them is armed, a detail we don't know yet, won't find out until after we wrestle them to the ground. Our only advantage is the surprise factor of dropping down from the ceiling. They never see us coming, not until my partner lands on one of them like an ungainly spider.

It's not until we're back in the station, processing our burglars, that I remember Diane is afraid of heights. And that, with the absence of guns, these burglars might have bludgeoned us with the same hammer used to smash the cash register. Things you never think about while you're doing it. Just considerations that creep in later, riding the coattails of "post-caper" nerves.

Back on the street, we cruise along slowly. Just one hour left to go, and maybe it will pass without incident. A thought that evaporates when we're flagged down by a weeping young woman standing at the curb. She nurses a swelling eye and speaks painfully through bleeding lips. A robbery victim, we learn. Attacked by a man and a woman who stole her purse, containing thirty-one dollars and miscellaneous IDs, and then fled in their car. She points to a green Plymouth heading down the block. It's all we need.

By legal standards, thirty-one dollars isn't much, not even enough to constitute a "felony theft." But the woman was alone, was on her way to buy diapers at the convenience store, and was beaten and robbed. Now she's crying, and counting on us to help. After a long night of frustrating wrongs, maybe this is one we can make right.

We take off after the Plymouth, which barrels through a red light and squeals around the corner. The chase is on.

Diane calls in the chase to our radio dispatcher. According to the department's rules, all car chases have to be approved first by a supervisor. This is because of the high number of accidents and property damage incurred when speeding cops are in hot pursuit. After scores of lawsuits from furious citizens whose vehicles were crunched, or worse, by zealous officers in high-speed chases, the department decided to draw the line. Which means that field supervisors (sergeants) will usually order a chase discontinued, unless the offenders are fleeing a homicide scene. For a thirty-one-dollar robbery, our chances for permission to continue the chase are less than zero.

Sure enough, as soon as we call in the chase, the sergeant is on the air, ordering us to cease and desist. But the Plymouth's heading down the expressway ramp, and we're right behind. And when the Plymouth skids crazily across three lanes, nearly taking out a pickup truck in the process, we know we're in for the long haul. So while our sergeant's shouts crackle over the radio, we keep going—two miles, six miles, almost ten—all the while imagining the stash of contraband that might be in our offender's car. Guns, probably. Maybe narcotics. Possibly the proceeds of a string of other robberies. It's enough to keep us flying down the road on our adrenaline high and our mission for justice.

Just short of the Skyway entrance that would take us in to Indiana, the Plymouth hits a patch of ice, swerves wildly before slamming into the guardrails. The hood flies open, smoke pours out of the engine, and Diane and I are out of our car with weapons drawn.

The occupants are dazed and, judging by the bottles that litter the car, more than a little drunk. With no resistance at all, the woman shambles out of the passenger side and leans passively over the trunk. The man at the wheel is so intoxicated he can't stand without assistance. While Diane guards the prisoners, I search the vehicle. There are no weapons, no drugs—only half a dozen liquor bottles and the greasy fast-food boxes of a week's worth of meals.

A search of the prisoners reveals the victim's thirty-one dollars, still neatly folded in a beaded change purse, as well as the accordioned plastic holder containing her IDs and snapshots of her two babies. As we handcuff the woman, she begins to cry. And explains that she didn't mean to do it, she just needed some money. Just enough to buy another bottle for her boyfriend, and maybe some gas for the car. But she never meant to hurt her baby.

"Baby?" Diane asks. "What baby?"

"My daughter," the woman sobs. "That's who we took the money from. I thought she'd just give it to me . . . never expected her to put up a fight."

"Your daughter? You robbed your own daughter?"

We settle our prisoners in the back of our car and start the long journey back to our district. The cassette clicks on and it's B. B. singing his last song of the night: "Nobody Loves Me But My Mother."

Nights like this prompt discussions between my partner and me. It usually starts off as a philosophical debate on why we do what we do. There are never pat answers, only a shared hope that sometimes what we do makes a difference. And even though the percentages aren't always in our favor, it's enough to keep us going. In between the lost souls and sad stories and surging highs, we actually do win a few, restore dignity or peace, and just a little faith to some people, sometimes. Which is all we need to keep going out there, doing it all over again.

As she approaches her thirty-first birthday, Diane tells me she's decided not to have kids. She's seen too much on the street, she says. No way she'd want to bring more children into this troubled world. And, given the danger of our jobs, why subject a family to that trauma? Which makes me think of my own family, and wonder for the billionth time whether I've hurt more than helped them.

She reflects on the way our work impacts the other parts of our lives. Her relationships with men mirror mine, and those of many other female cops. If civilian men are part of the equation, it's a situation that's almost doomed from the start. It takes a special man *not* to feel threatened, or insignificant. To keep a tight grip on his pride and his ego in the company of a woman who slings guns and slaps on handcuffs, scales walls and performs any number of other kamikaze stunts in the name of the law. Only a *very* special man could accept that. As Diane is quick to point out, we don't meet a lot of special men in this job. And because our off-duty time is also consumed by job-related activities, like court appearances and other mandatory testimony, there's not a lot of opportunity to explore other avenues searching for Mr. Right.

So, instead, we continue our madcap pace on the streets, suffer through unsatisfactory relationships, or accept the inevitable cop/cop relationship that at least guarantees dealing with a man who understands what you do, and why. Or we develop outside interests that quell the frustration and, for brief respites, allow us to forget the job for a while.

For Diane, it's the two horses she boards at a suburban stable. All of her free time and a good portion of her money is poured into their loving upkeep, and, on her days off, she can usually be found astride her favorite mount, a chestnut quarter horse who runs like the wind. Someday she'll have a ranch, she tells me. Horses and dogs and acres of rolling hills that are light-years away from the environment we work in. A place she won't have to fight the bad guys, or contend with the nightmares that come with what we do. That's the dream that sustains her.

For me, it's spending time with my kids. Exploring parks and countrysides and worlds that seem untarnished, offering another view of life. Parcels of shared time that seem too brief, never enough. For now, it has to be. Diane teaches them to ride her horses. Together, we take them on day trips, let them play at the beach and run along the dunes. It's a lazy pace that seems like sleepwalking, compared to our usual mode. But it's what we need to draw closer, gather strength from those times and each other. Enough to carry us through another night, another week, through pulsing nerves and the dark unknown.

19

Full-Moon Fever

Dispatcher: 1212? Double 12?

1212: Double.

Dispatcher: Double 12, the Candy Lady's at it again.
Security guard at the candy outlet store says
she broke in the back door, tried to swipe
a stack of candy boxes.

1212: What does he expect? It's the full moon, right?

Dispatcher: Yeah, time for her to make her "homemade
fudge balls." 'Specially if she's eaten a lot of
roughage.

It happens once a month. The moon is full, the tide
is high, planets shift, and the gravitational pull is
strong enough to bring every screwball out of the
woodwork, if only for one night. Any cop can tell
you there's more violent crimes committed, more
crazy incidents logged, and more babies born during
a full moon than at any other time. And any
emergency-room doctor or nurse who's witnessed
the results of full-moon fever will agree.

During one particular full moon, our night gets off
to an appropriate start. The roll-call sergeant is Elgin
Floyd, an older, easygoing guy who's been making
noises about retiring for the last year or so. Elgin's
the type who never hassles anyone. A low-key kind
of guy who's mostly content to go with the flow,

put in his time without fanfare or complaint. If he sometimes wears eyeliner to work, or sports the occasional pink manicure, no one mentions it. We all like Elgin, are in agreement that he's a stand-up guy, and anyway, who are we to judge? Everyone's got their own life.

On this particular night, though, Elgin has clearly crossed the line. When he strolls into the squad room, it's enough to quell the usual banter, enough, in fact, to shock the assembled watch into dead silence. Sergeant Floyd is wearing a bra over his uniform shirt, a frilly confection of rose-colored lace that contrasts nicely with the supervisory white. And exactly matches the beribboned garter belt that's fastened over his uniform slacks.

He reads through the watch announcements while everyone stares. Or, possibly, is wondering where he found the huge Minnie Mouse false eyelashes. The watch commander, a ham-fisted former Marine, enters the room and approaches Elgin quietly. With his crystal earrings glinting in the fluorescent light, the sergeant nods, listens to the whispered words. And looks confused, more than a little distracted, when he's ultimately led away by two of the desk crew. It's the full moon, and Elgin, it seems, has unofficially begun his retirement. And kicked off what will be a night to remember for the rest of us.

As the squads roll out onto the street, our dispatcher is already doling out multiple assignments. Disturbances, fights, gangs congregating, shots fired— everyone's out and ready to fight.

Our first call is a disturbance with a taxi driver. The passenger is waiting on the sidewalk when we pull up. Pointing to the annoyed driver, whom he's refused to pay, the man instructs us to shoot him. It's

Saddam Hussein, he tells us, the bane of mankind. The butcher, the defiler of life.

"Don't let that fake taxi ID fool you, Officers. It's Saddam. Kill him now—do the world a favor."

He himself is an Israeli national, the man tells us proudly. That's why he can identify this wretched dog. And when he refuses to pay his cab fare, we arrest him for theft of services and take him to jail, where he can amuse himself with all the other wretched dogs.

Our next call is a woman who needs help. It's her implants, she tells us. They need to be activated. Her parents, long deceased, never told her how to do it.

Implants?

The woman points to her head. "My communications implants. I can't communicate unless they're activated."

"Communications, huh? Then what you want is the FCC—the Federal Communications Commission. They're federal, we're municipal."

"Oh, thank you, Officer! And how do I find them?"

"In the phone book under 'F.' "

En route to our next job—a disturbance in a tavern—we're flagged down by a frantic woman. A very *pregnant* woman who tells us her water broke, her pains are bad—please help her. But before we can call for an ambulance, she lies back on the hood of the squad, screaming and grunting. No time for our rubber gloves now, because the baby is out, pushed with such force it's a bloody projectile lobbed toward Diane. While we wait for the ambulance, a crowd gathers for the free show.

"What'd she have?" one woman inquires. It's a boy.

"What you gonna call it, girl?" another inquires.

The new mother ponders this question.

"I ain't thought about it," she says. "All I had was a girl's name—Croatia."

Croatia? Like the Balkan country?

"I don' know. I jus' heard it somewhere and liked it. Ain't it pretty?"

"Yeah, girl, that's real pretty!" the first woman beams. "Y'all go ahead, name your son 'Croatia.' "

A man is staring at the bloody mess smeared over the hood of the squad.

"That's sure gonna fuck up the finish!"

"Naw, it ain't," someone else says. "When my homey got shot, blood was all over his ride. We washed it, buffed it out, it's alright now."

"That's afterbirth!" a young woman says knowledgeably. "Back in the day, they used to feed that to the warriors. Said it gave 'em strength and power."

"Don't look at me," the man returns. "I was just on my way to pick up some rib tips."

When the ambulance arrives to transport mother and baby to the hospital, the crowd disperses.

Next, we're sent to take a report for a stolen car. The incensed owner is screaming.

"Just bought the damn thing!" he rages. "Ain't had it more than a week—now they stole it!"

"What kind of car is it, sir?"

"A Baloobium."

"A . . . what?"

"A Baloobium. Silver, black interior, pinstripes on the sides."

"Uh, who makes the Baloobium? Ford? Buick? Olds . . . ?"

"Hell, I forget now! You mean to tell me you ain't never seen a Baloobium?" He snorts at our obvious ignorance. "I see 'em all the time. A real popular car. Guess that's why mine got stolen."

We take the report for the missing Baloobium. The man has no vehicle ID number, no license plates yet. Nothing that will identify his car. He offers to look in the house for his paperwork, but doesn't remember exactly where he put it. Still, according to departmental procedure, we're required to send a flash message over the radio. This ought to be good.

"All units in Twelve, all units on citywide, we have a theft of the auto, an auto theft just occurred at 19— South Sangamon," I begin. "We're looking for a silver vehicle, two-door, black interior and pinstripes—"

"What's the make of the car?" the dispatcher asks.

"It's uh . . . a Baloobium."

"Oh, too bad."

"You've heard of it?"

"Sure. Baloobium. Nice ride. My brother-in-law's got one."

Diane and I look at each other. And at the victim, who's returning from his house with the bill of sale. The one that says he took delivery of a two-door, silver Chevy Lumina.

The assignments come faster as the craziness escalates. We handle a battery victim at a taco stand. The customer wanted two chicken tacos, no lettuce, extra sauce. The owner demanded payment first, but the customer refused.

"No money, no tacos!" the owner screamed and, to emphasize his point, leaped over the counter and bit his face.

At the "El" train station, a man's been electrocuted. While waiting on the platform, he accidentally dropped a dollar onto the tracks. Budget-conscious, the man decided to retrieve it. The CTA supervisor who's called to the scene is more than a little annoyed. His comments indicate that ours is not the only profession where a hardened demeanor is part of his game face.

"Shit! You realize how much paperwork I'm gonna have to do?" he huffs, barely glancing at the charred corpse. "I'll be tied up here for hours! I was supposed to play golf in the morning, too! *Damn*!"

Later, we escort the victim of a "heinous battery" to the hospital. *Heinous* because of the third-degree burns she suffered at the hands of her boyfriend. He'd come home drunk and, even though he found her asleep—alone—was certain she'd been cheating on him. He beat her, stripped her, tied her spread-eagle to the bed, and plugged in the iron, which he planted firmly in her crotch. And left it there while she screamed and he went out to have a few more drinks.

Leaving the hospital, we're waved over by another squad car, two guys who've just handled a burglary at a meatpacking house. They hold up their spoils of war: a hog's head, minus skin, but with every other feature, including bulging eyes, intact.

"Is this great or what?" they laugh.

"What are you gonna do with it?"

"What else? Plant it in the captain's personal car."

More assignments, more craziness. On every other job, it seems, we're arresting someone. The lockup always does a booming business during the full moon.

"Don't you two have anything better to do?" the harried lockup keeper asks us. "Read a book? Eat bonbons?"

In the station it's a circus, with the desk sergeant

serving as unwilling ringmaster. People are thronged around the desk, talking and crying. Asking about their boyfriend's bail, their husband's charges. Demanding to see the captain, a priest, the mayor.

An agitated man pushes through the crowd.

"It's my vents," he wails. "I keep getting rays through my vents. The toaster, too. It's going to infect me, Sergeant, and I can't stop it!"

Filling out a bond slip for another anxious customer, the desk sergeant doesn't bat an eye.

"You tried aluminum foil?"

"Yes, I did. Plastic garbage bags, too. But the rays keep coming. I've been getting messages, too, sometimes, from the microwave. That's where the biggest rays come from. Mercury's retrograde, you know." He lowers his voice confidentially, leans closer to the tired sergeant.

"Elvis is coming back tonight. The planets are in alignment. He's been hiding in an old smelting plant, just outside of Gary, waiting until the time was right. Tonight's the night."

"No kidding?"

"Only I'll never get to see it if these rays keep clogging my vents!"

"You need a debogulator," the sergeant says solemnly.

"A *debogulator*?"

"Sure. They sell 'em at any Computer City. Zap those rays before you know it."

"Oh, thank you, Sergeant!"

On his way out of the station, the beaming man nearly collides with Booker, who is gingerly escorting a ragged, and very rank-smelling woman. It's the Candy Lady, another legend who makes her appearances only during the full moon. She's a vagrant who resides under the warehouse docks of lower Wacker Drive. Come the full moon, she hits the streets, propelled by some inexplicable urge to present "gifts" to random friends, including the police district desk staff. Her gifts come in the form of homemade "fudge balls," made the old-fashioned way. The *most* old fashioned way you can think of.

After procuring some candy boxes from the candy outlet store (sometimes by unlawful entry, sometimes by picking through the Dumpsters outside), she heads for the bushes and step two of her production phase, which includes a patented method known as "grunt and push." Once her "raw material" has been produced, it's a simple matter to roll it into balls and line them up in the pretty paper boxes.

Sure enough, she offers her wares to the desk crew while Booker signs in the arrest log.

"With or without nuts?" one cop asks, from the safe distance of the fax machine. He's upwind, unable to tell if the "fudge balls" are freshly made.

"No nuts this time," she says. "I been tryin' to watch what I eat. Nuts give me a spastic colon."

Booker leads her away, making room for two laughing cops and their latest arrestee. They picked him up on Lake Street, where he'd been harassing the whores and their tricks. He told the police he's in plumbing supplies and was just doing some business advertising, passing out cards and flyers to the surprised couples.

"Do I dare ask?" The weary sergeant groans.

"Spit sinks for the boudoir," the arrestee tells him. "The wave of the future for your higher-priced hookers. Think about it. If they don't swallow, it's gotta go *somewhere*!"

Outside in the parking lot, the wagon guys are swinging open the squadrol doors. Inside is a hand-cuffed man with dreadlocks, what looks like a chain saw, and a very large poodle. This time, I don't even want to ask.

The dispatcher chortles over our next job.

"You got a wand waver, corner of 16th and Blue Island." Great. A "wand waver" is a naked man.

"A few people are calling on this one. They say he's been out there for quite a while, waving his magic wand. Might even be close to sprinkling his fairy dust by now."

The man is doing more than waving his wand. He's pulling it, stroking it, doing everything but baton-twirling with it. Standing naked as a newborn at the intersection, his eyes are closed and his body is rocking rhythmically to the beat of a different thumb.

At this point, fatigue makes us benevolent. The night's been crazy enough without having to deal with Lord Godiva. We tell him to put on his clothes and go home.

"No clothes." The man smiles without missing a beat. "The better to praise God's glory. Naked we're born, naked we shall stay!"

"Not if you live in a northern climate," Diane says. We're both amazed by this guy's *exuberance*.

"That's *got* to hurt!" She whispers to me.

"Or else he's the Callus King."

The man refuses to stop. In spite of our warnings, he continues working himself, beaming at his own magnificence. Rubber-gloves time again.

We cuff him, reluctantly, and haul him down to the station.

"Uncuff me, Officer. Please. I was almost finished.

Something you *must* see. You girls would never forget it. It's wonderful."

"Uh-huh. Capture the magic."

He's escorted, wand-first, toward the lockup.

"Now what?" The lockup keeper asks.

"A man who moves to his own beat."

At the end of the night, when we're heading for the parking lot, the lockup keeper catches up with us.

"Whatever you guys do, don't *ever* bring me another nut like that guy! He made everybody back there sick!"

"Wouldn't stop his one-man symphony, huh?"

"No, but that wasn't the bad part."

"He refused to put clothes on?"

"Yeah, but it's worse than that. We caught him with his head in the toilet, 'bobbing for apples'!"

20

Stars in Bars

Dispatcher:	Alright, folks, it's about that time to head in to the ol' corral. Everybody stand by for the new crew.
Unidentified Unit:	You gonna meet us at the joint later on?
Dispatcher:	Depends on who's buying.
Unidentified Unit:	Nobody's buying, but you never let that stop you before.
Dispatcher:	Ten-four. Well, pour the first beer. I'm on the way.

It might be a phenomenon peculiar to gunslingers. If we examine history over any given period of time, we find that sheriffs, and cops, and anyone assigned to uphold the law have always had a designated place of sanctuary, a place where they're shielded from the eyes of outsiders and surrounded by their own kind. In other words, a cop bar.

A place where the lights are low, the laughter loud, and the yeasty taste of foaming beer is the perfect antidote for a long day's work. Wyatt Earp rested his six-shooters in such a place, tossing back whiskey and war stories with Doc Holliday. Marshal Dillon tipped suds with his deputy at Miss Kitty's saloon. And cops today retreat to their designated ginmill, the one off the beaten path (read: off the *civilian* path) where they can relax, regroup, and know that here, at least, is one place where everyone is the same.

A true cop bar is not the same as a bar *frequented* by cops. The latter is a place to hang out with the cop groupies, allow admiring citizens to buy drinks and, in general, mingle with folks who are mesmerized by the cop "mystique." Everyone wants to talk to cops: whether for instructions on how to beat a speeding ticket, or to pry for gory details of the latest crime, or simply to hang on the many war stories cops will spin at the drop of a drink. Cops are the last gunslingers, the knights who ride tirelessly into the fray, the last line that separates order from chaos. And, for the price of a beer, they're also great storytellers who spin tales that grow more amazing, more incredible with each telling.

A cop bar, on the other hand, is for cops only. It's not a fancy place—in fact, it would have to go some to be considered a *joint*. Most times, it's a nondescript building, often without windows or signs, that only the sworn brotherhood knows about. A place that might be accessible only through the rear door off an obscure alley. Once inside, you move into a murky, no-frills interior of a bar that features nothing fancier than shots and beers. There will be no designer water here, no wimpy hanging plants, and no pastel bottles with labels you can't pronounce. Instead, there's ordinary liquor served in ordinary glasses to ordinary men and women who just happen to be called upon to perform an extraordinary job.

This is the place to hang out, socialize, commiserate, lick wounds, or merely sit in companionable silence. War stories abound, as well as the latest jokes, department gossip, sports news, vacation chatter—

anything that spells downtime. There are no groupies here, nobody teetering on pedestals someone else
placed us on. Just a joint where you can be yourself,
with your friends, without judgment.

In my district, cops congregate at the Siren, a
joint in Greektown, obscured from the public eye by
a bland brick facade and an alley entrance. Inside,
the long stretch of oak bar is stained and scarred by
countless cops over several decades. The only decoration is stretched on the wall behind the bar—a
faded mural of a siren from Greek mythology, lur-
ing ancient sailors with her deadly song. Over the
years, bar patrons have lobbed pieces of melted sa-
ganaki at the siren, hitting her in various parts of her
breasts. The fossilized cheese still clings there like
lumpy melanoma, which prompted a female sergeant to place a donation box for breast-cancer research directly underneath. Since then, substantial
donations have been made to the American Cancer
Foundation thanks to cops willing to "toss some
cheese for a cure."

At the Siren, the television is usually flickering in
the corner, but nobody pays much attention. It's the
conversation that's the main event here. There's no
guy talk, or girl's chatter—just cop stuff that's shared
by all.

On one particular night, the wagon men, Phillips
and Baskin, are slouched on stools at the far end,
matching our dispatcher beer for beer. The conversation is heated and earnest. Michael Jordan will
never retire, states Baskin. Phillips disagrees, and
Baskin growls louder, citing games and stats and
soaring displays of skill reserved for the superhu-
man. The dispatcher sides with Baskin, and the debate rages on.

Some of the older vets are scattered around the smaller tables, discussing the police contract now mired in arbitration.

"I don't think we're getting anything this time," LeFevre announces, squinting around his beer glass. "I think those union reps might sell us down the river."

"Ain't like the old days," Cleary says. With over twenty-eight years on the job, he's one of the most seasoned vets in the Siren tonight.

"In the old days we didn't have a union or a contract," Phillips tosses in.

A few stools away, the field lieutenant's eyes are glued to the TV screen as he sips his bourbon. Right now, department politics don't interest him as much as his immediate agenda. They're about to announce the evening's lottery numbers, and he's got his tickets ready. Maybe this time he'll hit it.

Two rookies new to the district perch nervously at the other end, already aware of the pecking order of district seniority. They'd like nothing better than to bend elbows with the guys, add their opinions to the current conversation. But that won't happen until an invitation is issued from the "old salts." And when it comes, a nod from LeFevre and two foaming glasses pushed toward them, they bound over like grateful puppies. Young pups eager to hear the stories of the old dogs.

Diane and I are lounging at a corner table with a few other members of our watch, glad to relax after a hectic night. Our first call of the watch had been a "tender-age" missing child—a five-year-old boy who vanished from his backyard. When the parents went to work, he'd been left in the care of an older sister, who didn't remember the last time she checked on him, only that she'd fallen asleep. It was determined the boy had been missing nearly twelve hours—and it was well past dark when the police arrived. Twelve critical hours in which anything could have happened. A canvas of the neighbors, the familiar places the boy frequented, proved fruitless. In the face of the mother's hysteria, we had to fight for every scrap of professional composure. No one wanted to extinguish that faint spark of hope in her panicked eyes. But we were torn, felt that dizzy helplessness that comes when you know, from instinct or past experience, that it might be too late. There might not be anything you or anyone can do to help.

Flash messages about the missing boy were broadcast citywide, and all available district manpower was assigned to conduct a street-by-street search. Four grueling hours later, Diane and I found him, hungry, cold, but unhurt. He was in a laundromat, a place he'd wandered into because of the candy machine. He was starving, he told us, and a candy bar was better than nothing. Especially the chocolate with almonds—his favorite.

When the boy was returned to his parents, it was all either of us could do not to cry. This time, it was a happy ending. Something we don't get to witness nearly as often as we should.

So now, at the Siren, I let cold drinks and warm friends replace the fear that haunted us tonight. Push it out of my mind, the way cops are supposed to, and leave the job at the station.

"So what's up with the promotion list?" Hauser asks. Like all of us, he has taken the Sergeant Exam. It's a promotional test that's given every four or five years, and one that's always fraught with controversy. Before the ink is dry on the tests, the media is usually lambasting the department, citing unfair testing practices and discriminatory promotional policies. While it's true that cronyism, nepotism, and all those other boys' clubisms play a distinct role in promotion, there's not much recourse patrol cops have other than to continue to take the tests and keep on hoping. Since the latest Sergeant Exam results are already tied up in a class-action lawsuit, none of us are optimistic.

"Think of the money you'll save, not having to buy white shirts," Baskin chuckles from the bar. He's referring to the color distinction between supervisors and their blue-shirted subordinates.

"Hey, Loo," Hauser shouts to the quiet lieutenant. "Who'd you know when you made rank?"

"My wife. She used to be a drill sergeant in the army and told my bosses she'd kick all their asses if I didn't get promoted."

"*That's* a thought," Hauser grins. "My old lady sells cosmetics. Think that'll carry any weight?"

"Who says being a sergeant is so great anyway?" asks LeFevre. "Those guys are just middle management with all the same headaches. Me, I'd rather be a dick."

"You're *already* a dick!" Cleary chortles.

"Yeah, smartass. But those guys in the Detective Division make a bundle. More overtime than you can shake a stick at. All that court time—the *comp* time—what a sweet setup!"

"Who wants to look at dead bodies all the time?" Phillips, the wagon man, inquires. "Those guys that work in Violent Crimes, that's all they see."

"Violent Crimes ain't the only thing dicks work. What about Major Accidents? Those guys are dicks, too. Or Property Crimes." Cleary sucks the suds off a fresh glass and nods. "Now, that might be something to think about. A nice little gig in Property Crimes. Investigate some lady's missing necklace, a stolen computer or something, write the report, call it a day. Nice and neat. No blood, no gore, big money. I could handle that."

"So how come you never took the dick's test?" one of the rookies inquires boldly. Cleary spares him a narrowed look.

"Same reason I ain't wearing sergeant's chevrons, kid. Cuz I ain't related, I ain't dropping money, and my Chinaman's dead."

The conversations spin off in separate directions again.

"What about Youth Officers?" the rookie asks. "They're on the same pay scale as detectives, right? It's not that hard to get in there, is it?"

Diane shoots me a look that speaks volumes. Both of us took the Youth Officer Exam, both were offered the positions. And, after considering the higher salary grade, the better hours, the relative safety compared to our current jobs, we made our decisions. There was no way we could work with kids. We saw enough in what we did, the heartbreak and abuse and shattered lives. Youth Officers lived it, breathed it, were tied up in court arguing over it on a daily basis. I couldn't stand the constant parade of broken kids, or the nightmares, and my partner felt the same.

"It isn't easy, working with kids." Kilpatrick, who's been nursing a beer in the corner, steps over to our table. "Had a partner, a few years back, that transferred over to the Youth Division. Figured the hours were better, he'd be in plainclothes, nice neat job, and he liked kids. How bad could it be? Until maybe three, four months into the job."

Pulling up a chair, he settles near the rookie and warms to his story.

"See, Sammy—that was his name—he always liked kids. Had a son that got killed by a hit-and-run when he was around ten or eleven. After that, Sam was never the same. His only kid, y'know? Guess he figured, if he worked with them, that would be like getting a little piece of his own boy back. But it didn't turn out like that."

There's absolute silence in the bar as Kilpatrick continues. Some of the guys remember Sam, know where the story is heading. Curiosity is enough to keep the rest of us quiet.

"So Sam gets out there, starts working with the kids. Makes the rounds at Juvie Hall, seeing the kids who were locked up, maybe wards of the state because their parents signed over custody. Started spending a lot of time there, getting to know the kids. And couldn't figure out how their parents could throw them away—just give them to somebody else. It started eating at him.

"Then, he'd be called out on the bad cases . . . the child neglect, the bad abuse cases, the criminal abandonments, and I think it started working on his mind. Affected his judgment, you might say. In fact, he had a case once where three little girls—I guess they were between six and ten years old—had been left alone by their mother for a few days. No food, no heat . . . and the place they lived was a flophouse—filled with transients, drug addicts, you name it. The good part was that, although they were alone and hungry, these girls weren't molested or hurt. Which is something, when you think about what could have happened.

"So Sam brings the girls to the Youth Office, gets

all this food for them, warm clothes, warm blankets, everything they could want. And while he's waiting for the DCFS caseworker to show up, who should come waltzing in but the girls' mother? And she's demanding that Sam release her girls, shouting that he has no right . . . and Sam goes off."

Kilpatrick drains his glass and looks at the rookie somberly.

"That's all it took to push him over the edge. He jumped up out of the chair, shoved the woman out of the office so the girls couldn't hear, and might have slapped the shit out of her if the desk sergeant hadn't intervened. She filed charges, of course, and Sam was suspended pending Internal Affairs' investigation."

Another silence, humming louder this time, until the rookie dares to ask.

"So whatever happened to him?"

"He ate his muzzle," Kilpatrick says quietly. "Suspended, facing battery charges, 'conduct unbecoming an officer,' and whatever else they tacked on . . . and he couldn't understand it. Thought he was just doing his job. Just looking out for the kids. Maybe figured if he couldn't do that, there wasn't much else he could do. So he waited 'til his wife went to work one morning and . . . that was that."

"And no departmental funeral," Cleary tosses in gruffly. His face is stony but his eyes are glittering fiercely. "Didn't even get the respect he deserved. Maybe he got a little confused there, but, hell, don't we all sometimes? He was a good man. A damn fine man!"

"Say that again!" the lieutenant says, and raises his bourbon. "A hell of a man!"

More glasses are raised, and toasts are drunk to Sam, and to the untold others like him. Those who muddle along like the rest of us, trying to do the right thing.

Diane's eyes are suspiciously bright, and she ducks her head lower.

"Thought we came in here to relax!" she mutters to me irritably. "Didn't we deal with enough tonight?"

"Just another day at the office!" Hauser tells her. "All in a day's work, right?" His cynical smile doesn't begin to mask what's in his eyes, but this is one place where it doesn't matter. But the rookies stare at him, wondering about his cavalier attitude in the wake of Sam's story. *Game face* again. Hauser knows they're too green right now to understand it. That they're cops, like we are, and they have to learn. So, with a broad wink to the silent rookies, he swaggers over to Baskin, throws a friendly arm over his shoulder, and says, "My money's with you, man. I don't think Jordan will *ever* retire!"

21

COP-ulation

1237:	1237.
Dispatcher:	'37 coming in?
1237:	Yeah, Squad. We're clear from this job, and we'd like to request a "personal" at Cermak and Racine.
Dispatcher:	'37, aren't you working with that new little blonde rookie tonight?
1237:	All night long, Squad.
Dispatcher:	Then just make sure you don't make it *too* personal!

It's one of the questions cops are asked the most. Usually, right after the old standard, "Did you ever kill anyone?" comes the query everyone wants to know about: "What's the real deal with cops and sex?"

Thanks to an onslaught of cop novels, shows, and movies that glamorize this job, which make it seem that sexual activity ranks as our primary aerobic exercise, the public has an insatiable curiosity about our private lives. Maybe people believe there's a certain type of glamour there that might, by association, rub off on them. Or perhaps it's another residual from the "gunslinger" mystique. We carry weapons, we symbolize power, and, for many people, power equates to sexual attraction, which, combined with the glamour fantasy, packs a potent wallop. Suddenly, men or women who would be considered merely average in any other circumstances are, by virtue of their profession, *sexual* gunslingers as well, imbued with all the magnetism and prowess and raw carnal charisma that fuels thousands of civilian fantasies.

It's an absurd notion, when you think about it. Outfitting people with a uniform and a gun belt does *not* make them sexual athletes, or add to their repertoire of intimate "techniques." Wearing a badge does not increase sensuality, sensitivity, or include a foolproof formula for giving—or experiencing—multiple orgasms. The reality is that we're the same people in different clothes. But, as with most fantasies, reality has little to do with it. It's that romanticized notion of power, authority as an erotic trigger that keeps the public wondering, and asking.

Do cops make better lovers? The question to be addressed is, rather, are cops provided the opportunity to be more *frequent* lovers? Thanks to a curious public steeped in erotic fantasies, the answer is yes.

Sex is out there, literally in our faces, every day we hit the streets. It's not just the cop groupies, both male and female, who are legion. The public we serve provides us ample sexual opportunities during the course of an average day. For example, the police are called for a common complaint—perhaps "disturbance with a neighbor." They arrive, settle the dispute, and prepare to leave. The woman who called might linger near the squad car, expressing her thanks, her anxiety over the possibility of another dispute. And touches the officer's arm, squeezes his hand, maybe licks her lips while her eyes convey the unmistakable signals. The offer's been made—but whether or not that officer acts on it is his personal choice.

Other women or men might receive service from the police, note their names or badge numbers and, at a later time, call 911 to request that specific officer. When Diane and I became partners, there were a lot of callers who said simply, "Send the redhead and the blonde." As though we worked for the Chicago Police Escort Service and were the flavors of the day. And when we responded to those calls, there was no specific police service required—only another fervent proposition, however thinly disguised. Does that make us—any of us in uniform—more desirable? No. What it *does* is reduce us to objects. Forget the person behind the blue. A cop becomes a piece of ass in uniform, another notch on the sexual bedpost, distinguished by a badge.

It's not unheard of for male cops to walk into a job and find the female caller wearing nothing more than a smile. Or for citizens to express their "gratitude" for service by offering cops more "personalized" thanks. Some simply want to satisfy the curiosity of, as one woman explained to me, "what it feels like to go to bed with a man who drops his gun belt along with his pants."

When it comes to the more overt displays of sexual interest, cop groupies may be the masters. Cop-stalking campaigns are planned with the same skillful strategy as a general outlining his next battle. Cop groupies know which bars are frequented by certain cops, what their work schedules are, when they'll participate in an interdepartmental softball game or bowling tournament. A district barbecue? The groupies are there, lingering on the fringes. Interested, available, and waiting to be selected. A department wake or funeral? The bar closest to the funeral home is targeted and staked out, waiting for the lines of grieving uniforms who will surely stride through the doors in search of a stiff drink and some soft comfort.

Many cop groupies have no agenda other than to bag a cop. For them it's not about the person as an individual. Cops are viewed as symbols—sexy, glamorous, powerful, and, in their eyes, a trophy fuck. Like an airline pilot, a doctor, anyone in an occupation that, in the groupie's estimation, spells prestige.

One groupie, a regular at the district bars for most of my career, once explained what cop sex meant to her. It wasn't that the act itself was extraordinary, or the performance above and beyond others she'd experienced. It was simply the thrill. One look at the uniform, and she saw power. Danger when she looked at his service weapon. Authority and control and cocky confidence that, in a civilian male, might be construed as chauvinistic grandstanding; but in a cop, it was part of the package. Something about touching the untouchable that gave the experience a deliciously dangerous edge. A walk on the wild side so intoxicating, she was hooked. The *fantasy*—more than the reality—is what sustains her and the others like her who believe police are equivalent to gritty glamour and hot sex.

From a logical standpoint, cops may be one of the *least* likely professional groups to hoist on that sexual pedestal. A street cop's life is about negotiating life and death in the criminal fast lane, which leaves him teetering in precarious balance between stress and exhaustion. Shoot-outs, ambushes, and knockdown drag-outs with crazed felons may *look* glamorous on television, but in real life, it takes a heavy toll. Add to that the sleep that's forfeited for endless court appearances, rotating shifts, extra assignments, and you've got one exhausted cop . . . not the best candidate for sexual superstardom. But for the groupie, he's a prestigious notch, and for the cop who decides to partake in what's offered, it's a warm body in a cold landscape, and a reasonable way to relieve the stress.

Sounds cold, right? A jaundiced way of looking at what's supposed to be the ultimate form of interaction? Maybe, but that's the way some cops look at it. It's another symptom of that learned defense, the one that teaches you to bury any feelings that might sell you out. Emotional distance means you can get through almost anything reasonably intact. As your time on the job increases, you become more remote, more adept at masking feelings. Which is frustrating for cops' spouses and significant others who still expect a show of feelings, who don't understand the isolation that now encloses this person they love. It's hell on marriages—on any relationship, which would account for the soaring divorce rate among police. It takes a special person to understand a cop, and a cop's life—something we can't reasonably expect if we don't always understand ourselves.

How does a cop explain to his spouse or lover that other feelings have taken precedence now? That it's not about hearts and flowers, sentiment and shared feelings anymore, when each day, you wake up with the knowledge that (in the most basic street expression), "Some days you eat the bear, some days the bear eats you." And you're never sure, going out, which day it'll be for you, if you're going to make it back in one piece, or at all. But you'd go crazy if you processed that on a conscious level, that awareness and fear and fatalistic expectation, so you don't. You bury it, along with all the other feelings, and slap on your game face and go out there and get on with it. If you don't think about it, you won't feel it, not now, anyway. But it's still a source of anxiety, simmering just below the surface. And it's also an emotional trump card to be pulled out to justify buying into the cop/sex game.

For some cops, it becomes simpler to take the easy way. No commitments, no long-term attachments, just a little "slap-and-tickle" with the closest available body who doesn't care what's in your head, only what's in your pants, as long as you're wearing regulation police blue. What one cop referred to as "hips that pass in the night." The opportunities and assortment of available partners seem endless, and don't require anything more than a few standard lines, the price of a few drinks.

Cops learn, from that first day in the Training Academy and throughout their careers, that sex is a viable form of currency. It's there within the department and at all levels of job performance. Veteran cops regale eager recruits with countless stories of sex in uniform. The watch parties that are modern-day bacchanals of limitless booze and willing women. Sex on the streets, sex in the squad rooms, sex anywhere, anytime, because you're a cop, and it comes with the territory. So it's understandable that some cops buy into the fantasy as well. Why shouldn't they take advantage of something that's offered so freely? And they ask how cop sex is any different that sex in the boardroom, or sex in the political arena. Anytime it's available, and prevalent, there's going to be takers. In police circles, you learn early that it's very prevalent, there for the taking, providing ample opportunity to serve, protect, and *partake*. As one twenty-five-year veteran observed, "As soon as I put on the uniform, it was like somebody gave me a 'Get All the Free Pussy You Want' pass. And in twenty-five years, that never changed. I was the one to change . . . I just got tired."

Many people question the morality of cops. The term needs to be defined first—hard to do since, for most cops, one year on the street is all it takes to alter your views of what's right, what's *moral*. In a cop's world, there are no absolutes of right and wrong, no clear-cut black-and-white choices which guide our actions. After a while, it all bleeds together, and eventually it's gut feeling and instinct that determines what we do. Whatever works, with the least amount of harm incurred, is the path most usually taken.

For cops who witness the tragedies, the foibles, and the fall-out of man as a rational creature, who view the victims and the carnage and the absolute capriciousness of a life that can and does end at any time, we know that the only thing we can count on is this moment. This day is all we have, so we live it, and keep going, without apology. And with that perspective, who's going to sweat a random liaison now and then? Yes, there are innumerable groupies and other cop fans who offer themselves freely. Gratuitous sex? Absolutely. And a lot of cops take full advantage of it, feel it's their just due for the trade-offs we make. And have no problem justifying their behavior to themselves, or anyone else.

But there are others who feel it's small compensation for the lifestyle thrust upon us. They're not trying to justify anything. They know it's less about hot sex with a willing, if nameless, partner than just another form of escapism.

One of my male partners once explained, "It was one of those nights. I handled a homicide at the beginning that took me through the watch and into overtime. Innocent victim of a drive-by shooting. But she didn't die right away, and I was at the hospital with the whole family, watching them watch her die, feeling them look at me like I was scum because I couldn't stop it. Made me feel worthless.

"After that, I could have gone to the joint and drunk myself shitfaced. But then the old lady would start in on me when I got home. This particular girl happened to be in my face, and I took her up on it. There was no problem. And no bad hangover afterward, and cheaper than an all-night poker game."

Sex as a stress reducer is as common for some cops as sex to relieve boredom, sex to dispel anger, sex because it's there. Sex as a tool to facilitate release. Sex for any imaginable reason *except* as a way of developing intimacy. In lieu of "getting in touch" with feelings, the idea is just to touch, briefly, some body, without feeling anything but temporary respite, fleeting relief.

Just as some people don't view cops as sexual icons, there are plenty of cops who wouldn't look twice at a cop groupie, would never consider casual sex as a perk of the job. Not all of us are out there playing "grab-ass" with the closest warm body. Some cops are capable of maintaining some level of intimacy, remaining emotionally intact. It's not easy, but it can be done. These cops have good marriages and committed relationships. For them, there's no enticement in the prospect of a quick tryst. The point is that, in a cop's world, it's all about choices. Sex is there, if you want it. But whatever your decision, no one passes judgment, and no one's keeping score.

The other question everyone wants to know about is sex among the ranks. Ever since women have joined the force, taking their place alongside the boys in blue, the debate over female cops as glorified groupies, or "bimbos with badges" continues.

In the mid-seventies, when female officers were first allowed in the Patrol Division of the Chicago Police, a huge controversy erupted. Cops' wives were up in arms, demanding that the "man-stealing bimbos" be kept away from their husbands. Meetings and demonstrations were held, both at Police Headquarters and the Training Academy by militant wives willing to do whatever it took to preserve their men from harm's way, which, in this case, was a female partner. They signed petitions and marched on City Hall. The message they carried was simple: Women had no business working with their husbands. As females, they alleged, we were clearly unable to perform adequately as police, thereby endangering our partners. We were too emotional to handle the reality of the street, and would be incapable of acting in a stressful situation. And the most important issue of all, we had no business spending eight long hours with a man—their man—in the close quarters of a squad car. It was too much temptation, and there were bound to be disastrous results.

In the interest of maintaining some level of domestic tranquillity, the department allowed its male members to refuse a female partner—at first. All it took was a wife's angry phone call to the watch commander, and her husband could count on a male/male partnership. But it was a patronizing gesture, one that couldn't last. Women were joining the force in larger numbers, making gender exclusivity in assigning partners impossible, and impractical.

The old boys' club attitudes were still in full swing. They condescended to women, believed they couldn't perform as well, or at all, and held tight to the conviction that a woman in uniform meant a badge bunny who'd found a way to stalk cops—*and* get a paycheck. It took decades of experience before those attitudes began to change; they still exist among the older veterans. But since female cops are here to stay, then sex among the ranks will remain another hot topic.

I can tell you that cops, like professionals in any other workplace, date each other, have relationships that develop through shared experiences and common interest. Cops understand other cops, the lives we lead, the isolation that comes with the turf. Since a fellow cop is already part of the inner "us against them" circle to which we all eventually withdraw, he or she is a likely candidate for a relationship, either platonic or sexual.

Sex in the police workplace is as common as any other professional environment, and exists for as many different reasons. Anytime men and women come together, chemistry and the laws of nature dictate that it's inevitable, at some point, for some people to become involved. Which would make cops no different than anyone else who ever fell in lust, or gave in to fleeting temptation, or merely wanted to scratch a libidinous "itch."

But there's another side to sex among the ranks that has nothing to do with relationships or dating, or significant others, and it happens more than anyone can guess. But not necessarily for the reasons one would expect.

It starts out at the Academy. Anxious recruits are grouped together, forced to undergo a training regimen so mentally stressful, so physically taxing, that no one's ever certain they'll make it to graduation day. It's that "shared trauma" that bonds everybody— male and female—together. These people become your partners, your friends, your brothers and sisters, for whom you would (and someday, on the street, may have to) lay down your life. Friendship breeds affection which, sometimes, breeds more. Academy sex is not about promises and future dreams shared. It's an outlet and an exercise, and maybe a desperate grab for emotional salvation. As a recruit, you're a faceless grunt, expected to jump through hoops and perform on command. Sex becomes the release valve that vents that pressure, affirms that each "grunt" is a desirable, feeling person capable of physical bonding.

Through the course of your training, you hear the sex stories, the erotic escapades that never end. You watch some instructors select their "recruit du jour" from each new class, hear the comments and invitations from other instructors and veteran cops who troll the Academy for fresh young bodies. Sex is out there, all around you. And, like anything that's been overexposed, it loses its significance, becomes diminished. Eventually, you're not surprised, or shocked, by anything you hear or see. Sex with an instructor? What else is new? A random sampling of the bodies congregating in the men's shower room? Yawn.

You learn early that anything is possible, and nobody really cares who's doing what with whom. Your only performance that cops are concerned with is on the street, in the line of fire. Anything else is your own business. Your behavior, and how you choose to comport yourself, are guided solely by your personal beliefs. The decision to be a willing participant or a jaded observer is up to the individual. And by the time you make it through the Academy and out to the streets, you're well prepared for what comes next.

As a new rookie, or even a veteran cop transferring in to a new district, you're paired with a variety of partners, many of whom will be men, some who will inquire about your sex life, your availability, your willingness. Some guys are interested; others do it as a way to pass the time. Part of the unwritten boys' club rules of interaction with the new female partner. It's something you learn to expect, and to deal with.

When, as a patrol officer, you're finally assigned a permanent partner, a new type of relationship develops. He becomes your responsibility. Trust is the critical issue here, since both of your lives depend on it. This is the person who watches your back, is alongside you through it all—fights and shootings, ambushes and car chases. You learn each other's strengths and weaknesses, behavior patterns, personality characteristics. Just like a marriage, you say? It's *exactly* like a marriage—only more so.

You're with your partner eight hours a day, eight hours of being alert and watchful and absolutely ready for the unknown. And since the average beat cop experiences long periods of calm between the action, there's a lot of time to talk, and to listen. It's just a way to pass the time, but you learn more about your partner, his thoughts and observations, than even his wife might know. That's because you're a cop, too—and you understand what civilians can't. You cover his ass, keep him safe, prop him up, and make sure he knows he's somebody special. Because he *is* special—a regular guy in a Superman suit who protects you and the public, tries to do what's right, and brings home a paycheck to the wife and kids. Something you understand, since you're doing the same. And so he feels safe sharing with you those feelings he puts under wraps as soon as he gets home.

You learn about his family life. You know about his son's Little League championship and his daughter's struggle with algebra. You also hear the wife stories. Her plans to redecorate the family room, her bitchy excursions to PMS every month, how she complains when, on his two precious days off, all he wants to do is relax at home.

You learn enough about each other to fortify your friendship, develop a bond that's hard to describe. You face life and death together, and all that comes between, counting on this one person to bring you back alive. A heavy responsibility and, for some, an open door to the next level of intimacy.

It's been my observation that, for the majority of male-female partnerships I've witnessed in my career, it never progresses farther than friends. Your partner is like family, a relationship you value without violating. But with as many different value systems as cops out here, there are always those who chose to expand the relationship. Sex with your partner? Not usually. But it can happen. Or, if not your partner, then it might be someone on your watch, or your supervisor. Someone who's been there alongside you in the fray.

It might be just something else to do after a beer at the end of your tour of duty, a way of extending the cop camaraderie. And it might be the only thing that will get you through a harrowing night.

The lives cops lead are full of violence, deadly bursts of tension and danger that explode without warning. You witness a homicide—or are involved in one. Or you step out of the squad on your way to a call, and sniper fire takes out your windshield, your vehicle door—bringing the specter of death closer than you ever dreamed. You're involved in a fight in which your gun is wrestled away, which may now be used by your drug-fueled combatant to blow your brains out. In each scenario, you make it out alive, but not intact. Once again, you've faced down the demons, watched your mortality flicker and ebb, and lived to tell about it. But whom do you tell?

Can someone who's never been there understand the fear, the way the air presses out of your lungs when you realize this may be your last breath? Or the improbable thoughts that race through your brain as you stare at a gun bore aimed at your face? Who would know that feeling, and the draining weakness afterward, except someone who's been there? You need to reach out, connect, make sure you're still alive, that this circle of fear in which you reside is populated by others. You need the comfort, and reassurance that comes only from a fellow survivor. And because the job has taught you that all that exists is this special moment in time, you take your comfort where you can. Sex can be a powerful healer, and it's your *soul* that needs it now. When that happens, there are no strings or expectations, no emotional drapery to disguise the basic need. You've just traversed a deadly terrain. All you want now is to warm yourself at a friendly fire.

Stress-related sex can be the most comforting, and the least understood. You're coupled with someone in what's defined as the most intimate way, except that what preceded this act was more intimate than anything physical could ever be. You faced death together, and resumed your lives, an experience that few people ever share. You brought each other through that darkness, left part of yourselves behind, and celebrate what remains.

It's not about violating each other's marriages or relationships, usurping commitments, or expecting promises and picket-fenced cottages in the future. And for those who read this and are now convinced that female cops are cop groupies or husband stealers, here's something to consider.

Female cops work in what has historically been a man's domain. We're expected to perform what's considered a man's work without exhibiting any emotions or behavior thought to be "feminine." We witness our male counterparts develop the skills and defense mechanisms that will allow them to perform the job and ensure their survival. We see the game faces that hide unshed tears, the anger and frustration that translate to swaggering bravado. The groupie sex that's used as a bandage to hide deeper emotional wounds.

And somewhere along the way, by necessity, we develop some "male-oriented" characteristics of our own. In this job, where the weak are destroyed and detachment is necessary to protect the shreds that once were our hearts, we learn the man's way to survive. One of those ways is to take the comfort we need at the time that we need it, fully cognizant that it's only a moment in time, from which we move on.

Life on the street is a frenzied pace that requires all of our focus. There can be no looking back, no time for rumination, only the hope that in each moment, we do what's "right." A word for which, in our world, there is no clear definition or explanation.

Just like morals. Just like sex.

22

Trick or Treat, Fuck My Feet

Dispatcher: Attention all units in the Twelfth District and units on citywide. Be advised that Operation Angel is now in effect, vicinity of Madison and Bishop streets, at 1300 hours. Civilian-dress officers are on the scene. All marked units are advised to avoid that location and use caution. The time is now 1301 hours. This is Zone 13 radio in the Twelfth District.

Operation Angel. That's the prostitution sting that uses cops as decoy hookers. Every few months, the tactical lieutenant gets a brainstorm, decides it's time to do a sweep. West Madison Street, one of the most active whores' promenades in the city, is the perfect place to do it.

Locking up the hookers is one way to make a sweep, but that doesn't happen often. The Twelfth District doesn't have a woman's lockup, so the prisoners have to be trucked downtown via squadrol to Women's Central Detention. That ties up a squadrol for at least forty-five minutes, and the whores always bond out the next morning. So what's the point?

So when the tactical lieutenant decides his arrest stats might need a boost, make his unit look good on paper, it's time for Operation Angel. Trick out some cops (male and female) in trashy clothes to look like streetwalkers, put them out on the whores' stroll, and grab whatever prospective customer takes the bait. This time, it's the johns we'll be locking up, enough arrests to fill up the men's misdemeanor court docket and assure the department brass that we're doing our job.

Entrapment, you say? Sure it is. But the bosses justify it by the "criteria" that has to be met before the poor slob's arrested. For example, he doesn't drive up, ask, "Yo, baby, how much?" and then get dragged off in handcuffs, kicking and screaming. He's got to name a specific sexual act, and a price (i.e., "How 'bout a blowjob for twenty bucks?") Technically, it doesn't even have to be a sexual act, but if it provides the customer sexual gratification, it still counts. The definitions get very blurred here, but as long as the arrests are made, the lieutenant's happy, the watch commander's happy, the almighty district commander is satisfied that, according to statistics, he's got a district full of diligent, hardworking cops. And nobody would have it any other way. Why piss off the bosses? Shit rolls downhill.

It's Halloween, and here I am, Whore for a Day, out on the corner to target the lunchtime crowd: the truck drivers, factory workers, and passing tradesmen who might stop for a quickie.

It's freezing on this corner. Not surprising, since November starts tomorrow, so why am I out here in a flimsy chamois halter top and shorts so tight anyone on the street can read my lips? The tactical guys tell me it's the halter that'll do the trick. Just two small triangles of chamois, held together in front by a single buckskin thong. The chamois is like a second skin, thin enough to clearly outline my semifrozen nipples poking against the fabric like fingers desperate to claw their way out. Nothing is concealed in this getup. No weapon, no wire, nothing but what God gave me, give or take a few thousand goose bumps.

It's the shoes that kill me. You can't be a whore without ankle-strap heels, a notion that must be in the secret codebook of the street sisterhood. I'm wearing ankle-straps, flaming red ones with four-inch heels. Dr. Scholl would spin in his grave. It's hard to stand in them—much less walk—but then, whores aren't supposed to spend a lot of time on their feet. Not if they're any good.

I'm positioned on a corner with my lookout posted down the block. He's dressed as a telephone repairman, complete with utility belt, hard hat, and a metal lunch pail that holds the radio he'll use to call for my backup: four tactical officers in two un-marked cars who will swoop in on command to grab the john. My lookout is lounging on the stairs of a brownstone two-flat pretending to read the paper, and watching for my signal. Once the john's said enough to incriminate himself, I'll pat my hair and play with my left earring.

Mincing around on the sooty corner, I curse my shoes, the blustery wind, and the gaudy makeup I've spackled on for a "professional look." I wonder who originally thought up this whole operation. There must be a better way. Something that would be a lot more comfortable, like taking one of the squadrols and turning it into a pimpmobile. Remove all the po-lice decals, add heart-shaped windows and coach lights, paint it an appropriate color like hot pink or gold. Toss a mattress in the back, maybe a fake-fur throw, add a couple of decoy prostitutes, and drive over to one of the factories where the guys can't get away for lunch. Talk about curb service! You could make the same number of arrests in the comfort of your own wagon. Then I'd *really* be a wagon ho! And the operation could be renamed, something catchy, like "Meals on Wheels!" An idea with definite potential. I'll have to mention it to the tact lieutenant—if I live through these shoes.

A tan Dodge slows down so the driver can peer out. And then angles closer to the curb where I'm flaunting my goods.

"How much?" The graying man in the corduroy jacket is Average Joe Citizen. The scoutmaster out for a quart of milk and loaf of bread.

I sashay over and lean into the window, fully aware that if my buckskin thong snaps, he could get a concussion from the avalanche.

"What's your pleasure, sugar?" I remember to lick my lips invitingly. This guy smells like Doublemint and onions.

"Whattaya usually charge? I don't have too much money."

"What would you like?" I heave my chest in invitation. Or maybe it's the onset of double pneumonia.

His eyes shift to the rearview mirror. No cops around, no cars behind him. It must be okay.

"How 'bout a blowjob? Five bucks?"

Bingo! I signal, smile, and then step back, waiting for the cavalry. As they lead him off, I run one hand over my hip.

"You insulted me!" I scold him. "Only five bucks? What kind of cheap whore do you take me for?"

"I *love* leather!" The man in the yellow LeSabre inhales deeply. "Love the smell, love the feel. Love to bite it off your beautiful body."

"And how much would you love to pay?" I notice that this man is seriously into color coordination. Yellow car, yellow polo shirt, yellow car freshener. I wonder if his condom colors have been chosen accordingly.

The man's glazed eyes never make it past my collarbones.

"Depends. Do you do parties?"

"I might," I purr—hard to do when you're freezing.

"That's great, cuz I got these two girls working for me—you'd fit right in. See. . . ." He whips out his wallet, stretches out an accordioned plastic strip of pictures. "That is Dawn, and that's Stacey. The rottweiler's name is Ramrod, a real sweetheart! You like dogs?"

Two-or four-legged?

"A girl like you can make a lot of money. And this is a real sweet setup I got. The girls are dolls, the dog's *real* friendly. . . . I tell ya, instant cash flow!"

I examine the pictures. Stacey is nude, save for a studded dog collar. Dawn is more formal in birthday suit and leather boots. The pictures leave no doubt that both girls are animal lovers. No wonder Ramrod looks happy.

This will work. Charge the guy with pimping and pandering in addition to solicitation. I give my signal while the guy waxes poetic about silver leashes and golden showers.

When my backup arrives, I totter off. Shouts behind me, a car door slamming, and then—

"You fucking bitch! I oughtta kill you!"

I whirl around to see the tact car driving off, and the man now standing on the street facing me. He's got a snub-nosed revolver in his hand which he raises and, as I dive for the ground, pops off two rounds in the air. And then calmly gets back in his car and drives away.

My backup team returns, swerving around the corner on squealing wheels. They're all laughing, a joke I don't get.

"Are you *crazy*?" I scream. "That guy almost killed me. What the hell is wrong with you?"

"Don't you know who that guy is?" They're laughing to beat the band.

"Yeah, some crazy freak!"

"Close. That was Roy Ecklund."

"Who's he?"

"Lieutenant from the Vice Unit. Works Gambling."

"So, what—this was a setup? Make me look like a fool?" Now I'm really hot.

"No setup. He didn't even know we're out here. He's off duty."

"Then what's he doing over here?"

"Trolling, like everyone else. Looking for—ahem—a little action."

"You mean . . ." I'm trying to grasp this. The Yellow Man leather fetishist works Gambling? A lieutenant? Why am I so surprised? Given the sexual diversity of our department members, nothing should shock me by now. "He was serious? He had pictures of girls with dogs and. . . ."

Marty, the driver, shrugs. "Hey, everybody's gotta moonlight sometime."

"But why'd he shoot?"

"Dramatic exit. Fuckin' Roy is a cowboy, man. He was just yankin' your chain. Ain't he a pistol?"

They drive off, cackling like old hens. Roy's a pistol, alright. A yellow-wearing, leather-sucking, .38 caliber pistol.

The next guy has a novel approach. He's all business: double-breasted black suit, generic striped tie, nondescript four-door sedan, and hornrimmed glasses that might have been copped from Clark Kent. When I approach the car, he offers me a sheaf of papers on which a number of questions have been neatly typed. A preliminary health questionnaire, so Mr. Clean can screen his playmates?

"It's a test," he tells me. "You be the teacher and I'll be the student. Any question I miss, you can punish me."

I scan the columns of questions. One hundred per page, at least ten pages. "Impressive. This looks really professional, like a midterm or something."

"It *is* a midterm. I'm a history teacher, and I've been making up tests for thirty years." Behind the glasses, his gray eyes twinkle. "But you'll notice that this test doesn't pertain to history."

Another quick glance at the papers proves him right. Not unless the caloric count of the average ejaculation has recently been included in U.S. History. I read further. The fifty most popular positions in the *Kama Sutra*? (Are these wheelchair accessible?) A question about the best uses of semen, with multiple-choice answers: (A) a facial, (B) wrinkle remover, (C) cuticle softener.

"This is some test! Is there an answer key included?" Reading on, I note that all the questions are of an explicit and almost preposterous sexual nature, with answers that could exist only in this man's fantasy world. And a titillation factor that's kicked in, as indicated by his rising . . . interest. This guy's getting a freebie, and we haven't even begun price negotiations!

"No fair taking a test you made up yourself. You know all the answers."

"Oh, but I don't! I haven't studied at all! I've been a very naughty boy," he simpers. "Wouldn't you like to spank me? Spank me until my ass is cherry red! Please, teacher! I need to be punished!"

"*How much* do you need it?"

"A lot! Spank me, beat me, whip me. I have a leather crop in the backseat."

I roll my eyes. Has this guy forgotten I'm a businesswoman? Many more like him, and I could never afford these trashy clothes. Finally—

"A hundred dollars! Spank me for a hundred dollars. I want you to hurt me, teacher. Make me see what a bad boy I've been!"

When the tac team loads him into the car, one of them pockets the test.

"Just let me make about one hundred copies or so, so we can stuff them in the mailboxes at the station. Let the troops think it's a special deal on continuing education. You know what they say: 'Knowledge is Power!'"

Before they take him away, I lean into the window.

"Too bad a teacher like you wasn't around about twenty years ago. I would've *loved* to belt my algebra teacher, and I would've done it for free!"

He's old, so frail-looking, shrunken behind the wheel of his ancient Rambler, that when he pulls over I think he's going to ask for directions. Not too much of a stretch, since the V. A. hospital is only a half-mile away—a place that might suit his needs better than I could. His rope-veined hands tremble as they clutch the steering wheel. I'm sure he's not here to party.

"Excuse me . . . young lady?" The creaky voice has more rust than his car.

"Yes, sir?"

He adjusts smeared trifocals and looks befuddled.

"I think I'm lost. I—" Gesturing helplessly, he looks around.

"Looking for the hospital? You go down about five blocks to Damen and—"

"No, no." He pats the pockets of his standard-issue old-man's shirt—brown plaid flannel. "I had a list here, somewhere. Don't know where I put it."

Tufts of white silk protrude from his ears. I notice the liver spots that pepper the back of his neck like the Florida Keys. Poor old guy. Took a wrong turn somewhere and ended up in Pimp City.

"What is it you're looking for?"

Confused, he gapes at me through the greasy lenses. His cracked lips purse, then quiver.

"Grocery store," he says finally. "Wife sent me out to get candy for the trick-or-treaters. It's Halloween, you know."

"Right." *But the only candy you'll find around here is rock candy—the kind of rocks you smoke. Ten and twenty bucks a pop. I'm sure that's not the kind of candy Grandma had in mind.*

"There's no grocery store around here. But if you tell me where you live, maybe I can tell you how to get back."

The man grips the steering wheel tighter.

"I'm a shoemaker," he says finally.

"That's nice."

"Not shoe repair. A real shoe *maker*. Not many of us left, nowadays. Do you like shoes?"

"Wear 'em all the time,"

The old eyes travel the length of my body, down to my feet and back up in a thorough, lingering inspection.

"Pretty feet. Like a ballerina. I could make you some shoes, something lovely. You can wear them when you put your legs around my neck."

Oh, no.

The old man is beginning to wheeze, and it's white-knuckle time on the steering wheel.

"I have my own shop, you know. With a cot in the back. You could lay on it. I'd give you candy. And I could rub your pretty feet. Would you like that?" Behind the glasses, his rheumy eyes are glazing.

"A massage first, I think. Your arches, your heels, every little piggy. Splendid!"

I don't want to hear this. This old man is somebody's grandfather, with kind blue eyes and a thatch of white hair that probably flops over his brow when he works at his cobbler's bench, or whatever the damn thing is called. Someone's doting grandpa who tells stories, fixes toys, and passes out peppermints. And who, he tells me now with a very ungrandfatherly leer, wants to swab out my toe-jam with his throbbing dick. Gepetto unleashed.

When my backup arrives, they don't believe me. Mistake, they tell me.

No mistake. As they help him into the car, the old man shakes his head regretfully.

"I could have made you happy. Something lovely for your feet."

Sure thing, Pops. A loafer, maybe. Or something in a pump.

* * *

The wind is picking up now, much colder than it was before. As SuperHo, I prance a little, trying to simultaneously generate heat, look seductive and not fall out of my halter or these treacherous heels. I'm so intent, I don't even notice her until she's right behind me.

"You the *po*-lice?"

"What?"

"You the *po*-lice, huh?" A young girl—sixteen, tops—with scarred, skinny legs hanging out of a striped mini-dress. She's shivering, clutching at a silly feather jacket that looks like a fluorescent ostrich. Below drooping fingers of nappy hair, her doe eyes are curious.

"I could tell right off." Not like it's a state secret or anything, but I thought my cover was pretty good.

"You the only white woman on the street. Mostly black women be around here."

Oh.

"Them your real titties?" A casual question, like, "So, how 'bout those White Sox?"

"Why?" *Please, God, don't let this little girl be a customer!* Most of the whores working this strip fade when they see a decoy. So why else is this girl approaching me?

"They real nice. Some a these womens, they be doing the heroin"—pronounced 'harrow-ON'—"and they titties shrink into nothin'." She glances down the street with a practiced eye. "You should get a lotta tricks. These mens, they like them some white pussy."

Shivering, the girl pulls her jacket tighter against the biting wind. "My name's Twanna. What's yours?"

I almost say, "Officer." Her cheap glass earrings

are glinting in the midday light. "You can call me Diamond."

"Oh, yeah?" This is enough to make her smile. There's a gap where the two front teeth once were. The rest are chipped, crowded together at odd angles.

"Used to be a pimp named Diamond. Had a diamond set in his gold tooth. Real fly! Used to stay up in the 'jets."

"If he's a pimp, what's he living in the 'jets for?"

"Lot of money up in there. All them mens goin' in and out. Diamond had him some womens stayed up in there and all he did was collect the money. But he dead now. Romeo cut him up cuz he tried to take his women." Twanna smiles again and pats her bedraggled feathers. "Romeo my man. He gave me this cuz I'm his top bitch. Ain't it bad?" Preening, she does a half-pivot so I can admire.

"It's bad, alright."

"Yeah. He always do right by me, most times. Say he take care a me, I take care a him." She glances down the street again. No customers in sight.

"Know how else I know you're a cop?" She nods wisely, an adolescent sage with fifty thousand miles of street wear.

"You ain't got a wig on. Where you gon' keep your money if you ain't got a wig?"

"Where's *your* wig?" I return. She ducks her head sheepishly.

"Oh, I ain't workin' now. I just come over here to axe you somethin'."

"Axe away."

"Well, you know, you bein' the *po*-lice and all, I thought you can help me. See, I got this friend Keisha, and she got this job with the *po*-lice, say they pay good money."

"Twanna, you're not old enough to join the force. You have to be at least twenty-three and—"

"I don't wanna *be* the *po*-lice. I wanna *work* for them." She looks at me with eyes older than time. "These policemens, they have parties, and they like them some black girls. Sometimes boys, too, right? Keisha, she say some of the bosses—they the ones with the white shirts, right?—she say they get them a room at the hotel and they have them some girls brung in to party. Keisha say they likes 'em young. I'm thirteen, and I can do everything Keisha do— fuck, suck, womens, mens, whatever. Keisha say they always have food there, so if she hungry, they let her eat, *and* she gets money!" Twanna's eyes are shining at the wonder of it.

"So I figured, you the *po*-lice, you know some-body I can party with. So I can make me some money."

She babbles on, describing her skills like an ear-nest job applicant. Thirteen years old, and a résumé that would give the Mayflower Madam pause. It makes me sick.

"Twanna, stop it!"

"No, listen. I'm good. I can do anything. I got me a little son—for real, Office!—and I got to take care of him. So if you help me"—her eyes narrow sugges-tively—"I'll even give you some, if that's your thing. I can suck your pussy."

"Go home, Twanna."

"Hey, now—"

"Go. Get out of here!"

The doe eyes darken. "Why, you gonna lock me up?"

"No. I'm gonna kick your ass if you don't get out of my sight." I want to cry. I want to grab her and hug her, hide her from the life that's robbed her of being a child. And I know there are a million other Twannas doing—and being—the same thing. Almost immediately, I can feel it, the coldness descending that means I'm withdrawing to another place, somewhere behind that callous cop veneer so I won't have to think about this little girl and all the others like her.

"Why you say that? I thought we was cool." The gap-toothed smile settles into a pout.

"We *are* cool. That's why I'm telling you to get out of here. And if I ever see you out here, I'll lock up your ass for sure." She stares at me to see if I'm kidding. And turns away reluctantly, muttering just loud enough so I can hear.

"Raggedy-ass ol' white bitch! Think you somethin'! Nasty ol' heifer!" She waits until she's a safe distance, maybe half a block, before turning to shout.

"An' you ain't *all that,* neither! Funky-ass titties, probably ain't even yours!" And then she bolts, as fast as her stalkish, thirteen-year-old legs will carry her.

This is the man every mother dreams of for her daughter. The handsome rich one who arrives on his noble steed (in this case, an immaculate Mercedes 450SL), scoops up the fair princess, and rides off to a life of wealth and privilege in the kingdom of Suburbia. He's gorgeous, he's sleek, and he smells like money. It's not just the car, or the beautiful suit that's the wet dream of English tailors everywhere. The designer hairstyle, the elegant whisper of raw silk, the 24-karat glint at cuffs and tie—all are accoutrements of Ultimate *Babe* Man, Platinum Edition. If I were younger, I'd ask him to the prom. Now I'd like to know his position on prenuptials. And then I remember I'm Whore for a Day, and this handsome prince isn't here to take me to the ball.

I look into the bourbon-colored eyes, framed with impossibly thick lashes, and think, *How can you do this? You're handsome, you're loaded, you could probably have your pick of any female on the planet!* And then I see the wedding band. Mr. Husband of the Year ready to work out his kinks with a street whore. Now he's a pig for sure—a disgusting swine who ruts with whores, and risks bringing disease home to the wife and kiddies. Maybe that's part of the thrill for him. Now I'm all business.

"What can I do for you, sugar?"

His nostrils flare as he checks out the chamois. Please, not another leather fetishist!

"What will it cost me?" The voice is low, cultured, insinuating.

"Depends on your taste." I actually smile when I say this, without gagging. Quick—the Oscar nomination, *please*! He leers at me, licking his perfectly chiseled lips.

"How 'bout we sixty-nine, then you can eat out my ass?"

"And what do I get for that?"

He grabs my hair before I can jump back and yanks me through the window, toward his crotch.

"Eat this, you bitch! *This* is what I'll give you!" His other hand is digging around frantically. It's the one-eyed worm, engorged, purplish, and more than a little angry to be yanked so hard. No wonder it spits all over the luxurious leather upholstery, the steering wheel and part of my arm.

"I *said, eat it,* bitch!" My dream date from hell is gasping like a drowning man.

"*Eat this,* motherfucker!" My backup has arrived. Another one-eyed object, this time the barrel of a 9mm Browning semiautomatic, is pointed through the passenger window at the handsome prince's head. "*Police!* Take your hands off her and put 'em up on the dash. Try anything, and I'll blow your head off so you can suck your own dick!"

The handsome prince is not convinced. Or else he's seen too many cop shows, but either way, he opts to rewrite the script. And throws the car into drive and floors the gas, with me still hanging out his window.

Back at the station, the tac guys tell me to count my blessings. They *could* have shot out his gas tank, in which case it'd be Operation Angel for real, complete with harp and halo. Shooting out his tires was the next best thing. What's a few scratches and bruises compared to a command performance at the Pearly Gates?

A good point, I concede. And, after I wash off the blood, cinders, and shredded chamois in the women's locker room, I head back to the tac office, where Sweet Prince is being processed. "Aggravated battery of a police officer, solicitation, fleeing the police, resisting arrest. . . ." The list of charges goes on and on. But as far as I'm concerned, there should be something more. I owe this man a little something extra—to help him remember our precious moments together.

The address on his driver's license says Kenilworth—the rich man's paradise. It's a North Shore fantasy suburb of gated estates and enough collective income to start a new country. In one of those estates resides the wife of this man, who may be waiting for him right now, her spouse and bread-winner and whoremonger husband.

From the bench where he's handcuffed, the man's face is set in an arrogant sneer, which remains intact until my next comment.

"And of course you know, Mr. Dunbar, that our sergeant will be contacting your wife regarding the arrangements."

"Arrangements?" Arrogance melts into horror as the color drains from his face. "My wife? What are you talking about?"

This time, it's easy to summon the required game face.

"Just the minor details, like the charges you're being booked on, the time and date of your court appearance, and amount of your bail, I'm guessing. The usual information. Family notification is standard procedure."

"But it can't be. I mean, it's not necessary. I'll just call my lawyer."

The dour expression on our sergeant's face indicates that he's heard it all in his twenty years on the job. Which is why he merely shakes his head.

"You'll get to call your lawyer, Mr. Dunbar. But I have to call your wife. Like this young lady said, it's standard procedure. And besides, I'm sure you wouldn't want the little woman to worry about you."

23

Scratch 'n' Sniff

1561 D:	'61 David.
Dispatcher:	'61 David coming in?
1561 D:	Yeah. Squad, are there any female officers working tonight to do a prisoner search for us?
Dispatcher:	What've you got, '61 David?
1561 D:	We've got three females over here, mules for one of the dealers. We need one of our ladies to go through them.
Dispatcher:	Okay. Any units out there with a female to do a search for '61 David?
1523:	I'll slide by, Squad. What's their location?
1561 D:	We're on the southeast corner of Lotus and West End, right across from Austin High School.
1523:	Ten-four. On the way.
Unidentified Unit:	Don't forget to wash your hands!

Any junkie will tell you that heroin is better than sex. You fix up and—*bam!*—you're hit with a rush that's better than any orgasm Dr. Ruth can dream of. The warmth oozes through you, silkening your jittery nerves, and you melt, drip into the velvet chasm where soft and warm and motherfucking *fine* are the only feelings that exist. Definitely better than sex, they say. It's quicker, easier, nothing to fake—and you don't have to brush your teeth afterward. In fact, after a while, you won't *have* any teeth to brush, because sugar is a junkie's second-best friend. But appearances don't matter. Lady Heroin is an indiscriminate lover, inviting one and all to come ride the horse. She keeps only one secret from her legion of lovers, which is that there will *never* be a time with her that equals the first. The first high is always the best. It's such a complete sensory celebration that people spend years, money, lives chasing after it, trying to duplicate that first exquisite rush.

The detox center on 64th and Dorchester has enough addicts, both current and recovering users, to debate the notion of better living through chemistry. It's where the squadrols deposit the junkies found inert in doorways, spasming through seizures, or knotted in the bowel-wrenching agony of too much time between fixes. A place where both substance and alcohol abusers can detoxify, enter the twelve-step residential program, or just find a sympathetic ear.

The center is staffed primarily by recovering addicts/alcoholics, important because not only have they been there and done it, but also have a finely developed bullshit meter that can expose any scam the patients can think of. The program is supposed to be about getting better, not getting *over*.

For those who've never been there before, it's an unsettling place. The building itself is scary looking—a huge Gothic monstrosity, complete with crumbling stairs, a soot-blackened edifice and creaking shutters that bang against windows variously shattered or shaded by layers of filth. This is not a place to let the sun shine in until the demons are vanquished. And as long as drug sales are booming, it's an uphill battle.

For cops, making a run to the detox center is never a pleasant experience. Nobody likes this assignment: having to collect the slumping addicts off the streets. Every time you touch one of those filthy bodies with the oozing sores, you hope desperately that your rubber gloves are enough protection. You gather them up, gasping at the ammonia stench and other smells strong enough to tear your eyes, careful to turn your head. Invariably, you're showered with spittle from their chronic coughs, enough to have you scheduling regular TB tests through the department Medical Section. The possibility of contracting infectious diseases would make most people turn and run. For cops, it's all part of the job description.

The detox center is where cops transport those who inhabit the middle ground between jail and the morgue. They haven't committed a crime, and they don't yet require a toe tag. Where else do you bring the seventeen-year-old girl you find squatting in the filth of an abandoned building, rocking and scratching, plucking imaginary bugs off paper-dry skin? Vacant-eyed, her tongue hangs lax, savoring the sweet, metallic memory of her latest hit—the one she cooked up in the dirty bottle cap near her equally dirty feet.

Deborah Egan has been a junkie for years—six or more, she doesn't remember. She was running with the Vice Lords back then, partying, getting high. Enjoying the benefits that came with being the top bitch of a high-ranking gang leader. He bought her clothes, and drugs, and she was his woman. More drugs, and she was anyone's woman. The girl they called "Coffee Cake," because "everybody gets a piece."

Now, at seventeen, she's pushed aside, used up, strung out. Replaced by some younger, finer bitches who don't live minute to minute worrying about the next fix. So far, she doesn't have much of a rap sheet to speak of. A few arrests for solicitation—nothing serious. A girl's got to earn her dope money somehow. Whenever we find her, hunched over a curb, babbling and crying, we bring her to detox where, maybe one day, she'll stay more than a day or so. Exorcize the demons and reclaim her life.

One night, we get an anonymous tip to check an empty lot behind a warehouse. It's Deborah Egan, slumped against a tree. Nearby is a newborn baby, dropped or flung with enough force to smash its head. A trail of blood zigzags to Deborah, stopping at the congealing puddle between her legs. Her eyes are open wide—shocked by the experience of childbirth, or the final, fatal thrill provided by the needle stuck in her arm?

The 100 block of North Waller is a fool's paradise. Fools who snort, sniff, lick, or smoke cocaine—either lines of powder or rocks of crack. It's a buyer's market here, and it's all for sale, twenty-four convenient shopping hours a day. Nestled among the once-stately Victorian houses eroded by the hardship of ghetto life, just steps away from a children's playground is the domain of Starman: dealer, pusher, devil in disguise. His sentinels are posted along the street and around the empty lot adjacent to the building where his wares are sold. Their job is to direct the customers—and keep watch for the cops.

"All's well," they'll chant if the coast is clear, or "Five-O" when the cops are sighted. It's a wave of sound that ripples down the street, reminding distressed neighborhood residents that death is dealt among them in little plastic bags. Crack cocaine, or rocks, is the drug of choice in these parts, sold for ten or twenty dollars per piece. Cheaper than buying powdered cocaine by gram weight, crack is a bargain-basement high with a G-force kick. "G" as in, get some, gotta have more, gimme gimme, gone completely out of minds, out of bodies, graveyard bound.

Starman is shrewd enough to understand the first tenet of good business: Give the people what they want. Deliver a product that's satisfactory and reap the rewards. And if there's a way to cut corners, make even more money, so much the better. After all, how discerning can a strungout crackhead be? Starman's got it down to a science. He's got a team of workers who make the crack, a procedure that can be done in the kitchen, on a hot plate—anywhere you can boil water. It's a simple process. Measures of baking soda, water, and cocaine are mixed together, boiled into paste. When all the water boils off and the mixture turns from white to beige, it becomes crack, hardening into a huge chunk that's shaved into smaller fragments: "rocks."

The profits are unbelievable. One gram of coke, depending on quality, costs anywhere from one hundred fifty to five hundred dollars. Rocks are sold for ten and twenty dollars apiece, depending on size. It's possible to get a few hundred rocks per batch of crack, so Starman is in the money.

Most of his customers have never seen him. It's like going to see the Wizard, they say. You never get past the door. Money is handed through a hole in the door; the rock is passed back. No names, no faces—just efficient delivery of a product that's claiming more lives than the Vietnam War.

When we finally bust Starman, it's almost anticlimatic. After a year of gathering intelligence, a months-long stake-out, we bust him when he makes a stupid mistake, trying to elude us in a high-speed car chase after buying a bucket of his favorite chicken. Chicken he can't resist sampling as he starts up his Lexus. Greasy fingers have no advantage for getaway drivers. Starman loses control of his car, barreling over a concrete median, careening off a mailbox and into the wall of a dry-cleaning store.

For those of us who expected some larger-than-life Mack Daddy, he's a surprise. He's short, not quite 5'5", dressed conservatively in a subdued gray wool sweater and gray slacks. No gold teeth, no flashy ID bracelet with his name spelled out in diamonds. Nothing that shouts "Superfly!" Or even hints of how he makes his money. Only the satchel containing fifty thousand dollars and a pound of crack suggests his true vocation.

In his other life, Starman is Horace Purtell, distinguished gentleman and lord of a tasteful manor in Oak Brook, the very exclusive enclave that's home to the famous Polo Club and wealthy patrons of the arts.

"The house that crack built," my partner says, filling out the arrest report.

Horace/Starman is unperturbed.

"It's just business," he says. "If nobody bought it, I couldn't sell it."

"Guess that makes you eligible for the good-citizen's award."

"I'm like anyone else. I've got bills to pay, a family to raise. Kids in private school. . . ."

"Do they get to bring some crack to school for show-and-tell?"

"I don't give drugs to kids. I'm not a monster."

"Let me guess. You're the successor to Mother Teresa, right?"

After that, Starman exercises his right to remain silent. And sits impassively, unconcerned, waiting for his lawyer, a high-priced, nattily dressed attorney who arrives via Jaguar. With a glittering diamond stud winking in one earlobe, the lawyer starts ranting about the violation of his client's rights. Illegal search and seizure, police brutality, reckless endangerment, and a lot of other legalese to let us know he works hard for his very substantial retainer.

Starman knows he's going to walk, knows that, at the arraignment, bail will be negotiated and paid at warp speed. And everyone else knows why. Justice may be blind, but she's not deaf. When money talks, she listens. Starman's got enough money to be fluent in the art of conversation—especially one that prevents him from cooling his heels in a jail cell, or doing any serious time. Drug dealers are like the new power brokers in our judicial system, able to purchase freedom either by "direct deposit" or through substantial funds filtered through the right channels by their savvy attorneys. Because the judges, the prosecutors, and Starman's sharpie lawyer are, in one way, just like him. They've all got mouths to feed, bills to pay. Business is business. Their business, which is supported by ours. We gather intelligence, do the surveillance, risk our lives (and our health) to bring these people to justice. And after the best of our efforts, we have the opportunity to watch the case dismissed, or the arrestee given a token slap on the wrist, which means that he returns to the streets to resume his business. A frustrating loop of commerce that indicates there's something wrong with the system. Or maybe just that we don't understand the principles of the art of the deal. After all, we're only cops, not businessmen.

One night we're called to a disturbance in a tattoo parlor. It's a dissatisfied customer, creating such a scene the owner feels compelled to pull out his version of a "peacemaker"—a two-foot machete that's seen more action than we want to know about. When we arrive, the owner is standing on the counter, fully prepared to cleave the furious customer's head like a coconut.

"He was in here last night," the owner tells us. "Him and a few of his friends. He picked out a design, paid his money, I gave him the tattoo. Now he's back here starting trouble."

The customer, a husky young man in his early twenties, has a different story. He *never* wanted a tattoo; it wasn't his idea. He was just hanging out with his friends, getting buzzed. Nobody ever mentioned tattoos.

"So what happened?"

They'd been drinking, he says. A few beers, a few shooters, not too much. Then someone in the bar asked if he wanted to get high. He was already high, so what was a little more? He thought the guy was talking about smoking some weed. Instead, it was Quaaludes, a powerful depressant, enough for him and his friends. That's the last thing he remembers until he woke up today, with a life-sized tattoo of Felix the Cat prancing across his chest.

"What's your beef with this guy?" my partner

asks. "You picked out the tattoo, you paid for it, right? It's not his fault. Technically, we could lock you up for purchasing a controlled substance."

"Uh, I'm not the one who bought it. Somebody else did."

"And twisted your arm to take it, right? Sure!"

But the tattooed man's not willing to let it go.

"I didn't even know I was getting a tattoo, Officer. I think you should arrest him, too."

"On what charge?"

"What about 'damage to property'?"

The store owner lays down his machete and leans on the counter.

"Look, kid, I don't know what you're complaining about. I do nice work. The cat looks good—you should be happy. Look at it this way. Most guys your age are always looking for a little pussy. You already got yours."

At Cook County Hospital, the pace is always hectic. Having the best trauma unit in the city means that the ER sees a constant parade of shooting victims, accidents, every conceivable injury where life and death hang in delicate balance. Their success rate in the treatment of critical trauma patients is better than most hospitals, but no one can play God all the time. There's only so many miracles to go around.

We handle a traffic accident one night that's bad enough to qualify for a miracle, with enough carnage to sicken the most jaded veteran cop. A man and his wife were coasting along, oblivious to the posted speed limits and the icy pavement. Fifty miles an hour, sixty, and then floored for the ultimate speed thrill. They never saw the red light. A truck

coming through the intersection braked—too late—
crashed into the car, and then skidded across two
more lanes of traffic before smashing through a restaurant's plate-glass window. The man, the truck
driver, and four patrons of the restaurant were killed.

Trapped in the wreckage of the car, the woman is
moaning, slipping into the clammy grip of shock.

"The baby!" she screams. "Where's the baby? I
want my baby!"

Baby? There is no baby, so we assume she's referring to her husband. We concentrate on helping the
rescue team free her from the wreckage, until a bystander steps forward. He points to where the baby
is—across the street, now impaled on a fence post
after being projected through the windshield on impact. Apparently, a restraining infant car seat was
not high on her parents' priority list.

The woman is rushed to the Cook County Trauma
Unit, unconscious, nearly bled out from a crushed
artery. This will require a miracle of the highest order. While she's hustled off to surgery, we notify her
family. They arrive in groups, huddle together sobbing.

The woman's brother lingers in the hallway, talking with the police.

"I can't believe it, man. Just can't fucking believe
it. A couple hours ago, we were all together partying. My brother-in-law's birthday." *And death day.*

"I *told* him he should lighten up. Sometimes
enough is enough, y'know? But he wouldn't listen."
He brushes away the tracking tears. "He liked his
coke, my brother-in-law. Just a little toot now and
then, just enough to get off. But tonight . . . he said
he had a right to party. His birthday and all."

And?

"So him and my sister...they were doing 'freezes.' Rubbed baking soda on their gums, then snorted a few lines. Said it felt like their heads were inside a block of ice." He scrubs a hand over streaming eyes. "Said there was no high like it. Just too cool for words. In fact, that's the last thing he said to me. Looked at me with that goofy stoned smile and said, 'This is too cool for words.'"

There are three of them. Three young girls hand-cuffed together, slouched in sullen defiance against the school wall. Each dressed in baggy jeans and oversized sports jerseys, they look the same, down to the purplish black lipstick and black nail polish. These girls are junkies, mules for Royal, a West Side drug dealer who uses them as an extra perk for his preferred customers. When a girl delivers the dope, they can get high and get lucky at the same time. Depending on how luck is defined, that is. These three are at the bottom of the food chain in the dealer's harem. Their scarred, skinny arms are a road map of past drug pleasures, and the pallor of their gaunt faces looks more embalmed than au courant. Not quite fifteen years old, and they're the walking dead—just a needle and a spoon away from the final rush.

Some tactical officers picked them up in the schoolyard, just past midnight, but this is more than a curfew violation. The Narcotics Unit has intelligence regarding Royal's latest drug shipment—a substantial amount of brown heroin—"Mexican mud"—smuggled across the border. Which means that Royal's mules will be out making deliveries.

The tac team calls for a female officer to search the

girls—standard police procedure. When I arrive the girls are quiet, waiting in the shadowed schoolyard.

"This is Corazon, that's Letitia, this one's Luz," a tac cop says. "Who do you want first? Your choice."

My *choice* would be not to do a search at all. No one likes to search a junkie. In addition to the lesions, oozing sores, occasional body lice, and body odor that would fell Attila the Hun, there's the matter of hidden surprises. Like hypodermic syringes that they secrete on their body or in their clothing. It's easy to get stabbed by a needle that's hidden in someone's waistband, in their armpit—all the places that you have to pat down because they might also hide weapons. Gloves don't offer much protection. Disposable rubber surgical gloves that protect you from the sores and filth are no match for a sharp needle, or razor blades. Thicker gloves are out because you need the sensitivity in your fingertips to find the contraband drugs.

Junkies are resourceful when it comes to hiding their drugs, female junkies even more so. They're clever about concealing their stash either *in* their body or on it. Besides being hidden in every body orifice, they put the drugs in wigs, taped to the earpieces of glasses, in armpits, between toes, behind ears, under breasts, behind knees, and anywhere else they can think of. Needles are stashed in socks, waistbands, backs of collars, hems of pants, in bras, underpants, sanitary napkins. All of these are places that have to be searched—carefully, cautiously, thoroughly. One puncture from a tainted needle, and I'll be on the AIDS clinic mailing list.

I search Luz first, then Letitia, and find nothing—unless scabies count as contraband. Corazon has a small pipe in her shoe, and a tiny, foilcovered chunk of what appears to be hashish. No heroin is found, no cocaine.

Corazon is placed in the unmarked tactical squad car for transport to the station. The other girls are uncuffed and ushered toward my car. It's well past curfew now, and these two women-children need to be taken home.

"I *told* you I didn't have nothin'!" Luz glowers. "You gonna give me back my kid now or what?" From his squad, one of the tac cops produces a plastic carrier seat holding a sleeping infant and places it in her scrawny arms.

"That's your baby?" I can't believe her wasted body could support such a biological function. "How old is it?"

Luz glares at me defiantly. "Ain't none of your business."

"No, it isn't." The baby has managed to sleep through this drama. It has black, wispy curls and a rosebud mouth laxly embracing the nipple of an empty bottle.

"Your baby is beautiful, Luz. You should be proud."

The girl's face softens. "*Es mi hijo, Pablito*. My son, Paul. He's three months old."

"Don't worry about the kid," one of the tac guys advises. "He's clean. We already checked the diaper. No dope."

Luz reverts to her previous snarl, cradling the baby protectively. It's the standard Madonna-and-Child routine we've seen a hundred times before. The model junkie dope-running mom who hides the drugs in the baby's diaper. This time, thankfully, both mother and son are clean.

I bring Letitia home and leave her in the custody

of her semi-sober father. And am nearly to Luz's house when she starts to scream.

It's the baby, she wails. Something's wrong. He's cold, he's not breathing. Holy Mother, Jesus—*some-body!*—help!

Now it's blue lights and siren over to Loretto Hospital, where the ER staff confirms the worst. The baby is dead, has been dead for an hour or more, judging by the degree of lividity—the postmortem pooling of blood in the body. His tiny body is unblemished, with no external signs of abuse or disease. Only an autopsy will determine the cause of death.

Several days later, I find out what happened. And learn that the tac cops had been wrong. The baby *wasn't* clean. He was just most unfortunate to have a mother more resourceful than the average junkie mules. When Luz knew the cops were coming, she'd dumped the heroin—three ounces of it—into the baby's bottle, where it mixed with his formula. And then she submitted to a lengthy search while her baby lay contentedly in his carrier, sucking his bottle, ending his brief life.

We've all heard the media's public service announcements about "joining the war on drugs." For those of us out here in the trenches, it feels like Armageddon. The advance of this ruthless enemy will claim more lives, leave behind devastation wrought with a puff of smoke, or a needle and spoon. Weapons with a kill rate efficient enough to project the bleak statistics. Our kids are dying with spikes in their arms, babies poisoned in pursuit of the Almighty High—enough drug-related deaths to equal or surpass the fatalities of military wars. Except, in this war, there will be no cease-fire, no truce or armistice when we all get to go home and resume our lives. Not unless the horsemen who usher in this fearsome Apocalypse, like Starman and Royal and all the drug dealers, are taken off the streets, tried, and *convicted*. A cherished dream of cops, enough to keep us out there fighting for it. Fighting for our kids, fighting for their lives.

24

The Whiz Quiz

Dispatcher:	2422? Beat 2422?
2422:	'22.
Dispatcher:	Got an Officer Skilling ridin' on your car today?
2422:	Ten-four. That's me.
Dispatcher:	Okay, pal. We just got a message from your station desk. You're supposed to take a ride over to the medical section, report to the Drug Testing Unit.
2422:	Great. Just what I need to make my day.
Unidentified Unit:	I got two words for you, Skilling.
2422:	Yeah? What's that?
Unidentified Unit:	*Poppy seeds!*

Nobody said we're saints. When it comes to using alcohol and drugs, cops are just like anyone else: some do, some don't. As for who gets caught, the same answer applies. Drinking on the job is a problem that, until recent years, was never even considered a problem. It was part of the package, the logical extension of the macho boys' club mentality. You put in your eight hours, then hit the tavern. All the guys did it in the name of fellowship or camaraderie, or just to avoid going home for a few hours longer. You had a few drinks, a few laughs, traded some war stories with your fellow cops. Commiserated in a

circle of fraternity removed from the public eye.
Nothing wrong with stopping off at the district cop
joint. There, at least, among your brothers in blue,
was acceptance.

Bending elbows with other uniforms served as a
political lubricant as well. Tipping suds with the
bosses in a convivial atmosphere could keep you off
someone's shit list, portray you as a "stand-up guy,"
even pave the way for cushy assignments or future
favors. Not a bad return for just a social drink every
now and then.

The next step is therapeutic drinking: drinking as
stress reduction. It's a rough tour of duty—drink to
forget. You handle a teen suicide—drink to forget. A
particular boss is on your ass and, no matter what
you do, he won't back off—drink to forget. After a
while, you forget everything—*why* you're drinking,
how much you're drinking, even *that* you drink. It's
an integral part of your life, as much a part of the
job as your gun and star, drinking *while* you work,
after work and, for those on the afternoon and midnight watches, having a few *before* work.

Pretty soon you're spending the better part of
your work day riding a bar stool in some cop-
friendly joint. Many supervisors will look the other
way. After all, drinking among the ranks is a well-
established department tradition. And since it's just
as likely to be a sergeant or lieutenant on the neighboring bar stool, what can they say? Cops in glass
houses.

In recent years, top-ranking police officials were
forced to address the problem of alcoholism among
the ranks. Too many cops under the influence were
smashing up the company cars, inviting public scrutiny with continued drunken antics, botching assign-

ments, and falling woefully short of their police duties because they were too pie-eyed to function. The media was in an uproar and the department's dirty laundry was starting to show.

Time to throw the public a bone.

Police counseling referral services were initiated. The very same type of counseling center that I anticipated working at, in the earliest stages of my career. What I didn't know then—and didn't find out until later—was that these centers are manned strictly by civilian social workers.

Typical problems that were targeted for treatment were stress reduction, grief counseling (for the period after a shooting, or the work-related death of a coworker) and, yes, even alcohol-abuse counseling.

Any cop deemed to have a "noticeable" drinking problem could now be referred for counseling rather than receive disciplinary action. It was perfect. Total a squad car after an interlude with Johnnie Walker? No problem—go for counseling. Almost shoot your partner because you're too drunk to aim? Don't worry about it—here's the referral. The department likes to think that it's progressive enough to recognize that alcoholism is a disease—and how can you punish someone who's *sick*?

Ironically, the task of identifying and referring cops with drinking problems falls to the immediate supervisors of these officers—the same sergeants, lieutenants, and captains who might be on the next bar stool. The guys whose perspectives might be a little skewed, especially if they're viewing the world through the bottom of an empty glass. The drunk leading the drunk.

As far as the quality of the counseling services provided went, the general consensus of the participating patients agreed it was less than helpful. For the cops who actually *did* show up for their sessions, it wasn't exactly a therapeutic atmosphere. Typical civil-service bullshit, they reported. Just figureheads collecting their very substantial paychecks. It didn't help that the civilian counselors had no inkling of the types of situations cops face, or the multitude of stressors that are *internal*—problems that exist and fester *within* the department, *because* of the department. The counselors were oblivious, and content to toss out a few pat statements, some standard touchy-feely psychobabble as relevant as a fortune cookie.

One officer referred for counseling couldn't control his drinking. He was the only survivor in a gang shoot-out in which his partner, who'd been a close personal friend as well, had been killed along with four civilians, including a two-year-old child hit by stray bullets. The surviving officer had descended into an emotional hell, unable to sleep or eat, victim of recurring visions of his dying partner, the bullet-ridden baby. Drinking was the only thing that erased the grisly images—temporarily. He was *glad* to be referred to counseling, welcomed anything that might help him through this anguish and pain.

At one of the counseling centers, he was given endless forms to fill out, with pertinent questions like: "name of high school attended" and "mother's maiden name." After slogging through the paperwork and enduring an interminable wait in the drab lobby, he was finally led into his therapist's office. A therapist who snapped gum and looked not very much older than his youngest daughter, who jiggled her platform-heeled feet relentlessly while she interrogated him.

"Why did you want to be a policeman? How did

you feel about your father? Did you ever have inappropriate feelings about your mother? Do you like women? Are you angry?"

Angry—and on the way to furious. He suffered through a half hour of it, listening numbly to the endless questions. Number of siblings? Any sibling rivalry as a child? Any residual hostility? When she got to the one about his service revolver as an extension of his penis, he walked out. She'd never even asked why he was there, he said later. Never even asked what happened. And he wasn't about to waste his time with some teenybopper Dr. Freud-wannabe.

For their part, the counseling staff provided what they felt was expected of them. Nobody believed they were actually going to make a difference. Everyone knows that cops are essentially crazy—look at their high suicide rate! So the counselors went through the motions. In that their own political connections had placed them in a gravy job, raking in fifty thousand-plus a year, they weren't required to do much. A few perfunctory sessions, a little paperwork to make it look kosher, and the cop in question was back on the street, in the tavern and buying the next round. But *for appearances,* the department could officially say that it takes care of its own.

Drug usage among the ranks was met with considerably less tolerance. There were some cops who'd been getting high for years, enjoying their drugs of choice with confidence. They were the police—who was going to bust them? As long as they were careful, not too obvious, it wasn't a problem. When driving around on routine patrol got boring, why not light up a joint? The supervisors wouldn't catch them—they were in the taverns.

A few lines of coke every now and then? Why not?

It increased concentration, added a little zip to the day. Amphetamines? Helped you stay awake on the midnight shifts. A dangerous practice, and one inadvertently fueled by the job. Windows of opportunity opened every time you went out on the street. Bust some small-time dealer with a few ounces of marijuana, inventory *half* of it. The dealer won't snitch. Cocaine, uppers, downers—it's all out there if you know where to look. As the police, it's your *duty* to confiscate it.

Other cops had a fix in with street dealers. For a regular supply of the merchandise, *and* a little cash thrown in for good measure, the cops stayed high, the dealers didn't get busted. It was a problem that threatened to run rampant until the department began its drug-testing program.

For three months before the testing began officially, announcements were made at district roll calls and in special department bulletins. The message was clear: Judgment Day is coming; time to clean up your act. If you were doing it before, time to give it up. Three months was plenty of time to clear your system of residual drugs, to give everyone a fair shot at "pissing clean." But there were still a stubborn few who refused—or were too high—to see the writing on the wall.

The testing selection was set up on a lottery-type system, using each officer's six-digit employee number. Numbers were selected randomly by the Drug Testing Unit personnel each day, on each watch, round the clock. Any working officer could be called in at any time during his tour of duty for a drug test. The procedure was simple. The testee would report to the medical section, fill up a specimen cup, and wait for the good—or bad—news. But before taking the "whiz quiz," the officer was obligated to answer some standard preliminary questions. Any drug usage at this time? Prescribed medications currently taken that might affect the test results? Any illegal drug usage in the past?

In the beginning, the drug screen was rudimentary. Mostly, they were looking for marijuana and cocaine. For those die-hard drug users who failed to heed the department's three-month warning, an unpleasant surprise was in store. Anyone who failed the whiz quiz ("pissed hot") was suspended immediately, pending termination. *Adios* to future career plans, *sayonara* to a civil servant's pension.

After a month or so of weeding out, the troops were not happy. Friends, partners, stand-up guys were being dumped, and for what? A little reefer, a taste of coke every once in a while? Big deal!

It was time to get creative. Cops are people who build careers on covering their asses. Who can elevate the art of subterfuge to new heights. And who, whenever the shit hits the fan, never let a little thing like rules and regulations get in the way.

In a very short time, the department grapevine was buzzing. Some of the more ingenious cops had done their homework, and were ready to pass it along. There were ways, and there were *ways* to beat the whiz quiz. One surefire method is to stop at a hot-dog stand or bakery before reporting for the test. The recommended snack? A hot-dog bun with poppy seeds, or any kind of poppy-seed danish. The poppy seeds show up on the drug screen as a narcotic—and ruin your test. Enough to put the testing personnel in a snit because now they have to reschedule your test. But it takes two weeks for the poppy/narcotic traces to leave your system. Two weeks for you to lay off the bad behavior and ace your test.

Some cops swear by the cleansing tea available at health-food stores. It's fast-acting, effectively neutralizes a wide range of drug traces, and comes highly recommended—full-page ads in *High Times* and other counterculture magazines. Allegedly, it's the same tea used by professional athletes to beat *their* whiz quiz.

As time went on, department members became more savvy, more creative in beating the test. But that creativity wasn't limited to the lower ranks, or in simply beating the test. Manipulation can go both ways. In the spring of 1996, several civilian employees of the police Medical Section were taken into custody by Internal Affairs, interrogated, and subsequently fired. The charges involved switching or altering drug-testing results for a group of officers taking the sergeant's promotional exam.

A promotion list had been made of the sergeants-to-be as dictated by their Chinamen—promotion ensured by one of the three C's: cash, clout, or coochie. A few token officers would be promoted by actual test scores, just enough to make it appear on the up-and-up. The rest would be dumped, regardless of how well they scored. Rigging a hot whiz quiz was one way to do it. No one was particularly surprised by the news. Or the announcement that was made soon after, by embarrassed department officials who stated that a new, more reliable type of drug testing that involved hair analysis would be instituted, to prevent future discrepancies.

The troops knew better. The powers that be would continue to promote their favored officers, and ax anyone without the necessary connections, just as the ranks would continue to find ways to beat the system—whichever test they used.

As for the unfortunate pawns who were fired? No one was particularly surprised by the news. It was too bad, some said, that it was civilians who took the fall, since the orders had come from the upper echelons. On the other hand, something like this would *never* have happened to a sworn officer.

Cops know how to cover their asses.

25

Vertical Patrol

Dispatcher: Units in the Twelfth District, units on citywide,
              we have a ten-one, a ten-one officer down at
              1209 Racine, fifth floor. Beat 1227 is calling a
              ten-one, officer down at that location. All
              available units be advised of shots fired. First
              unit on the scene, let us know what's going on.

On paper, it must have sounded like a great idea.
Low-income housing for as many as 130 families per
building, families that could share a sense of community without bearing the obvious stigma of pov-
erty. Design the buildings to mimic the Gold Coast
high rises along Lake Shore Drive, with a few modi-
fications, of course. Cinder-block walls instead of
textured silk wall coverings, concrete floors in lieu of
pastel terrazzo.

So what if the project dwellers didn't have much
money? At least, their buildings could look like those
lofty penthouses with the breathtaking Lake Michigan view. Sort of.

The building architects must have broken their
arms patting each other on the back after the City
Council approved their designs. High-rise structures
with a plot of land around each for parking lots, and
a playground for the kiddies. The theory was that,
even though these buildings were erected in the most

crime-ridden areas of the city, the kids could enjoy a safe place to play while their parents kept a watchful eye out from the apartments above.

The problem was that each building had fifteen floors, which didn't allow for much parental supervision—not unless you're peering through some high-powered binoculars. And if you did happen to notice something questionable involving your child—say, a fast transaction with a drug dealer, or a chance encounter with the neighborhood pedophile, there wouldn't be much you could do in the way of intervention. It's hard to get down fifteen flights in a hurry—especially when there's only two small elevators, each just a bit larger than a phone booth, and neither of them in working order very often. Which is to say, only in months with "X" in them, which is about as often as the Housing Authority maintenance engineers awaken from their white port stupors and attempt to fix something.

Once the high-rise "jets" were inhabited, the architects realized they'd made a few major boo-boos. The space designated for kiddie parks was too small, and no parents felt safe leaving their kids there when gangs were bopping on every corner. You could get shot just walking out of the building. To let children play alone would be an outright sacrifice to the gangbanger gods. And the physical placement of the buildings was nothing short of brilliant, if you were trained in sniping and high-powered weaponry. From the higher levels of the Robert Taylor Homes, or Rockwell Gardens, or the notorious Cabrini-Green, a sniper could pick off a rival gang member, an innocent bystander, the windshield of a police squad—anything he chose, without being detected.

There are other glitches in the jets that never

showed up on the drawing board. In some buildings, the apartments are entered from an outdoor balcony, motel-style, that spans the width of the building. A nice touch for the Gold Coast wealthy, a bad idea for the inner city. Too many bodies got tossed over the railings during domestic disputes, gang fights, or the random Saturday-night "get outta my face, mutha-fucka" attitude that went too far. In no time at all, the Chicago Housing Authority agreed to the wisdom of adding steel mesh on the balconies from floor to roof, making the buildings appear to be what their residents had felt all along: cages of crime and violence, where staying alive is a job *and* an adventure!

In their infinite wisdom, the Housing Authority developed a tacit policy for apartment assignment, determined by frequency of police encounters. The peaceful families with little or no history of distur-bances are assigned the lower floors, a convenience which means they don't have to heft groceries or laundry up a dozen or more flights. The frequent of-fenders are given the higher-floor apartments, which does nothing to curb the cycle of violence. Climbing ten or more flights several times a day is enough to give *anyone* an attitude. Toss in some liquor, drugs, and a mouthy mate who won't do right, and it's time to call 911.

For cops assigned to a project beat, it's vertical pa-trol every night: stairs and domestics, stairs and burglaries, stairs and guns, stairs and stairs. The first two commandments of patrolling the jets are to *never* take the elevator, *always* wear a safety vest. And for those who don't share an appreciation of wildlife, it's a good idea to spray your shoes with insecticide before going up those stairs, so you don't leave with more than you came with.

There are no words to describe the onslaught of feelings a cop experiences when entering the jets for the first time. It's the darkness you notice first, a perpetual gloom that comes from insufficient light sources, windowless halls, and lobbies that look more like grim tunnels than a residential building. Rank smells, mixed with the stench of industrial-strength insecticide, are strong enough to gag you. You learn to breathe through your mouth, creep carefully up stairwells littered with garbage, and worse. All you want to do is take care of business, and get out quickly. This is a dangerous place for cops who come as peacemakers, but arrive as targets.

You fight back the nausea, the flutter of fear each time you enter those dark hallways. Fifteen dark and secret floors of eyes watching, untold crimes waiting to happen.

For residents here, there's a pervasive despair that comes from living in daily fear. Crime is as much a part of the project experience as the strong gang presence, poorly maintained facilities, nearly intolerable living conditions. With gunshots popping throughout the night, even during the day, just stepping out on the balcony is a risk. Living here means there are no simple household chores. Trips to the laundromat are an invitation to burglarize your apartment. And *if* you are burglarized, the subsequent repairs to your door, or locks, or shattered windows won't be made immediately. Maybe not at all. With "property damage" incidents occurring on a daily basis, it's all the building maintenance people can do to keep up. Most times, they slap a sheet of plywood against a shattered window, advise the tenant to fix his own broken locks, or else just stay at home to protect what's his.

Female residents know better than to carry a purse—another open invitation. Cunning thieves slouch near the building entrances, watching for easy victims. Simple to pick off the lady who's just cashed her welfare check, or to snatch the groceries from a woman struggling with the burden of packages.

Nothing is easy here, not even the business of being a child. Playgrounds meant for carefree fun are the domain of gang members and dope dealers. Tiny people with ancient eyes staring out of children's faces linger on the fringes, witnessing the atrocities of a life few can comprehend. Injury, drugs, and shootings are commonplace here, part of the bloody terrain these kids call home. Some families struggle to break the cycle of despair, work desperately to find a better life. Others become victim to the despair, and victimize others.

Eleven-year-old Latrell Daniels was one of those who planned to find a better way. He never noticed the cockroaches or the squalor. He was a dreamer, his mother said, always had his head in the clouds. Latrell *was* a dreamer, but he hadn't made it to the clouds. Not yet. Not until he got a pair of Air Jordans, the creme de la athletic shoes, so he could be just like Mike. He'd be airborne for sure then, soaring toward his dream of being an NBA All-Star, the next world-famous Chicago Bull.

Dream on, his mother told him. With four kids to feed, she was lucky she could buy him shoes at all. Air Jordans? Why not a Cadillac? The likelihood of her being able to afford either was the same.

But Latrell was an enterprising kid. Nothing was going to interfere with his dream. He started working around the neighborhood, carrying laundry, washing cars, hauling stock for Mr. Artese, at the

Italian grocery on Taylor Street. It took a while to save up, longer than he expected, but he kept on striving toward his goal.

His dream came true on a Wednesday. The gray skies and persistent drizzle didn't dampen his excitement as he proudly walked home, laced into immaculate red-and-black high-tops. He couldn't wait for the rain to stop so he could get out on the court and shoot some hoops. Go in for a layup, dazzling everyone with his vertical leap. Hang time like no one else but Mike. In these shoes, he could do anything. Drive the lane, go airborne for a sweet fade-away jumper. . . .

Lost in the rarefied air of hoop dreams, he never saw the boys who lingered near his building's entryway. Didn't see them move toward him, barely heard their muttered "Yo, Blood . . ." The last thing he remembered was a flash—and finally, the sensation of flying.

A first-floor resident called the police. She'd heard a shot, she said. A scuffle near the stairwell. She was too scared to peek out. What could she have done anyway, an old woman like her? Them hoodlums would kill her just as soon as look at her.

We find Latrell crumpled in the stairwell. He's conscious, just barely bleeding from the .22 slug lodged near his spine. The new shoes are gone, stolen from feet that will never fly again. Latrell doesn't know that yet. Even as he's carried to the ambulance, he's talking—about basketball and glory, and being like Mike.

The call is a domestic on the twelfth floor, the Braddock apartment, a family known for fighting. On any given night, the gin starts talking once the sun goes down, and somebody cops a major attitude. That's when the brawling starts. Some shouting first, a few tossed punches—and then it's time to get serious. Furniture's upended, windows broken and, if the neighbors complain, they're dragged into the mix.

We wait for our backup before starting the climb. Experience has taught us that, for this family, two cops are never enough. The apartment door is ajar when we get there, the scene inside one of surprising tranquillity. And, once we determine what's happened, it's enough to penetrate the toughest game face and chill us to the bone. Mrs. Braddock is at the stove, complacently tending to a sizzling frying pan. Seated at the kitchen table are the three Braddock sons, aged twenty to twenty-four, busily wolfing a plate of pork chops. Their father sits with them, neither eating nor drinking from his can of beer. His eyes are open, staring, but he doesn't say a word—silence bought by the large serving fork that protrudes from his chest.

"What happened?"

Oddly detached, Mrs. Braddock waves a dismissive hand.

"Them boys, they always be clownin'!" Completely flat-lined emotions. Numbed by apathy, or the drinks she's been nursing all afternoon?

"Who did it?"

"Jamal," the middle boy, she tells us. Her words slide together in a drunken mumble.

"His daddy started jumpin' salty, got up in his face. I *told* him don't be startin' no mess. Now look!" She waves vaguely toward the table, barely suppressing a belch. Judging from her hundred-proof breath, I wonder how much of this scenario she actually

comprehends. One of the male cops approaches Jamal.

"What happened, man? He threaten you? Come
after you?"

"Naw." Busily sucking pork marrow, Jamal is
nonchalant. "Just didn't feel like listenin' to his
mouth. I ain't fightin' tonight."

"So you killed him instead."

"Didn't mean to. But he wouldn't shut up. I was
tryin' to concentrate."

"On what?"

Jamal spares us an incredulous look, points to the
portable TV blaring in the corner.

"The football game, what else? Cowboys just in-
tercepted in the end zone, man. This is some *serious*
shit!"

As Jamal is handcuffed and led away, his brothers' attention barely wavers from the game. And
when the detectives and evidence technician arrive
to process the crime scene, his mother is sprawled
across the couch, snoring loudly. When asked direct
questions about the homicide, the remaining brothers
simply shrug, with puzzled or blank expressions.
Whatever happened was between Jamal and Daddy,
they said. Everyone else was watching the game.

A call to 911 reports a rape in progress in the projects, first-floor stairway. It's the kind of call we get
all the time—sometimes a crank, many times an invitation to what becomes an ambush. This time, it's
for real.

The victim is a fifty-five-year-old woman who's
slumped on the filthy stairs. The offender, described
as "a young punk" is gone, ran out the back entryway.

The woman is dressed in baggy sweats, with fresh bloodstains around the neckline of her shirt. Waving away the hands offered to help her up, she adjusts her cracked eyeglasses instead.

"I ain't hurt!" she tells us when we radio for an ambulance. "Don't want to go to no hospital." What she *does* want is for us to find the man who jumped her.

"He got my lotto tickets!" she says, lisping around toothless gums. "Jumped me when I was comin' back from the grocery store. Had a knife. Pushed me down, grabbed my purse, then figured, he got him a woman here, he might as well get him some. So he unzipped his pants, shoved that thing in my mouth." She proceeds to describe her attacker, so I can send a flash message on the radio.

"Attention units in Twelve and citywide, I have a flash on a rape that just occurred, 14— West 13th Street. Offender is a black male, medium build, approximately 5'9". Light complexion, mustache and goatee. Wearing a blue knit cap, black jacket, dark pants. Offender fled on foot from this location in unknown direction. He's wanted for aggravated criminal sexual assault, is armed with a knife. Authority of Beat 1227."

The woman sits, nodding as she listens to the crackling police radio, the dispatcher's quick acknowledgment.

"How long you think it'll take to get him, Office?"

I don't have the heart to tell her there's probably a hundred guys fitting that description around these parts. And that the odds of apprehending him are not good—not when his direction of flight is unknown. Since more than thirty minutes have elapsed since the attack, he could be on the other side of the city by now.

"I couldn't say, ma'am. Depends on how far he's gotten."

Shaking her head, she gives us an owlish look.

"I don't think he gone too far, Officer."

"Why's that?"

She points to the stairs. It's a bloody penis—or what's left of it—still clamped between a set of dentures that gleam like pearls on the grimy concrete.

The intersection of Roosevelt and Ashland, in the shadow of the high-rise jets, is always busy. Traffic surges from the hospitals of the West Side Medical Complex, the juvenile courts buildings, and all the businesses north of Taylor. It's the perfect corner for a smash-and-grab.

The thief loiters in the bus stop, waiting for his prey. Usually, it's a woman driver, alone and a little nervous to be in the 'hood. She's thoughtlessly left her purse on the seat next to her, an open invitation for crime.

With a brick or small bat concealed in his jacket, the thief watches. The light turns red, some unwitting female eases her car to a stop, and *bam!* Her passenger window is smashed and her purse gone in one savage spray of flying glass.

It happens all the time. Thieves and junkies in need of quick cash know a photo op when they see one. Break the window, take the money, and run. What could be easier? Over and over, the residents of the area watched it happen, but never did much in the way of intervention. It didn't pay to get involved.

You never knew when one of those fools would be toting a gun. In this neighborhood, apathy can keep you alive.

Twin sisters Brenda and Brianna Oakley didn't share this philosophy. Just eight years old, they'd seen plenty of smash-and-grabs, many executed while the girls walked home from school. They lived in the jets and knew all about the hustlers and thieves. They'd seen neighbors burglarized, friends cut down by random gunfire. Knew what havoc the combination of drugs and anger could wreak on a community. It was a plague of violence that sickened them.

Passing the intersection after school one day, the twins saw Redbone, one of the local thieves, a twenty-year-old man with a pocked face and an expensive habit. They looked at him and decided to do something about it—that this was the day to make a difference. Petite girls with delicate features, the sisters looked more like china dolls than crime stoppers, but that didn't stop them. After a whispered consultation, Brenda approached the bus stop.

Redbone never noticed the little girl. He was too busy focusing on the older lady in the silver Audi pulling up to the light. When he smashed out the window, Brenda dropped down behind him, using her body and her school backpack as a stumbling block. Whirling around with purse in hand, Redbone tripped over Brenda and went sailing, crashing into the steel light post and knocking himself out cold. While Brianna ran for help, Brenda sat on the thief—all fifty pounds of her—just in case he came to. Making sure this was one who wouldn't get away.

The shaken victim was grateful, astonished by the girls' bravery. After the squadrol carted Redbone off, she pressed a twenty-dollar bill into each girl's hand.

"You're heroes!" the woman gushed. "Your parents should be *very* proud! Where do you live?"

Brianna, the quieter twin, gestured toward the closest high-rise.

"Oh, I see. Well, you make sure to tell your mama what good girls you are, alright?" The woman had thought, briefly, that she might escort the girls home, express her personal thanks to the parents. But the *projects*? She was a woman alone with a shattered car window. Why invite more trouble? Time for Plan B.

"Officer, you'll take these girls home, won't you? Tell their parents how brave they were?"

"Sure thing, ma'am."

On their ride home, the twins are excited. It's the first time they've been in a squad car, so we take a leisurely detour, letting them play with the lights, squawk the siren, giggle over the loudspeaker.

"You guys were pretty tough out there," I tell them. "Gave that bad guy the ol' one-two KO." I hold up giggling Brenda's scrawny arm. "Ever think about being a prizefighter when you grow up? I bet you could knock out Tyson!"

Instantly, the girls are serious.

"We don't know *if* we'll grow up," Brianna says solemnly. "Mama says Jesus can call us home anytime." Her dark eyes challenge me to dispute the statement. She's another of the "ancient children" who live here, a street-smart mini-sage calmly accepting reality. Neither Diane or I can say a word.

At their apartment, Mama has plenty to say. She's pleased the girls took action, angered that they accepted a reward.

"You did what you were s'posed to—that's it's own reward! Why you think you should get money for doin' right?"

My partner intervenes.

"Ma'am, your daughters were very brave. They did something most grown people wouldn't do. The lady they helped just wanted to thank them, that's all."

"Saying 'thank you' would've been enough. I'm the one got to raise these kids, Office. I don't want them thinkin' every time they do right, money's gonna fall from the sky. Ain't no use fillin' their heads with foolish dreams."

"You've done a fine job with your girls, ma'am. They know what's right and wrong, and they did something about it. You should be proud. They're just little girls. Nothing wrong with dreaming once in a while."

"You think so? Well, let me tell you somethin'!" Her arms cross in a defiant stance. "Up in here, dreams ain't gonna cut it. The only thing we got is what's real. Livin' today, cuz there's no tellin' about tomorrow. In this place, that's the only thing that's real!"

It's another Christmas Eve on Chicago's West Side, the eighth year I've spent working the projects beat, and my sixth year with Diane. Another holiday spent together on the West Side, waiting for the battles to start and gunshots fired. We cruise slowly around the winding road that circles the four center high-rises of the ABLA projects. Despite the bitter cold, people are still on the street, slouched against walls or clustered on the corners. There are no happy revelers here, only wary faces that fade into the shadows when our squad car approaches.

The only place that's brightly lit is the liquor store

on Roosevelt Road. Here, an endless parade of customers ensure that the proprietor, at least, will enjoy a very prosperous Christmas. Outside, groups of men drink on the street, passing the bottles among them. Cheap liquor gulped down to toast—or forget—this special night that will fuel the fights to come later on.

There are few celebrations here. The struggle of basic survival leaves little energy for anything more than a passing acknowledgment, and a wistful longing to—just once—be someplace better, someplace where dreams come true. Streetwise kids here don't believe in Santa Claus; experience tells them if he *did* show up, some hoodlum thugs would probably steal his sleigh.

"Kids are at your mother's tonight, right?" Diane asks idly. By now she knows the family drill. Since we've been partners, every Christmas, every New Year have been spent together, most of them on the street. On the rare occasions that we didn't work, she was with my family, eating the turkey, ripping open the gifts, and feeling the same *unreality* that I felt. What a lot of cops experience once they've seen this other world.

Even when you're removed from it, when you tell yourself to leave the job at work, it invades your life. You watch your kids trim the tree and remember the watchful eyes of *other* kids—the ones who populate these buildings. Only it's not Santa they're watching for, or the advent of reindeer. They might be watching the police arrest their father, or waiting to see if, this time, their mother will make it home from the grocery store without getting robbed.

So no matter how merry the holiday at your own home is, it's tempered by your feeling that this must be the fantasy, this cheer and goodwill and festive Christmas dinner. The stuff that sitcoms are made of, where everything's bright and perfect. You know it's not a perfect world—you're out there in it every night. And despite your best efforts to leave it behind, escape for a while in the warmth of your family, it's still with you, darkening the edges of your special day. It's a nagging feeling, hard to describe unless you've felt it. But you slap on a smile and bluff your way through it—still another version of your game face—and the family never guesses.

But Diane knows. She's felt the same sadness, and knows, without asking, what's in my head. She knows my thoughts and covers my back and, I realize, for the millionth time, how lucky I am to have her. She's more than a friend, better than a sister. Thoughts I've never told her, but she knows that, too. Lucky for us, words aren't necessary. Most cops are adept at hiding their feelings; in our case, we're also adept at reading them.

The crackling radio transmission snaps me out of my reverie. The job is someone else's assignment, but we're close enough to go in on it. It's in the high-rise at the far end of the complex, and we're there, beginning the twelve-floor climb before anyone else arrives on the scene.

It starts out as a simple domestic. He's drunk, she's mad, both are spoiling for a fight. "Get this bitch outta my face!" "Get that nigger outta my house!"

He's *glad* to leave, he tells us.

" 'Bout fed up with that funky-ass ol' heifer."

Hands on hips, the woman watches him go, gloating over her small victory. Peace restored, almost.

At the apartment door, a chromed 9mm automatic drops out of the man's waistband, clunks on the floor. After that, it's a free-for-all. Simultaneously, the man and my partner dive for the gun. Eager to get in the act, the woman tackles me, using the momentum of her 250 pounds to launch us both out on the balcony. Rolling, straining, the frenzied struggle slams us against a wall. Clothes rip, teeth chomp, pudgy fingers claw in a stranglehold.

Bucking, I roll over, on top, as the first shot is fired. Doors bang open; neighbors rush out. Another shot fired. More bodies join in, kicking and punching.

"Ten-one!" I scream into the radio. "*1227— Emergency! Officer down, 12— Racine!*"

I don't know who's been shot, or if Diane is still alive. Boots are aimed at my head and back, stomping relentlessly. The taste of blood, a pulsing wound, soft-focus diffusion as pain blurs my senses. Thunder in the distance? It's our backup units, pounding up the stairs. Shouting, muffled screams, and then uniformed bodies through the muffled haze.

"Oh, no! Oh, Jesus Christ! Where's that fucking ambulance? Get 'em up here *now!*"

Whoever it is sounds frantic. It doesn't matter, I want to tell them. I can barely feel the pain.

Calm now, floating, drifting. Peace restored.

26

Reflections in a Silver Star

1262 C:	1261 Charlie.
Dispatcher:	1261 Charlie comin' in?
1261 C:	Yeah, Squad. Stopped at the hospital on the way to work and got an update on the girls.
Dispatcher:	How are they doing?
1261 C:	Better now. Going home in a couple days. And they both said to thank everybody for all the cards and flowers.
Unidentified Unit:	Did you tell 'em we miss 'em and want 'em back?
1261 C:	Yeah, but get used to it. Diane won't be coming back at all.

I'm very lucky. By police standards, my injuries are negligible: some broken bones, a skull fracture, a three-inch gash carved in my leg with someone's kitchen knife. At the hospital ER, it's a good-news–bad-news deal. When I regain consciousness, my sergeant informs me that Diane is alive. But, while she wrestled for the gun, it discharged, shooting her in the hand. Nerve damage and the loss of two fingers, which means her police career is over.

Her wrestling partner was more fortunate. After being shot, Diane *still* managed to grab the gun and fire off a round. The man was shot in the thigh, enough to stop him until our help arrived, not enough to do permanent damage. Which is the topic of the *other* news that filters to us as we lay in the hospital. The man has contacted a lawyer, it seems, who's wasted no time in filing suit against the city in general, and the police department in particular, naming Diane and me as the offenders. The charges listed—"police brutality, grievous personal injury, excessive use of force, pain and suffering"—are all the usual allegations one would expect for what will become a million-dollar "nuisance suit."

It's another of those phenomena that occur when dealing with opportunistic criminals. They know a photo op when they see one. Once they incur an injury, a lawsuit is the best way to bring in some major bucks. Any less-than-scrupulous lawyer is happy to handle it, since they know that the city will settle out of court for an amount large enough to keep everyone happy. Better that than risk another media attack featuring yet another unfortunate citizen who was "brutally maimed" by the police. That this unfortunate citizen almost killed a cop doesn't figure into the equation here. Although Diane is now permanently disabled, she's still alive. He didn't kill her, the man will testify. He was only trying to protect himself against her savage and unjustified attack. Which means that, a year or two down the line, the corporation counsel who represents the department's legal affairs will tire of the defendant's relentless badgering, and dip into the city coffers for a fat settlement.

It's happened before, and will continue, as long as there are criminals savvy enough to understand that with the right lawyer, the right story, and a *lot* of leverage from "brutality" publicity, they can transform a police encounter into a cash cow.

But I'm not worried about that. There are other things to think about, worry over as I stare at the ceiling. Christmas Day in the hospital brings my family here, with the same fear-pinched faces and the same haunted eyes I had once, on that long-ago Easter Sunday. This time, it's my father who stands at the foot of the bed, watching me fade in and out of consciousness. In a morbid way, we've come full circle. While he watches me, he's not wondering, as I once did, why anyone would continue to do such a dangerous job. He doesn't assign the same blame I did, passing judgment on me for exposing the family to this pain and fear. He *knows* all the reasons because he's been there. He understands how hard it is to leave the cop's life, once you begin. But the unshed tears he winks away tell another story.

I'm his daughter, his baby girl. He still wants to protect me, save me from what's out there, the same dangers from which I try to shield my own boys. It's an emotional tug-of-war. A cop's awareness tempered by a parent's anguish. A legacy he unwittingly passed on to me.

So they gather around me, my family and children, each hiding their private pain. Brave attempts made at normal conversation, feeble jokes, worried silence while they watch my eyes drift closed again. Finally, a nurse gently suggests they leave. There's nothing they can do here now. With the medications, and the injuries, I may be sleeping for hours. So they go, these cop's kids, to a home where there's no mother to serve the pumpkin pie or pass the Christmas gifts.

Later, they'll tell their grandmother that the only Christmas gift they want is me—uninjured, and at home. Another gift I can't provide. And they'll cry

alone, when no one can hear them curse the life, and
the job, and me for doing it.

Drifting in and out of filmy sleep, my thoughts
blend dreams and reality. Hard to accept what I
know is real, that my partnership with Diane is over
now. The end of the "Dynamic Duo," I think sadly,
watching her sleep in the next bed. Her arm and
hand are bandaged heavily, while the other arm is
fed through intravenous tubes. She's deeply medi-
cated now; but even in sleep she's restless, her good
hand moving fitfully over the bandaged one. More
than once, she frowns, or moans. Not from the pain,
I think, but from the bitter knowledge that invades
her dreams. That there's no going back to the life for
her, not to what she was, is *still,* or to what we were
together. It's good that she sleeps. She needs the rest,
and the respite from the fears and questions that will
come later. Like, *now what?* After years spent
pumped on adrenaline, streaking along the good-
guy-bad-guy fast track that became an existence
instead of a job, *now what?*

She knows how badly she was hurt. After the surgery to repair what was left of her hand, she was conscious enough to understand what the doctors told
her. What she already *knew.* No more being a cop,
of course. Extensive physical therapy that might, if
she's lucky, restore some feeling to her hand. She was
still young, they said, and healthy enough to make a
full recovery, whatever that meant. Recover the
physical capabilities that were destroyed in a single
shot, or her whole lifestyle? Or maybe recover
some sense of value regarding the sacrifice she made.
Did it make a difference out there? Did she—do any
of us—make a difference, enough to justify this loss?

More tough questions that I can't answer, can't

address while my head pounds and the medication offers merciful oblivion. Sleep now. I'll think about the nightmares later.

The healing comes slowly. Medication keeps the physical pain at bay, prevents us from thinking too much about the deeper emotional issues. The parade of visitors begins, friends and associates who come bearing flowers, funny gifts, good wishes to cheer us on. It's no surprise that it's our coworkers who are the easiest guests. Injury is part of a cop's life, accepted without question. When it happens, you simply deal with it and go forward. But it's guaranteed that other cops will be around to see you through it, keep you laughing until you're back out there with them.

With them there's no pinched faces and unspoken fears. Beneath the wisecracks and ribald jokes are respect and support. Understanding that it could have been any of them in this situation, that this time they got the break. It's a tight bond of comradeship, a cop comfort zone offered to any of the "brotherhood." The best therapy to get us through this time, and the difficult days ahead.

In between the visitors, Diane and I talk. There's much to be said, more that neither of us can find words for. Unspoken questions drift between us. Does she blame me? Was it my fault? Was there something I could have done, *should* have done that might have prevented this? I've replayed the scenario— what I can remember of it—a thousand times in my mind. Each time, the answer is the same. Nothing I could have done. It was that one "critical moment" that other cops have described, the one that happens faster than a heartbeat and alters the rest of your life. The one for which no blame can be laid, unless it's on the whims of fate or the scheme of the universe. *Some days you eat the bear, some days the bear eats you.*

Diane understands this, and, eventually accepts it. Years of concealing her feelings means she can keep a stoic face, accept endless visitors without a crack in her emotional armor. Nothing to do but go on, she says calmly. And see, finally, what life is like beyond the CPD.

But she still cries. At night, after nurses have administered the last injections, and the sounds of my even breathing tell her I must be asleep, she cries in the dark. Frightened, bitter sobs that she tries to muffle, but I can hear them, feel them, because I'm crying, too. Alone but together, each in our own beds, separated by fear and circumstances that neither of us could stop. She wonders about an uncertain future, if what she did was worth it. I try to imagine going out there again, doing what I do— what we used to do together. Only this time I'll be alone, and wondering if anything matters anymore.

I remember Vaughn's bitter words from my rookie days. *"It's not like we're making a difference out here. Only thing you can do is be careful and cover your ass."* I once thought this outlook was cynical. Now it seems prophetic. Am I on the way to becoming like him? Nothing feels the same anymore. Before, I thought we stood for something. I knew why I went out there each night. The old people, the kids, the countless victims needed me—and all of us who kept them safe.

Now, the only thing that's clear to me is the image of Diane, bleeding on that project balcony. Will I see her assailant's face in every person I encounter? Assign the blame to every gunman—*anyone* that I arrest? I can't be objective now, not with the flood of bloody images still fresh in my mind. Maybe time and perspective will change that. Or maybe this is just another part of being a cop. Another one of those changes I didn't anticipate, but experience just the same.

All I know for sure is that I have no partner now—and that means everything changes. Another long process begins: finding someone I can work with, someone I trust with my life. And finding a way, within myself, to go out there and do what I did before. And convince myself that it matters.

27

Dogs and Stand-up Guys

Unidentified Unit:	Hey, Squad! Is the department passing out blow-up dolls to everybody working one-man units?
Dispatcher:	If they are, it's news to me.
Unidentified Unit:	I just saw '24 ridin' around— looked like he had a big blow-up dummy sittin' next to him. It had a uniform on and everything!
Second Unidentified Unit:	He must be working with Reinhardt tonight.

I got a taste of it early on. The departmental phenomenon known as the "dogs"—the lazy, complaining, chickenshit slugs who can weasel their way through a workday without breaking a sweat. The people nobody wants to work with, but everyone does, sooner or later. And when you do, you never forget it. It's eight hours spent praying that nothing will happen while you're with this dog, no hot call that requires teamwork, because your ass will be out there alone. Some dogs are lazy, others are thieves; but all of them are the nightmare of decent, hardworking cops.

You hope there'll be no burglary reports to take. While you're interviewing the victim, your dog partner might be in another room, on the pretense of "checking the premises," but covertly cleaning out the drawers. A rape report? The most sensitivity a dog can muster is to sneer at the terrified victim and drawl, "Why'd you call the police? He forget to pay you?"

If there's an in-progress call, like an armed robbery or a gang fight, the dog does a disappearing act. But he'll be the first one on the scene at a "burglary just occurred. . . ." Especially if it's a warehouse or a place of business. "Just occurred" means the burglars are gone, the premises are open, and the owners haven't arrived yet. Which, to the dog, is tantamount to announcing, "Attention, shoppers! Time for the blue-light special!" And blue-light it he does to the crime scene; where, as the first car there, he has carte blanche to help himself before anyone shows up. Why not, they figure. The missing inventory gets written off on the owner's insurance, and who's to say how much those nasty burglars made off with?

During one memorable incident, the dog in question screeched up to a meatpacking house where the loading-dock door had been pried open. As the first unit on the scene, he knew what to do. And filled the trunk of his car with sides of beef, stacks of prime porterhouse, slabs of ribs that would make Fred Flintstone proud. A whole lamb, as much pork as he could carry. What didn't fit in the trunk was tossed in the backseat, and *then* he stole a tarp to cover it all.

His plan was to take a fast report from the astonished owner ("Jesus Christ! They really cleaned out the meat this time! Usually they just grab the money!") and then make a quick detour out of the district and to his house for a speedy drop-off. Which probably would have worked—except for one thing.

He was in such a hurry to get home, he decided to blow a few red lights; something police have been known to do, but usually with the lights and siren on. He omitted that minor detail, which was how he got broadsided by a late-model Thunderbird just half a mile from home.

Luckily, he was unconscious when they brought him to the hospital, so the inevitable interrogation by his furious supervisors was delayed. The demolished squad was towed to the police auto pound, whose enterprising cops discovered enough meat to supply their upcoming July Fourth barbecues, family picnics, even Christmas dinners. And while everyone was enjoying seconds of succulent ribs and inch-thick steaks, the auto-pound guys were toasting their generous benefactor with one simple line: "Every dog has its day."

For those who think that dog cops are morally bankrupt, allow me to set the record straight. Many of them *do* have a deep religious affiliation. They worship at the Temple of the Almighty Dollar. According to them, anything's okay if you don't get caught. Why waste one of the many opportunities cops encounter everyday? It's one of the perks of the job, isn't it? A shooting victim on the street? Go through his pockets before calling the ambulance; beat the paramedics out of some easy cash. A burglary investigation at a jewelry store? *Somebody's* wife and girlfriends will be getting diamonds for Christmas this year.

To a dog, dead bodies are the perfect prey. They have cash, wrist-watches, assorted jewelry. The trick is to make sure they're *really* dead.

Dog cops are the bane of the department, the ones whose moral bankruptcy shames and diminishes cops everywhere. While the rest of us are out there, serving the public, trying to do the right thing, or as close to right as the situation dictates, the dogs are out there serving themselves. Everyone's worked with a dog sometime, and everyone's got a story to tell.

When I come back to work, there's a period of adjustment while I try to find a partner to match my work style. It isn't easy. Most of the hardworking cops already have partners. In my unit there are no rookies, only the partnered teams and the leftovers, the ones who "float" as fill-in manpower. Which means they've put their "cowboy" years behind them and are content to coast toward retirement. Or, even worse, it means they're the dogs.

At the Siren one night, a few friends sympathize with my partnerless plight. It's tough being "single," they agree. Nobody wants to work with the leftovers. Since all of them have been there, at some time, they're happy to share their "dog stories."

Campioso, who now has nineteen years' seniority, recounts one midnight watch nearly a decade ago. He was partnered with a twenty-five-year vet who prided himself on his doggishness. Their first assignment of the night was a call to "meet the landlord." That usually means a landlord-tenant dispute, but this time, it was more. There was a strong odor coming from the third-floor apartment, the landlord told them as their squad car pulled up. He tried to get in, but the door was chained.

The punch of carbon monoxide hit them as soon as they entered the vestibule. The dog cop turned to the landlord.

"You better wait outside, sir, until we investigate. If it's a suicide, it could be really unpleasant."

It didn't take much to kick the door in. The resident, a thirtyish man, was indeed at home, in the kitchen, slumped facedown in front of the open stove. Which was enough to send the dog cop into action. While Campioso opened windows, his partner checked the man's pulse.

"Dead!" he sang out happily, because he'd just noticed the fat wallet bulging from the victim's rear pocket. And was just removing it when the "corpse" rolled over.

"What the hell are you doing?" the dead man screamed. "Gimme back my wallet!"

"You stupid prick! You're supposed to be dead!"

The fight was on. The victim grabbed his wallet, and the cop grabbed the victim. They rolled on the floor, thrashing, struggling for the wallet. With a fifty-odd pound advantage, the dog rolled on top of him. And was just about to deck him when—

"Oh, my God! He's alive! You saved him!" The landlord stood in the doorway with a dazed expression, either from the residual fumes or the miracle he'd just witnessed. A dead man resurrected by the Chicago Police! Thank God they knew CPR!

Like most people who witness a phenomenal event, the landlord wanted to share the wonder. And called the district commander, the superintendent's office, the mayor, and the newspapers, both neighborhood and citywide. The media was *always* trashing cops! This time, let them write something positive. Let the city know there are still cops who care.

The following month, Campioso and his dog partner were awarded department commendations in recognition of their "heroism, outstanding service, and exemplary actions taken in the face of tragedy." A few gilded sentences were thrown in about being role models, lifesavers, all that good stuff.

"Fuck *that*!" the dog cop growled. "I'd rather have the money!"

"That's still possible," Campioso told him. "You can always write a book."

"About saving that prick's life?"

"No. About your miraculous new method of CPR. You can call it the 'right hip-pocket massage.' Guaranteed to resurrect the dead!"

Dog cops don't limit their offensive behavior to the people we serve. They're happy to share it with coworkers, too. A shifty dog might offer condolences to another cop suffering through a painful divorce. "You're better off without her," he'll say. "She was nothing but a bitch anyway!" Two days later, he's spotted hustling the bitch into a cheap motel.

Dog cops are not gender specific, and exist at all levels of the department, regardless of rank. Their one redeeming quality is that, by comparison, they make everyone else look like a "stand-up guy;" men and women who serve the department conscientiously, with honor and courage. A lot of stand-up guys are out there; cops with integrity, cops who go the distance and a mile or so more. But however many of the good cops are out there, they'll always be overshadowed by the creeps, the complainers, the slugs, and the thieves. Bad cops make good press. Because there are no boundaries for corruption, dog cops exist and flourish, feeding like parasites off unsuspecting citizens.

A dog patrolman is a headache, but a dog supervisor is a nightmare. You can always tell off another cop, even refuse to work with him. Try that with a supervisor and you'll have reserved seating on his shit list for the rest of your career, *and* earn a reputation as a troublemaker with all the bosses. The truth is not a necessary component for gossip, and, on this job, word travels fast.

Sipping his beer at the end of the bar, LeFevre recalls just such an occasion. Assigned to a job of a "woman screaming for help," he learned that his sergeant of the night, a female, was riding as his backup. She was new to the district, just one month out of Sergeants' School, but already known as a first-class dog.

At the house, a distraught woman met LeFevre and his partner at the door. She was morbidly obese, he explains, naked except for the towel she held in a futile attempt at modesty. A quivering Shar-Pei of a woman, crying hysterically about her man.

"He's dead!" she sobbed. "One minute we were having fun, and then—" A fresh onslaught of tears. Emotions strong enough to create seismic ripples through the layered flab. The woman was beside herself. They attempted to comfort her, LeFevre says, find words that would somehow soften this tragedy. No guy can stand to see a woman cry.

In true dog fashion, the sergeant, who was also on the scene, contributed nothing. Her lips were curled in a noticeable sneer as she eyed the porcine flesh, wobbling now like tapioca.

The woman led them into the house, toward the bedroom and the body of the recently departed. Also naked, the expired man was as thin as she was fat, not more than 130 pounds stretched over a six-foot-something frame.

They'd been making love, the woman said. He was thrashing around, moaning, really getting in to it. At which point, LeFevre remembers, the woman had managed a proud smile. And then he quit moving. Just stopped—just like that.

Before they could say "cardiac arrest," the sergeant stepped forward.

"*How* were you making love?" She snapped a double wad of gum. "This sounds fishy to me. Maybe you're trying to cover up a homicide!"

"Oh, no! I love him! I'd never do anything to hurt him!"

"Then show me what you did. Otherwise, we'll have to lock you up for murder. Show me *exactly* what you were doing when he died."

It was enough to dumbfound all of them, LeFevre said, shaking his head. As mentioned earlier, ignorance knows no bounds. Sobbing, shuddering, the woman protested—but ultimately complied when the sergeant barked more orders, threatened life in prison. Wallowing on top of the body, she wriggled around until she was seated firmly on his face. A face that was completely obliterated by yards of spreading flesh. Mortified, the weeping woman hung her head.

As far as he was concerned, LeFevre tells us, they had no business there. The poor guy suffocated. End of story. But this dog sergeant wouldn't leave it alone. She called in an evidence technician and ordered him to take pictures of the "crime scene," with this poor woman still astride the cooling corpse. Told her the film would be "analyzed" by the Homicide detectives and, if it was determined to be a murder, they'd be back.

Later, LeFevre heard that the sergeant added those pictures to her "personal collection." Big laughs, she said. Great stuff to pass around at watch parties, or in the bars after work, occasions when the dogs get together to howl. What she didn't understand was that, for all the cops on the watch who *weren't* dogs, there is still such a thing as "pack behavior," and respect for certain codes which she clearly violated. And, after word of that incident got around, no one was willing to work with her, or provide her with any kind of backup. A harsh form of street justice, but enough to send a powerful message.

Just coming into the Siren, an old-timer named Meechum hears the end of LeFevre's story, and has one of his own to add. As a twenty-year man, he's seen plenty of dogs come and go.

One night, he says, he was paired with a dog named Reinhardt with the reputation of falling asleep as soon as he got in a squad, which earned him the districtwide distinction that "he never met a coma he didn't like." For the first two hours, he snored, waking up just in time for his coffee break. And conveniently dozed off again when the jobs start rolling in. Which was fine, as far as Meechum was concerned. Most of the calls were "paper jobs," those that require only a written report. It was better that Reinhardt kept his dead ass in the car and his sticky fingers to himself. With luck, Meechum figured, he might sleep through the entire night.

The jobs continued at a steady pace. It was just like working alone—peaceful except for the snoring, drooling, and occasional gaseous clouds that let Meechum know his partner was still alive.

Strangest thing, though, Meechum recalls, was that the guy had almost an atomic-clock precision, some internal mechanism that reminded him when it was lunchtime. Reinhardt woke up, snorting and belching, asking when they were going to eat. About that time, Meechum started wondering if there were any countries in the free world presently conducting lobotomies. If so, he was willing to donate Reinhardt as their poster boy.

After lunch, Reinhardt was just about to nod off again when the call came. "1221?"

"'21."

"'21 go to Cabrini Hospital for a pickup. The name is Stevens. It's a transport to the medical examiner." The morgue.

"Don't you want a wagon for that? We're a cage car."

"I know, '21, but all the wagons are tied up right now. And this one's supposed to be a baby. Ten-four?" A dead baby.

"Yeah, okay, ten-four."

With that news, Meechum relates that he fully expected his partner to go beyond coma, somewhere closer to suspended animation. But surprisingly, he perked up.

"Oh, good, the morgue!" he chirped. "Haven't been there in a while." And looked as excited as if Meechum had told him they were en route to an "open-door" job at Fort Knox.

The baby was just one month old, a victim of Sudden Infant Death Syndrome. Thankfully, the parents had already left the hospital. Nothing is more difficult—or more heart-wrenching—than separating parents from a dead child. The tiny body was wrapped and shrouded in a black plastic bag. Meechum carried it back to the car, trying to forget what he was holding. His partner, of course, elected to stay in the squad.

At the morgue, though, Reinhardt was a different man. He leaped out of the car before Meechum could even park it, and sprinted through the receiving doors. And then vanished—what he did best—while Meechum took care of police business.

Afterward, he tracked Reinhardt down in the lounge area, where he was deep in conversation with Mosetta Ralston, one of the morgue attendants.

"That's a great outfit, Mosetta," Meechum heard him say. "You just get that?"

"Just last week." She smiled. "Ain't it pretty?" She executed a quick pirouette.

"Yeah, and it don't look like there's any bullet holes, either."

"Naw. Just a little blood, but, shoot! I know how to get that out!" She ran a reverent hand down her sleeve. "This is an Adolfo!"

"No shit! I guess a better class of people are dying."

"Car accident on Lake Shore Drive." Mosetta smiled. "You should've seen her! From the way she was messed up, I thought sure this would be ripped or something, but no, I got lucky. Just a little blood is all."

"Overdoses are probably the best," Reinhardt said. "No bullet holes, no rips, everything nice and clean, most of the time. That's how I got me a Valentino jacket one time. Some River North dentist decided to off himself. Almost the same size as me. Ten bucks in alterations, and I had me a killer jacket! So, what have you got for me today?"

Meechum watched them walk to the back of the room and a row of lockers.

"Not too much of nothin'. Been a slow week for men's stuff. Mostly gunshot victims with holes everywhere. Although I did save you a real nice pair of dress shoes. They're Stacy Adams, I believe, just like new. Let's see now, what size are you again? A nine and a half?"

* * *

Some dog-asses are of the opinion that there's nothing wrong with mixing business and pleasure. And that, when the opportunity presents, one can certainly provide for the other. Sergeant Sean Bayliss, sitting at a side table, recalls his days in the patrol unit, and the dogs he encountered. The one who stands out, he says, is Stanley Beckerman.

Stanley, we're told, was a man well acquainted with the sweet sound of opportunity knocking. He'd been a wagon man for twenty-two years, an assignment he cherished almost as much as his life's blood. The squadrol assignment had been very, *very* good to him.

In addition to the never-ending parade of stiffs who provided money, jewelry, and small appliances, there were the "burglaries just occurred," the drunks and derelicts along Madison who—God bless 'em!—had just cashed their monthly welfare checks and were now passed out under the viaduct after a celebratory bottle of cheap wine. Stanley had eyes like a fox and magic fingers. He could *smell* money, lift it from an unsuspecting mark without them noticing a thing.

Stanley's home was furnished with proceeds from past squadrol capers. The walnut dining-room set that his wife cherished had come from a burglary at a furniture store. His son's Firebird was outfitted with a pricey sound system recovered from a stolen Lincoln Continental parked in an office building's lot. Well, okay, *technically,* it wasn't stolen; but when Stanley started yanking out the CD player and speakers, the car alarm went off. When the not-quite-sober security guard came bounding out of the building, Stanley told him he'd foiled the car thieves, who'd made their escape with only the sound system. But at least he'd saved the car. The owner was grateful, and Stanley and his partner received department honorable mentions for that one.

But money and possessions weren't the only perks Stanley enjoyed as the fruits of his labor. There were the prostitutes—those along the Madison whore's stroll who knew Stanley and his partner very well. And knew enough to give them freebies on demand if they expected to stay on the street when business was booming.

But Stanley wasn't a greedy man. Most times he was happy to let the hookers keep working—as long as they split their take with him. It was only fair. He was upholding the law, they were breaking it. Why not meet somewhere in the middle?

And as for freebies? Sometimes, climbing into the back of the wagon with a ripe and willing whore just wasn't enough. Stanley was a considerate guy, generous to a fault, and he wanted to share the wealth with his friends. He did this by hosting men-only parties that featured some of the better whores as the evening's primary entertainment.

Usually, those parties were held at a cop bar, Bayliss recalls, or the back room of a pool hall—which was okay, but not the comfortable surroundings Stanley would have preferred.

When his wife announced that she was going to Wichita for a few days to visit her ailing sister, he thought, why not? Why get blown in a sleazy bar when you could get deluxe treatment in the comfort of your own home? He was sure that gossiping neighbors wouldn't be a problem. There was nothing unusual about some of the guys coming over for a poker game. With the drapes drawn, who'd know the difference?

On the night of the party, everything was perfect. The bar was stocked with a selection of beer and liquors contributed by an unlicensed tavern owner as a gesture of goodwill. The chips, nuts, and food had been supplied by an distraught grocer who reported a break-in to Stanley while his partner "investigated" the premises. The entertainment—six giggling prostitutes well-lubricated with a combination of beer and Valium—were delivered in a guest's van, backed discreetly into the host's garage.

And the house itself, recently redecorated by Stanley's wife, never looked better. The expanse of cream-colored carpeting stretched from the elegant satin-brocade sofas to glittering glass étagères that held her impressive collection of Murano glass. With the sleek background of heavy silk draperies and ornate crystal lamps that prismed sparkling colors, Stanley thought the place looked like a ritzy bordello. Much better than the usual cop-bar dive.

The party began. Bedrooms were assigned according to activities. Straight sex in one, blowjobs in another, the group stuff in the master bedroom, which boasted a king-size bed. Other guests gathered in the living room, watching the show provided by the two unoccupied whores. They staggered around, bumping, managing a tipsy grind or two while they tossed off their clothes and swilled more booze. To the drunken cops, it was a performance equal to Gypsy Rose Lee. When they watched the girls do each other, it was enough to rouse them to action. So what if the bedrooms were occupied? Nothing wrong with the rug. The randy guests formed a train, clumsily mounting the women in turn, while the beaming Stanley looked on. This was one party they'd remember for a long time! As host, he couldn't be prouder.

So when one of the guys yelled that it was Stanley's turn, he staggered forward with a determined belch. As the host, as a cop, he had a reputation to maintain. But staring down at the drunken, dripping women, he decided he didn't want sloppy thirty-seconds. And pulled one of the whores up, and bent her over the brocaded sofa. He was a wagon man, why not be a back-door man? he mused. When Stanley thrust against her, the guests cheered. And when he had trouble entering his chosen path, one of the guys tossed him the dish-detergent bottle from the kitchen. Lubricant or soap, what was the difference? As long as it's slippery. Stanley squirted a generous dollop and rode to glory.

Later, when he thought about it, he figured he should have known better. It must have been the booze clouding his brain. Otherwise, it *surely* would have dawned on him that what he'd done was a crude version of a soapsuds enema. And while he humped and his friends cheered, the hooker was seized with dreadful cramps. When she shrieked and tried to pull away, Stanley the swordsman held on, chortling at his prowess. Screaming, she clawed at the sofa, twisting frantically. The guys thought it was part of the show.

Finally, she jerked herself free—but it was too late. A geyser of freshly churned shit shot out—on Stanley, on the opulent upholstery, the elegant drapes, and across the creamy carpet as she ran for the bathroom. But en route, she blasted out another fusillade. Diving out of the line of fire, several cops collided with the crystal étagères, sending them and Mrs. Beckerman's glass collection crashing to the floor.

Bayliss and his partner were summoned on a "woman screaming for help" call made by neighbors who'd spotted the yowling woman staggering naked through the streets. Even drunk, she'd had enough sense to make her escape out the bathroom window. After what had happened, no way was she going back into a roomful of men with *guns*.

At Stanley's house, the festive atmosphere had definitely fizzled. Some of the guests, disgusted and nauseated by what they'd witnessed, had left. Others had simply vomited on the ruined carpet. A few were passed out in the steeping puddles, unaware that the party was over. Stanley himself was outside, hunkered down on the front stoop, hoping the fresh air would bring him some clarity. How could he cover his ass this time?

"Wife's gonna kill me!" he moaned to Bayliss, shaking his head sadly.

Surveying the wreckage from the threshold, Bayliss's partner tried to lighten the mood a bit.

"Maybe you can tell her the shit hit the fan?"

But Stanley was beyond humor. "She's gonna kill me," he repeated. "I'm dead meat."

The screen door banged open and Stanley's partner lurched out, covered with suspicious yellow curds. He tossed a fraternal arm around his pal, his partner, his coconspirator. They'd been in tight spots before. This was just one more.

"Don' worry 'bout it, Stan!" he slurred. "We'll figure somethin' out."

"Yeah?" Stanley squinted at him through bleary, bloodshot eyes. "Like what?"

The partner flicked a yellow curd off his beer-soaked sleeve.

"Hell, I don' know. What about gettin' a puppy?"

28

Brass Monkeys

Dispatcher:	Okay, 1411, I'll start you off with a couple of jobs—
1411:	Hold on, Squad. We're not clear from the station yet. We gotta go back upstairs and stand inspection.
Dispatcher:	Didn't you have inspection before roll call?
1411:	Yeah, but then the deputy chief showed up in the station and ordered us to do it again.
Unidentified Unit:	Do *what* again?
1411:	Who knows? Maybe they're training us for the Rockettes!

Some think it's an issue of color. Whenever cops are promoted, they leave behind the blue shirt and silver star of a patrol officer and move into supervisory white and gold. It's a clear distinction meant to separate the brass from the working class, establish an interdepartmental "us versus them" climate that suggests that, once you make rank, you're a different—and better—person. Forget the people you sweated in the trenches with, the ones you depended on to cover your back. You're a boss now, one of the elite. A different breed. Time to separate the men from the brass.

Promotion to a higher rank means you return to the Academy for Sergeants' School, or Lieutenants' School, where you learn how to be a boss. There's more department policies to study, more paperwork to complete, and those unwritten but still important rules to learn about dealing with the troops. You're warned never to let empathy soften you, or cloud your ability to make command decisions. And for God's sake, forget the needs of the street cop. You've got more important things to think about, like keeping up appearances, maintaining an image for *your* bosses—and for your Chinaman, who got you that white shirt in the first place.

Making rank is a feat to be proud of. And however you achieve it—by relation, clout, sex, or the old-fashioned way, paying someone off, or even those cases where you've worked hard and actually earned the promotion—you're all the same now. You're one of the brass, ready to ascend the lofty levels of the police ruling class that range from middle-management sergeants to the rarefied air of "exempt rank"—the district commanders, area chiefs, assistant deputy superintendents. Those are the *real* power elite, a group so exclusive they get their own car and driver, and a special stylized version of the police badge: a gold-colored star with long, narrow points, each topped with a small ball. Brass balls to replace the ones they lost as they came up through the ranks.

Like any ascent to a higher elevation, the air up there, mostly the gusty self-importance of the blowhards you're surrounded by, can make you dizzy. It can distort what's real and, until you're acclimated, affect your ability to function normally. It doesn't matter. As one of the brass, you're not expected to be normal. It's okay to be as power-hungry, insidious, close-minded, and self-promoting as you want to be, as long as you look good doing it. Just remember that the eyes of the city are on you now. But don't worry. This is a department built on clout and cronyism. What good is being a boss if you can't enjoy it?

If bullshit walks and money talks, you've got a smooth ride for the rest of your career. Unless, of course, you get too greedy, or draw some negative attention to yourself. But as long as you keep half a wit about you—which is about as much as many bosses can muster—that's not likely to happen.

A lot of people—civilians, mostly—assume that the best job on the department is police superintendent. He's the top cop, the big cheese, the one with *all* the marbles. The guy who's supposed to be above reproach, who can pretty much do what he wants, when he wants it, without any cop in his jurisdiction to stop him.

The superintendent is the figurehead, the cop poster boy selected by the mayor after much input by the money people—the power brokers of the city who pay big money to make sure the top cop is someone who'll mold the department to serve their needs. Forget seniority or merit—two concepts mutually exclusive with the promotional process. The right man for the job is someone who will parrot the policies fed to him by the covert powers that be. He's the department mouthpiece, the spokesman for the troops, and he's also the convenient sponge to sop up any shit the mayor steps in.

Whenever the mayor is lampooned by the media for police-related issues, who gets the blame? Unfair hiring practices? Not enough minority promotions?

Cops on the take? It's *his* fault, says the mayor. The superintendent, the top cop. Any problems, blame him. Any praise, see the mayor.

In the history of Chicago's police department, there have been some great superintendents, willing to go out on the limb for the troops they led. Top cops who represented us in the best possible way, with intelligence and dignity. Unfortunately, there have also been a few of the other kind for whom the demands of the job were a professional and personal struggle.

The factors to be considered when choosing the superintendent are varied. He should be functionally literate, although department history proves that's a negotiable point. Able to speak whole sentences—a skill the mayor is still working on—since he's the guy at the press conferences, the media witch-hunts, and happier occasions like awards ceremonies. Most important, he should be politically correct in *appearance*. In Chicago, political correctness is dictated by the prevailing social climate of the city. Pressure from the black community, spearheaded by some heated anti-department diatribes from the Reverend Jesse Jackson? Time to install an African-American superintendent.

Uproar from the Hispanic community, whose demographic numbers are gaining in the city's population? (*What about us*, they demand. *We've been ignored too long!*) *No problemo*. The mayor won't ignore their needs any longer, not when the Hispanic vote comprises a hefty chunk in the mayoral race. And quickly appoints the city's first Hispanic superintendent. Cops know what other people don't—that the superintendent's job is not the glamorous power trip some civilians might imagine. It's a job fraught with pressure, treachery, and uncertainty every day of his office. He jumps according to who pulls the strings, and his tenure can be terminated at any time. Who needs stress like that? With the rising numbers of minority groups that are gaining strength, demanding a departmental voice to represent them, cops are taking bets on just how politically correct the next superintendent will be. We figure that, in order to satisfy everyone, it's going to be a Arabic/Asian female transsexual lesbian single-parent quadriplegic. Bonus points will be awarded for a terminal infectious disease currently at the forefront of social consciousness.

At the lower departmental elevations, a boss's job security is less precarious. All that's required is to be semifunctional, a political team-player, and a skilled fence-sitter regarding controversial issues. Other than that, it's a piece of cake.

In spite of the clout-heavy and the power trippers who clog the upper ranks, there are plenty of bosses who are stand-up guys. They never forgot what being at the bottom of the pecking order feels like, and they don't turn their backs of the lowly patrol officer. To them, being a supervisor just means same shit, different uniform, and a higher tax bracket. They're understanding, they're approachable, and there's *never* enough of them to go around.

For every stand-up boss, there's an equal or greater number of the *other* kind. The shaky ones who can't make a command decision and will deny having made one if there's any repercussions. And swiftly place the blame elsewhere, sending someone down the river in their place. The frenzied carnage of the 1968 Chicago Democratic Convention is an excellent example of command decisions gone awry.

Some supervisors see their rank as an extension of their genitalia. Their metaphorical balls swell every time they pin on their captain bars. Which is why they have no qualms about dabbling in sexual harassment when the mood strikes. It's a powder-keg issue that's only begun to be a department problem in recent years. It's *always* existed, but not until recently have victims had some legal recourse. Most of the victims are reluctant to take action. There has to be a witness to the action, someone who's willing to testify in court. Since most cops are concerned about covering their asses, that's not likely. Testifying against your boss brings some ugly thoughts to mind, such as reassignment to a combat zone, furlough selections, and day-off requests denied for the rest of your career, and the place of honor on the shit list of a vindictive boss planning a career-long vendetta.

Some cops learn about this firsthand. A cop named Karen once recounted the problems she and her partner Denise had experienced. Over a period of years, they'd both been sexually harassed by a particular supervisor who spent his tour of duty masturbating in his office, usually while drooling over the pornographic playing cards he'd brought back from Vegas. Every time he saw either Karen or Denise, in the hallway, near the desk, in the parking lot—*anywhere*—he'd make one of his disgusting comments. At first, it was just lewd observations about their respective anatomies, crude, childish remarks you'd expect to hear from adolescent boys. A fifty-year-old commander was another story.

They chose to ignore him, hoping he'd stop. He didn't.

Next, he progressed to the next step: lurid propositions. He was *very* explicit, describing positions,

actions, favored latex novelties, and some group action with a Shetland pony. And didn't seem to care
who heard him when he spoke this way. The women
were nauseated. It was time to take some action.
They consulted attorneys and representatives from
the union, all of whom told them the same thing:
Unless they had witnesses who would be willing to
testify against the captain, they had nothing. He was
a boss. Who'd believe their word against his? The
women had already polled their coworkers. None of
them would agree to do it. Some even thought they
were insane to suggest it. This boss was the Clout
King. His relatives and friends had been in the upper echelons of the department since the first paddy
wagon. He could bury anyone who tried to take him
down. Needless to say, this did *not* bode well for a
sexual-harassment case. There was nothing for
Karen and her partner to do but ignore him, stay out
of his way, or transfer to another district. Except
that he was the one who approved all transfers.

The turning point came one night when he called
the two women into his office and shut the door
with an ominous leer.

"Forget working your regular car. You're my drivers tonight," he told them. "Both of you."

"You can't do that—"

"The *hell* I can't. It's a command decision. And
you two have to follow my commands, get it?" He
was nearly drooling at the prospect. Obviously, he'd
decided it was time to abandon his sticky playing
cards for some real-live action. But his years in the
upper ranks had made him forget one critical point:
that partners—especially ones who'd worked together as long as these two had—develop a kind of
radar that lets them communicate without words,

protect each other from impending danger. Without so much as a single glance, they each knew what the other would do.

Karen let out a piercing shriek—loud enough to be heard by the desk crew just outside his office, and the entire building as well.

"Captain!" she screamed. *"Please! Fuck me! Fuck me now! I need it! Hurry!"* A tortured moan, and then: "Oh my God! Is that all you've got? What a *chipmunk dick!* Where's the magnifying glass?" And then she smiled serenely at her sputtering boss.

He was livid. They'd never seen him this way, purple-faced, bulging-eyed, and, for once, completely speechless.

Denise took advantage of the opportunity to get her two cents in.

"Oooooh, what's this?" Slight pause. *"That's no cold sore! Nobody gets 'em down there!"*

The captain sent the women back to their assigned car. Not as an admission of defeat, but an act of caution. If they were crazy enough for that performance, maybe they'd both gone completely bananas. And you never knew what a truly crazy woman might do—like call his wife, or put a bomb in his personal car. Anything was possible. But it didn't mean he was going to let it slide. They'd made a fool of him in front of his staff.

Karen and Denise waited for vengeance that never came. A transfer to a war zone, foot patrol in the projects, "lost" paychecks—but it never happened. The captain was like a snake, biding his time, waiting to strike. And like any snake worth its scales, he was willing to wait for as long as necessary. In this case, it was a year.

The women were responding to a ten-one on the

other side of the district. They were a long way off, but taking a shortcut through the University of Illinois Circle Campus would cut their travel time in half. A campus security cop, parked in his little beige Chevy, waved as they flew by. U of I cops monitor Chicago Police radios, listen to the calls that might be pertinent to their domain. Sometimes they even tag along on our hot calls—not because they have any authority, but for the thrill of the chase. Just to watch the "real" police in action.

This was one of those times. Intent on following the women, another security cop came squealing around the corner, with no lights, no siren, and no control of his car. On impact, he was doing about seventy—enough to crush both vehicles against a concrete stanchion, which almost split the women's squad in half.

It was two weeks before the captain showed up at the hospital. He'd made his inquiries, knew how long it would be before either one of them was coherent enough to understand what he had to tell them. Smiling like the cat who reamed the canary, he stood near their traction apparatus, close enough to be heard over the hissing oxygen. And waved a paper in front of their bandaged faces with a triumphant smile.

It was a SPAR form, a special department missive filled out by supervisors to initiate disciplinary action. In this case, he was recommending a *minimum* suspension of fifteen days for both Karen and Denise. As self-appointed investigator of their accident, he'd listed a number of infractions for which they now must be punished. All fictitious charges, of course, which no one would question—one of the privileges that come with rank and heavy clout. The charges included "failure to wear a seat belt," "reckless driving," "driving under the influence of controlled substances" (he'd found Denise's zinc cold lozenges in the car), and a raft of similar garbage. It didn't matter *what* the charges were. He was the captain, and he'd see to it that they got their suspension time.

As he was leaving, he sidled close to Karen's bed, leaned down, and peered through the gauze at her one good eye. And waited until she focused on him before delivering his exit line.

"Chipmunk dick, my ass!"

During one particular period, a female rookie was assigned to her new district. Newly graduated, she still had the wide-eyed wonder of someone ready to save the world. She also had a body men would die for. In no time, the guys in the station had established a betting pool on who would have her first. Why else would she be there, they reasoned, with a body like that, if she didn't share the wealth? A lot of cop groupies join the department, just to be closer to the men. They figured she was one of them. She was curvy, she was luscious, and just naïve enough to get her mind as well as her body fucked.

The captain knew a good thing when he saw it. And quickly appointed her his *personal* driver—the one who chauffeured him around the district whenever he felt like playing plantation master. Except this time, it wasn't the troops he inspected. And arrogantly decided that, as captain, his discretion and any sign of class or decency were optional.

They had their first encounter in the captain's car, parked under the expressway. While traffic roared above them, the captain loosened his trousers and the recruit bowed in her first command performance. After that, it was anywhere—alleys, empty lots, the deserted parking lot of a grocery store on midnights. More than one beat car happened upon the captain's car, steamed and rocking with the power of rank. Activities which might have continued indefinitely, except for one thing.

Someone dropped a dime. Some disgruntled cop, with an ax to grind or a taste for vengeance, called the captain's wife with some news of interest. News that prompted her to hire a private detective, who then tailed the captain on his extracurricular adventures for more than a month. Supplied with dates, locations, and some very sordid pictures, the wife took action. After filing for divorce, she stormed the superintendent's office, insisting on some disciplinary action for her wayward mate. Demanding accountability for allowing an employee, a high-ranking police official, to carry on such behavior, destroying their marriage *on company time!* And then she delivered the one that got their attention. She threatened to feed the media some very explicit and tasty tidbits. The magic words that meant it was time to soothe some ruffled feathers.

The captain received an "official reprimand." Which basically meant the big boys upstairs called him in for a little sit-down. Told him to keep his dick in his pants for a while until his crazy wife stopped foaming at the mouth. And from now on, take his bimbos to a motel, at least. Somewhere he could cover his ass. That was the extent of his disciplinary action, all that could be expected for one of the anointed elite.

The female officer received a thirty-day suspension for "conduct unbecoming." On her return, she was reassigned, sent to a district at the farthest geographical point in the city from her home. Now a woman's lockup matron, she's not required to wear a gun, make her own decisions, or do anything more than follow orders. Which, thanks to the captain's early tutoring, is what she does best.

Some supervisors would never use their rank for sexual gain. They're too busy thinking of new and creative ways to mess with the troops, for no particular reason other than that they can. It's a sadistic little power trip that begins when the gold star is issued.

And then there are those who everyone agrees is simply a jerk—and would be one regardless of occupation. The type of person with a multidimensional personality: a malcontent, tyrant, and certified pain in the ass.

Captain Bailey was one of those. A crusty old geezer and former Marine (who was rumored to be two years older than dirt), Captain Bailey refused to retire. His ability to reason had gone the way of his waistline—many years before. He executed his watch command like Captain Bligh in gold braid. Always one who enjoyed a good argument, he didn't always require a second party to do it. He was often seen tottering down the halls, muttering and complaining to himself. As a stickler for details, Captain Bailey insisted that rules be followed to the letter—or, at least, his interpretation of them.

Any cop caught without his uniform hat could expect disciplinary action. Take one minute more than the standard fifteen for a "personal" (copspeak for "coffee break") and he'd have your ass in a sling. Caught smoking in public view, and you'd be looking at suspension time.

Captain Bailey held uniform inspection every Wednesday. According to the rules and regs, that's standard procedure—but most bosses don't do it. They're realistic enough to know it's a waste of time. The important thing is having a full complement of functional manpower. So instead of a formal inspection, they're more likely to toss the troops a cursory glance at roll call—make sure everyone's basically in blue and able to stand upright. Got your gun, your star? Fine. Next order of business.

But Captain Bailey insisted on the whole nine yards. He'd line up the entire watch at attention, and inch along the rows in slow scrutiny.

"Pearl buttons? What the hell is that?" he'd shout, peering at someone's shirt. "Are you some kind of goddamn fairy? Sergeant, write this man up!" The sergeant, obliged to trail along behind him, ran interference for the confused cop.

"Uh, Captain, those aren't pearl buttons. Must be the way the light's hitting them. They're the regular white plastic."

Farther down the line, he was bellowing again.

"Look at that hat! Your goddamn *sprocket* is crooked!" This time, nobody said a word. No one had the faintest idea what a hat sprocket *was*.

As the captain made his way down the line, he carried a pair of steel balls, about the size of ping-pong balls, which he squeezed and rubbed and fondled. His "worry balls," he called them. He'd brought them from Korea, where he'd served in the war. They were supposed to reduce stress, provide an outlet for pressure. As long as he could play with his balls, he could handle anything on this job. His balls kept him sane. He was never without them.

One day, after the captain had been particularly

crazy, some industrious and unknown officers decided it was time for some payback. And while the boss was busy in the executive washroom, they crept into his office and glued his balls together. Not just any glue. The industrial strength stuff that guarantees togetherness in this lifetime and the next for any objects it makes contact with.

According to the desk crew, stationed just outside the captain's office, shouts could be heard all over the building.

"*My balls!*" he roared. "Somebody fucked with my balls!" He thundered into the hallway, eyes bulging, worry balls now affixed—permanently—to one meaty paw.

"I'll find the motherfucker, whoever did this! Nobody's gonna fuck with *my* balls and get away with it!" With veins popping in a face gone purple, the outraged captain lined up the desk crew for immediate inspection. Anyone with the faintest *suggestion* of glue was in deep shit. Unable to find the culprit, he got on the intercom, screaming about his damaged balls. And exercised his absolute authority by demanding that everyone—every single employee assigned to the district, including those on other watches, on days off or on furlough—*must* submit a report about the gluing of Captain Bailey's balls. All future days off would be canceled, all requests for compensatory time off denied until the guilty party came forward.

In his dreams.

A sheaf of reports was submitted, all of them titled: "Captain Bailey's Balls." Copies of these reports mysteriously made their way to other districts and other units for the ongoing entertainment of the rest of the troops. And all were consistent in their opening statement, that time-honored department tradition: "Reporting Officer has no knowledge of this incident."

The ball-gluing culprit was never found. Eventually, Captain Bailey's balls were separated from his hand, but not without great difficulty and some heartfelt cursing. The damaged balls were subsequently replaced, and would remain in the protective custody of the captain's right pants pocket until the day he retired.

29

Burnout

Dispatcher:	1271? Squadrol 1271?
1271:	'71.
Dispatcher:	Take a ride down to the river, the access road off Morgan.
1271:	Let me guess. A floater, right?
Dispatcher:	Ten-four. We got a few calls on this one. They say it looks like a male body, dressed in brownish clothes. Don't know how long it's been there. See if you can fish it out, bring it to the morgue.
1271:	Or maybe, if we throw enough rocks, it'll float over to the Thirteenth District's side of the river. Let *them* fish it out!

The years are passing now, faster, it seems, than I can count. My tenth anniversary as a cop, then the twelfth, and I don't know where the time is going. It's a time-warp syndrome not uncommon to battle zones, and that's what it is out on the streets.

Nobody can say we weren't warned. Not that it made a difference at the time. We were young; we were cocky, we never believed it would happen to us. We didn't know then that it happens to everyone. But it creeps up, a gradual process that's so insidious, you don't recognize it until it's too late. So, in the beginning, we were willing to squander our innocence on mean streets, offer up our green youth and fresh ideals as a sacrifice to the gods of harsh reality. What we got in exchange was less—and more—than we expected. You wake up one day with a chill in your soul and a nagging sense of disorientation. You know where you *are*, you just don't know where *you* are. You wonder who that person in the mirror is with the thousand-yard stare, and where the time's gone, and how you got here. It's burnout, the occupational plague that numbs your soul, armors your heart and leaves whatever remains to carry you through the rest of your career.

Most cops will say it's necessary, an emotional armor that protects you from what you encounter each day: pathetic victims, helpless babies abandoned by indifferent parents, true evil in the form of criminals without conscience. Names you don't remember, images you can't forget since you see it all in replay, in your mind's eye and on the street.

You remember the victims, some of the criminals, but most times, have no idea what happened to them after your brief encounter. You're a cop, not a social worker, and there's no time for follow-up or leisurely case studies. You arrest a criminal, never knowing whether he'll be convicted, or ever spend a minute of the sentence he deserves behind bars. That attempted suicide you talked down from the expressway overpass? You saved a life that day; but there are other days, other times, when you're just not sure. After a while, it all starts to look the same, because it happens again, over and over, a hundred times, a thousand. The names and faces change but the horror's the same: good versus evil, and guess who's winning?

It wasn't supposed to be like this, the helplessness

you feel while you're out there, trying to stem the tide. You were *supposed* to make a difference. Instead, you made a trade. Your heart, your conscience, and everything you believed to be right and just, for a paycheck and a pension. You're being paid to see how people hurt each other, butcher children, prey on the elderly. To witness the scene of a bloody accident and go tell some waiting family that Daddy won't be home for dinner. Daddy won't be home *ever*.

You wear your star on the left side, over your heart. To protect what you love, or cover what's been torn out? You notice the chill first. A warning breeze that waves cool fingers in the early days of your career. But you're busy then, so engrossed in your work that you ignore it. You're a crime fighter. You're holding the demons at bay. Just doing your job. But six months into it, you begin to question. By then, you've seen enough to wonder if anything *ever* changes. After a year, you haven't a clue. And you feel a little colder.

Experience teaches you that there are people without conscience, with no moral mechanism that prevents the wrong they do. People who will, without qualms, commit whatever acts necessary for their own satisfaction or gain. Without guilt, or feeling, or fear of reprisal. Some of them get arrested. Others wear uniforms and badges.

Cops are exposed to conditions that demand adaptation if they're to survive them. And learn to cope the best way they can, protecting themselves as they protect the public. There are many different ways of handling the stress. Some cops simply leave the job, or take an early retirement. Some drink or drug. Others commit suicide. And those who remain become what the public calls "hardened."

"You've changed!" family and friends tell you, but you don't believe them. Not you. You're not the one who's changed—it's everyone around you. You're still the same person with the same beliefs, same hopes . . . aren't you? You wonder why your family, or your friends, don't understand the things you've seen, the places you've been, the things you try to tell them. The things you can *never* tell them. They'd never understand. But cops do. Cops have been to the same places, seen the same things, felt the same pain.

When you look around one day and wonder where your friends are, *who* your friends are, you know what the answer is. You don't have any friends who aren't cops—something you didn't plan. Something that just happens.

It's not as easy to socialize with civilians now. That's how you think of them—"civilians"—anyone who isn't a cop. A term that reinforces that "us-them" line of distinction between yourself and the rest of the world. Civilians look at a cop and think "law enforcer." Cops look at other cops and think "survivor." Civilians don't know what you know, have no idea what it's like. And, if they had any inkling, would ask how you can do it each day, every day, something you often wonder yourself. But you do it.

You keep crazy hours, work 'round the clock. Drag yourself to court appearances and depositions after a full night's work, trying to function on broken sleep—an hour here, two more later. Trying to have a normal life. Normal? You don't even know what that is anymore. You gave it away when you pinned on your star. Something only other cops can understand. So your circle gets smaller.

Your personality dictates how you'll cope. Some develop a razor-sharp sense of humor, gallows hu-

mor. Laughter can get you through *anything*. Others
become more philosophical, or more laid back, or
more obnoxious. All behaviors that bear some sig-
nature from the job.

What's interesting is how your occupation affects
every part of your life. Your pre-cop friends have
faded, and your personal relationships take on an
odd new twist. To anyone outside your blue circle,
you're a cop first, anything else later. Not a woman,
not a mother, not a friend. You're referred to as "this
cop neighbor of mine," or maybe, "my *cop* girlfriend," or "this *cop* friend I have." As though you
can't be defined by anything other than the job you
hold. A disturbing thought, one that you fear might
be true.

You learn that wearing a uniform puts a different
spin on how men look at you. Forget the femininity
aspect—who'd believe it from someone toting handcuffs and a semiautomatic? Mention "cop" and men
see you as a power symbol, a potential conquest.
Hey, Officer, baby! You're not just another warm
body, but a body *in uniform*. A novelty fuck.

At a party, someone happens to mention that
you're a cop. What follows immediately is the "uh-
oh" phenomenon. The women think, "Uh-oh, she
must be some kind of macho dyke." The men think,
"Uh-oh. Do anything to make her mad, and she'll
shoot me."

Time passes. Without realizing it, you *become* your
job. It's little things that you don't notice at first,
but your family is quick to point out to you. Unconscious things, like sitting in restaurants with your
back to the wall. Reading the crowds in the shopping mall, or the movie theater; watching for the guy
who might be the purse snatcher, the pickpocket.

Casting a wary eye on any adult who involves himself with children—the concerned priest, the persistently cheery scoutmaster.

There are things that you internalize, even anticipate unconsciously. It happens all the time out there; why couldn't it happen to you? You see a robbery victim, an old lady without friends or family. There's fear in her eyes, loneliness, and more. It's the same numbness that's gripping you. And you think, *This could be me someday.* Or you find the man who's been dead so long, he dripped through the ceiling. The nightmares that follow feature *you* as the puddle, you as the forgotten old soul.

The first time you attend the funeral of a fellow cop killed in action, there's a sense of surrealism, as though something inside you refuses to plug into the events around you. This was your friend, your co-worker. Someone who'd laughed and sworn and sweated with you through the best times, the toughest. You're not ready to let him go, or acknowledge the unspoken message that his flag-draped coffin punches home: This could be you one day. The streets are a voracious animal that devours us. One cop is like another—it doesn't matter which one's next. But you shove it out of your mind. That's the only way you can go out there face each day that might be *the* day, the one where fate steps in, disguised as a bullet or a knife, to remind you that no one's immortal. But you don't think about it. Just numb yourself a little more. Try not to feel the pain of weeping victims. Look away from the hurt and dying. You're a seasoned veteran. A cop, just doing your job.

Years fly by. The job takes a physical toll, tallied in broken bones, countless injuries. All part of a cop's life. Every day, the police Medical Section is filled with hurt cops reporting their latest injuries. The waiting room looks like pilgrims on the way to Lourdes, filled with mangled, damaged bodies in casts and bandages, on crutches or canes. But no one's expecting a miracle here, or even a sympathetic word from the jaundiced police doctor.

Injured on duty? What else is new? You're the police—get over it! Broken arm? So what? A steel plate in your shattered ankle? How long before you bring your malingering ass back to work?

You learn to live with pain and injury. To *laugh* about it with other cops. There's nothing else you can do. It's part of the deal.

At home one night, you switch on the TV. A little tube time, some light diversion. A special news bulletin is blaring about the suicidal maniac who's barricaded in some cheap motel. A guy who shot and killed his wife, and is now threatening to take himself out. It's a name you recognize, a guy who was in your class at the Academy. A cop.

The reporter announces that, after working the midnight shift, the cop went home and killed his sleeping wife. No motive is given for the murder, but coworkers who were interviewed acknowledged he'd been "stressed" lately. Which was all anyone was willing to say, in keeping with the cops' code of silence. After the shooting, he locked himself in the motel room, indifferent to the efforts of a crisis negotiator. But he's got an agenda before he eats his gun, one last act that, somewhere, someone might understand. So he calls his district commander with a final message:

"I tried to be a good cop, but I just can't take it anymore."

* * *

Over the years, you see more cops hurt, killed at the hands of the public we serve. Cops with families, old or young, some just starting their careers. People you loved, people you counted on. There is no eulogy, no words eloquent enough to dilute the pain and the frissons of guilt that reach every cop. This was a friend, a coworker, someone who did what you do. Dead now, and you couldn't stop it. So you go to the funerals, join the ranks of the other uniforms assembled to pay last respects. Prayers are said, speeches lauding the fallen hero.

The mournful sound of shrilling bagpipes and muffled drums means that the Emerald Society has arrived, the official police pipe-and-drum corps who perform at all department funerals. Police officials comfort the grieving family, present them with the folded flag as the coffin is lowered. Which is, you think, the worst moment of all. Because that's when you see it, the little boys or girls—the children of the dead officer. Even as they're watching Mom or Daddy being put into the ground, they're eyeing the troops around them. An impressive display of solidarity and brotherhood in immaculate dress uniforms. It's an awesome sight, one that burns in their memories and kindles a dream.

You can see it in their eyes, a tiny spark that means you're looking at a future recruit. They'll follow one day. Honor the memory of their slain parent and become a cop, too, so they can squash evil and change the world.

To a kid, it's still simple. A clear cut distinction between good and bad. Join the good guys, wipe out the bad. What could be simpler?

There's nothing you can tell them. Nothing they'd *believe*. Like how they should really think about what they're getting into. How it's not just a job— it's a *life*. One that's tough on your body, bad for your soul, murder on your heart.

30

One for the Road

Dispatcher:	Everybody out there tonight, use caution. Be very, very careful.
Unidentified Unit:	Okay, Dad.
Dispatcher:	I'm not kidding, you guys. We don't want another night like last night.
Unidentified Unit:	Don't worry. I've been real careful since I was a kid. My mother used to pack Trojans in my lunch box.

There's tension in the air tonight, heavy as a leaden shroud. No joking as we assemble for roll call, none of usual insults. Only subdued voices murmuring over the chilling news.

Two cops were killed tonight. Two young partners, one of them a rookie, made a routine traffic stop. It was nothing special—just a broken taillight. Nothing that would warrant what would happen next.

When the driver got out of the car, they led him around, pointed out the cracked plastic lens. Just a friendly suggestion that he might want to get it fixed. Neither cop noticed the passenger who slid across the front seat, aimed the automatic pistol that spat a licking flame of blue death. The senior partner was killed instantly. The rookie, who'd been shot in the neck, back, and hip, bled to death before the ambulance arrived.

The incident happened earlier this evening on the Southwest Side. A place considered a "good" neighborhood of quiet, peaceful streets. It's the second instance of cop killing this month, fueling a blood lust among the street gangs who boast they're the best, the baddest. Cop killing carries status, more prestige than twenty drive-bys.

It's an outright war on the streets now. Gang members, young punks anxious to make a name for themselves are out there, waiting. Hunting the hunters. In police districts across the city, the troops are anxious. Use caution, we're told. They're trying to kill us out there.

I notice that even the wagon men, burly old-timers whose bellies eclipse their gun belts, are strapped into their safety vests tonight. They know what we've all seen—that no one is exempt from the danger. The watch sits tensely, grim-faced, waiting for the night to begin.

It doesn't help that we have a new sergeant acting as our watch commander tonight. He's just transferred in from a North Side district—hiding out, actually, from a sexual-harassment claim. The brass downtown thought a transfer would be in his best interests, some place where he could lay low until the dust settled. Why not the West Side, in a district so dangerous that he could do more than lay low. Just step outside at the wrong time, and he'd be *laid out!*

After a quick rundown of car assignments, the lieutenant surveys the room.

"Guess by now you've all heard what happened

tonight," he begins with a phony, inappropriate smile. "Two of our guys got capped. I don't have to tell you what that means." *No, you don't, jerk. Most of us here are smart enough to figure it out.*

Stroking his substantial gut absently, he pauses, enjoying his captive audience. Or trying to figure out a few platitudes to toss at us. None of us want to hear this. Just get on with the roll call, let us get to work—and away from this pompous slimeball who's been a desk jockey for the past fifteen years.

"There's some young motherfuckers out there who think they're bad," he continues, still grinning. "Wanna try and prove just how bad they are. So if you find yourself in some shit out there tonight, don't hesitate. You know what to do. Don't put your ass on the line—just do what you have to. You can worry about explaining it later on." He chuckles, shaking the jowls that frame his bloated face. "Better to be judged by twelve than carried by six!" Still chuckling, he takes off his glasses and waddles out of the room.

"Glad he enjoyed himself!" one of the guys mutters as we file out. "At least *one* of us had a good time."

"Probably had to get back to his office for some *real* laughs," his partner returns. "Like reading the obituaries."

On the way to the front desk to pick up my radio, I meet Booker near the lockup. With manpower down and a lot of people on the medical roll, assignments had to be shifted again. Booker is the assigned lockup keeper tonight, which he looks less than thrilled about.

"Stinks worse than a sewer in there," he mutters disgustedly. "And we got a full house, too. I'd rather be on the street."

"No, you wouldn't. It's like Kuwait out there.

Only thing missing's an air strike, and that might be coming next."

"Yeah, well, I'd feel a hell of a lot better if *you* weren't out there." His dark eyes are sober enough to underscore his words. "Why don't you tell 'em you're sick? Take time due and go home?"

"Like they'd let me? You know how short we are tonight. They've got me working with a rookie!"

"*That* makes me feel better!" A wry smile, but his hand moves to cover mine. "Listen to me, okay? I just got a weird feeling about tonight."

"And I got a feeling if I don't get my butt out there, Captain Bligh's gonna have it in a sling!" But I squeeze his hands tight. This is the friend who's been with me since the beginning. You can't have a history like ours without looking out for each other.

"I'll be okay. Promise." A quick wink. "And you'll like working the lockup. All the bologna sandwiches you can eat. Raisin bread so fresh, the raisins are moving." It's an old joke between us, referring to the "refreshments" provided for the prisoners. But he's not smiling.

"I wish you wouldn't go. I just got this *feeling*. . . ."

My partner tonight is Carl, a rookie so new his checkerboard hatband is still clean. He's boyish and enthusiastic—excited, he says, to be working a project car. They didn't have projects in his training district. But he's ready for them, ready for anything. *Was I ever this green?*

We roll down darkened streets that are deceptively calm. Even the weather matches my mood. This January night is brutally cold, with a vicious wind that savages the brittle landscape.

Carl likes to talk. He maintains a running monologue, before and between the assignments that carry us through the early-morning hours. Why he wanted to be the police, his adventures in the Academy, the indecision over his choice of service revolver—Colt or Smith & Wesson? No—definitely the Ruger! I hear it all as the night drags on. I can't ever remember feeling that enthusiastic. Hearing it now is amusing, and poignant. It's also the only thing that's keeping me awake.

"1235? Beat 1235?"

" '35"

" '35 takes a disturbance with the son–15 West Wilcox. Complainant's name is Mitchell, on the second floor."

"Ten-four."

"Oh–and, '35? We're getting a few calls on this one. Same woman called before, said it was her boyfriend."

"Maybe the son's also the boyfriend."

"I guess it beats the singles' bars."

When we get to the location, Carl hops out of the car in full regalia. His nightstick, his flashlights, three extra speed-loaders clank together on his squeaking gun belt. Because I'm the driver tonight, he's also carrying the radio, proudly in charge of all our communications.

Upstairs, the complainant is irate. It's her son Melvin, she says. He ain't here now, but it don't matter. Can't do nothin' with him, or any of the hoodlum friends he brings around. She raised that boy herself. Gave him ever'thing she could—and now look. He's in the streets, runnin' with the bad boys.

Using guns, drugs, who knows what? It's a mess, is all. Nineteen years old and thinks he's grown.

"If he's nineteen, he *is* grown, ma'am. Old enough for him to be out on his own if you don't want him here."

"Never said nothin' 'bout puttin' him out," she sulks. "Just want him to act right. Show me some respect. You the *po*-lice. Can't you make him act right?"

"What do you mean, 'act right'?"

"You know. Show a little 'preciation for all I done for him. Spend a little time with me, 'stead of out there with those hoodlums. Won't do nothin' but get hisself killed, out in them streets. Leastways, up in here, he knows his mama love him."

While the woman rambles on, I'm scanning the apartment. It's a cramped little place—just a room with a bed, and a galley kitchen off to the side. A single closet covered by a curtain. Barely enough space for one person, and certainly not big enough to qualify as an "apartment."

"Your son lives here with you?"

"Uh-huh."

"Where's he sleep?"

"In the bed—where else?" She snorts when Carl and I exchange a look.

"He my child, Office. I been sleepin' with my baby since the day he was born—"

I never hear the rest. There's a shout behind me, a crashing blow that sends me sprawling facedown on the floor. It's Melvin, the loving son who's been crouched behind the closet curtain. The son who, while his mama watches, proceeds to bludgeon me with a bat while Carl stares in frozen horror across the room. Instinctively, I curl into a fetal position, try to shield my head from the relentless blows. Bones crunch, blood spurts while my partner simply stands there.

"Carl! Shoot him! Shoot this son of a bitch! *Do something!*" My anguished plea is all he needs to spur him to action. He turns on his heel, this brand-new, ready-for-anything, Ruger-toting rookie, and races out of the apartment. Taking his weapon, our radio, and my only chance of survival right along with him.

Melvin lowers his bloody bat. Here's one cop, but the other got away. Went to get reinforcements, maybe, enough to take him down. Better take off before they get back.

Dropping his weapon, Melvin grabs a jacket and makes it to the door before he remembers something. He swaggers back to me with a confident sneer. Cops carry guns, and he's decided to take mine. Trembling, squinting through the liquid red, I give it to him.

The shot blasts through the tiny room. Melvin staggers, pitches toward the doorway, crashes down the two steep flights. After that, my senses blur, swim with the mixture of cordite smells, the hot metallic taste of gushing blood, and Mama screaming somewhere.

My body is a pyre of pain, a flash fire that devours me. It's easy to surrender to it. They're gone now, everyone's gone, so I don't have to worry. Nothing to do now but close my eyes and fade.

Dreams, visions, blessed warmth. Sergeant Woods: "Keep your eyes open . . ." Booker on the Academy firing range, diving after his ammo. Diane and I laughing together. "We're cool!" First-day antics with Manny. "You and me, we're gonna work out fine." My first day in brand-new blues. Pinning on the star. Lost children, newborn puppies. Laughter. Screams. Muffled voices.

"Are you a Catholic?" An anxious face hovers above me. Cotton wrapped voices that barely reach through the clouds.

"Officer, you're at the hospital. Are you a Catholic? Do you want a priest?"

Filmy shapes move around me, touching, pressing, barking orders. Tubes, machines, a throbbing computer heartbeat that matches my own.

"Code Blue! Code Blue! Paddles? Okay, everybody—*clear!*"

Funny, how frantic they are, when I feel so peaceful. Floating around them, above them, lulled by the beat of the pulsing monitor. A lugging pulse that trips and slows, smoothing finally into a thin flat line that lets me fly away.

Epilogue

Back at the Training Academy again, only this time I'm at the Medical Section for a command performance. I'm not in uniform today, but instead, dressed casually: casual clothes, casual shoes, casual crutches. The medical director has requested my presence one last time: to sign the papers that will end my police career. The departmental powers that be decided my injuries were too extensive, too debilitating to continue to carry out the duties of an officer. In short, I'm now one of the walking wounded who needs to be jettisoned in order to make way for the next wave of able-bodied young warriors.

As usual, the waiting room is packed with the sick and injured, all waiting to see the doctor. And it's the usual mix of cop faces I see: some bored, some anxious, a few catching a quick nap before they're called in. Fresh-faced rookies, cynical vets, they're all here, all going through the motions that the department dictates. Some things never change, I think.

Other faces come to mind: the people I've loved and hated, laughed with and wept over. People who will remain with me no matter how far my steps take me away from this building, from this police life.

Diane, my beloved partner and dear friend, was placed on duty disability after her shooting. After the frantic pace we kept, her new life took some getting used to. She lives quietly in Michigan now, on a rolling spread with horses and dogs and sunrises that never fail to thrill her. A precious gift, she says, after years of stalking evil in the night.

My erstwhile training officer, Vaughan, trained another recruit after me—briefly. His name was Alonzo, and he wasted no time in setting Vaughn straight. Nobody knows all the details, but word is that Vaughn nearly got killed in a shoot-out at a warehouse burglary. Except that he was hiding in the squad car at the time while Alonzo went inside, and the slug they removed from him was department-issued police ammunition.

Alonzo's not talking, other than to say that he merely went after the bad guy. In a rare flash of wisdom, the department stripped Vaughn of his training-officer status and returned him to the Deuce, where he's permanently assigned to a project car.

Booker Dubois is now *Sergeant* Dubois, a meritorious promotion he received after consistent outstanding police work: a stack of honorable mentions, several department commendations, ten lifesaving awards, and community-service distinction. He currently heads a specialized gun task force and is completing studies for his master's degree in criminal science. He and his wife now reside with their daughter and two sons in a splendidly refurbished Victorian in the gracious Kensington area.

My thoughts scatter when my name is called. The medical director's secretary summons me in to the inner sanctum, gestures to a single form on the coffee-stained desk.

"The director's still at lunch," she tells me in a

bored voice. "Must've got tied up, I guess. So just sign that paper; then you can go."

"That's it?"

"What else?" Noting the crutches, she struggles unsuccessfully to curb the impatience in her voice. "I got a lotta things to do, y'know?"

"Yeah, but. . . ." *Sign the papers and go. Sixteen years of service, tears, heartbreak . . . sign the papers and hit the bricks. There's* real *cops out there who deserve her attention. I'm nothing but a statistic now.*

The pen feels like a cold sword that severs all ties. One scribbled gesture serves as the last rites of my police career.

"You'll be hearing from the pension board, I guess," she says vaguely. "If not, give 'em a call. . . ." The last words are lost as she bustles out of the office.

So much for a big send-off.

I hobble out to the parking lot, where a squad of grunting, sweatsuited recruits are suffering through calisthenics.

"Listen up, you mutts!" barks the sergeant who stands glowering over them. "Get your goddamn asses in gear. Y'all wanna be the *po*-lice, you got to *work* for it!"

It must be the glare of the noonday sun that has my eyes welling. Lucky I remembered to wear shades. Preserve my game face. Blinking back the burning sting, I direct my crutches toward the car.

Everything changes.

And some things never change.